Suzanne & George

Warmest regards,

Bob

LOOKING BACK
THINKING
FORWARD

OKLAHOMA CITY
NATIONAL MEMORIAL & MUSEUM

THE OKLAHOMA CITY NATIONAL MEMORIAL & MUSEUM

Looking Back. Thinking Forward.

DEFINING THE OKLAHOMA STANDARD

BY BOB JOHNSON AND KARI WATKINS
FOREWORD BY FRANK KEATING

SERIES EDITOR: GINI MOORE CAMPBELL

OKLAHOMA CITY
NATIONAL
MEMORIAL
MUSEUM

All proceeds from this
book will be donated to the
Oklahoma City National
Memorial Foundation
for the maintenance
and preservation of The
Oklahoma City National
Memorial & Museum.

This book is dedicated to the families of those who were killed, those who survived, all who were changed forever by the Oklahoma City bombing and to all whose selfless and compassionate responses created hope amidst chaos.

FOREWORD VIII

ACKNOWLEDGMENTS X

INTRODUCTION 2

LOOKING BACK BY BOB JOHNSON

1. AN AMERICAN TRAGEDY—
   9:02 A.M., APRIL 19, 1995 4

REFLECTIONS BY RON NORICK 16

2. THE OKLAHOMA STANDARD 20

3. A NATION MOURNS 32

4. THE IMPORTANT ROLE OF THE MEDIA 38

5. MEMORIAL PLANNING 42

REFLECTIONS BY CATHY KEATING 60

REFLECTIONS BY PHILLIP THOMPSON 64

6. DESIGN SELECTION METHODOLOGY 68

7. MEMORIAL MISSION STATEMENT 74

8. SURVIVOR TREE 78

9. AVOIDING POLITICAL AND NON-POLITICAL
   CONTROVERSY 82

10. ASSEMBLING THE MEMORIAL AND
    MUSEUM SITE 90

11. INTERNATIONAL DESIGN COMPETITION 96

REFLECTIONS BY HANS AND TORREY BUTZER 114

12. SYMBOLISM OF THE MEMORIAL COMPONENTS AND CONTINUED RELEVANCE OF THE FENCE 120

13. NATIONAL MEMORIAL DESIGNATION BY CONGRESS AND THE CHALLENGES FACED 134

14. FUNDING OF THE MEMORIAL AND MUSEUM 140

REFLECTIONS BY POLLY NICHOLS 144

15. DEFINITION OF SURVIVOR 150

REFLECTIONS BY RICHARD WILLIAMS 154

16. GROUNDBREAKING AND FENCE MOVING CEREMONIES 158

17. MEMORIAL CONSTRUCTION AND DEDICATION 162

REFLECTIONS BY ROWLAND DENMAN 182

18. CREATION OF THE MUSEUM 186

REFLECTIONS BY HARDY WATKINS 190

19. DEDICATION AND IMPORTANCE OF THE MUSEUM 200

20. WORLDWIDE PILGRIMAGE TO THE MEMORIAL AND MUSEUM 212

REFLECTIONS BY KAREN LUKE 218

THINKING FORWARD BY KARI WATKINS

21. LEADERSHIP INVESTED 224

22. A CLASSROOM 232

23. THE SECOND DECADE 236

REFLECTIONS BY SAM PRESTI 242

24. CHALLENGES AND RESPONSIBILITIES 248

REFLECTIONS BY BOB JOHNSON 252

EPILOGUE BY JON MEACHAM 263

EPILOGUE BY LARRY NICHOLS 271

APPENDICES

I: THOSE WHO WERE KILLED 275

II: MEMBERSHIP OF MEMORIAL TASK FORCE 284

III: ORGANIZATIONAL STRUCTURE OF MEMORIAL TASK FORCE 293

IV: MINUTES OF JULY 26, 1995 ORIENTATION MEETING OF MEMORIAL TASK FORCE 297

V: MEMORIAL MISSION STATEMENT AND APPENDICES 302

VI: INTERGOVERNMENTAL LETTER OF UNDERSTANDING 313

VII: PRESENTATION TO CITY COUNCIL OF OKLAHOMA CITY REGARDING CLOSING OF FIFTH STREET 318

INDEX 324

FOREWORD

Frank Keating
Governor of Oklahoma, 1995-2003

April 19, 1995, is a day that rocked the world and in American history it will be remembered as the day America lost its innocence. Lives were lost. Families were shattered. A community was devastated and changed forever. Although it was tragically the ending for 168 beloved men, women, and children it was also the beginning of the most compelling story of faith, love, hope, and healing, which started just moments after the bombing of the Murrah Federal Building and continues 25 years later. A centuries old prayer, The Prayer of Saint Francis of Assisi, reflects the spirit of our journey:

Lord, make me an instrument of your peace

Where there is hatred, let me sow love

Where there is injury, pardon

Where there is doubt, faith

Where there is despair, hope

Where there is darkness, light

Where there is sadness, joy

O Divine Master, grant that I may

Not so much seek to be consoled as to console

To be understood, as to understand

To be loved, as to love

For it is in giving that we receive

And it's in pardoning that we are pardoned...

This encompasses the Oklahoma that we know. This helps define the "Oklahoma Standard" that the world continues to know. The Oklahoma City National Memorial & Museum safeguards this by Bob Johnson and Kari Watkins beautifully documenting the 25-year journey as told in the following pages.

ACKNOWLEDGMENTS

Bob Johnson

Without the support and encouragement of my wife, Gennie Johnson, I could not have completed the process of establishing the Oklahoma City National Memorial & Museum. Gennie was always supportive on the many occasions on which I carried home the emotions, difficulties, and challenges of our memorialization efforts. I will be forever grateful for her patience, understanding, counsel, and sacrifice during our six-year memorial journey.

Words cannot express the value of Karen Luke's many contributions. Despite going through chemotherapy during the difficult early stages of the memorialization process, Karen was always there for sound guidance grounded in sensitivity and balanced judgment. Without Karen's devotion and leadership throughout the memorialization journey, our prospects of success would have been significantly diminished.

In February 1996 the Memorial Task Force appointed by Oklahoma City Mayor Ron Norick did not yet have paid staff, but because of the anticipated media focus on the memorial planning during the approaching first anniversary of the bombing, we commenced a search for a communications director. Our search led us to a perfect candidate, namely Kari Watkins. She had been the news producer at KFOR, the local NBC affiliate, the communications director at Sonic Corp., and she had just completed her MBA at Oklahoma City University. When we interviewed Kari, we told her we could only afford a part-time employee, and, without hesitation, she said that would not be a problem. On March 1, 1996, our new "part-time" employee started working 12-16 hour days. Rarely has she varied from that exceptional work ethic, and on many occasions she has exceeded those hours.

Hiring Kari proved to be one of the most important milestones in the evolution of the Memorial and Museum. She always seeks perfection and brings out the best in all with whom she works. My very close working relationship and daily conversations with Kari during a five-plus year period will always be among the highlights of my life. She is intelligent, compassionate, creative, courageous, tenacious, driven, and savvy. I would be remiss not to reiterate "tenacious". In 1998, Kari became the Executive Director of the Memorial, and she has been a constant guardian of a commitment to maintain and operate the Oklahoma City National Memorial & Museum at the high standards established during their planning and creation. Without Kari's extraordinary organizational skills, devotion, drive, and ability to orchestrate media relations and events, the Memorial groundbreaking ceremony, the Memorial dedication, the Museum dedication, the annual anniversary ceremonies, and so many other Memorial and Museum ceremonies and events could not have been elevated to the high standard she achieved. Kari has been the lynchpin that allowed us to attain excellence on all fronts. It was my great honor and privilege to work with her.

The Oklahoma City National Memorial & Museum would not exist without the continued support provided by Former Oklahoma Governor and First Lady, Frank and Cathy Keating. From the telephone call I received from Cathy six days after the bombing to the completion of the Memorial and Museum, they helped us in so many important ways. Without Frank Keating's extraordinary effort to complete our capital campaign, we might have struggled to achieve funding of the Memorial and Museum free of debt.

Former Oklahoma City Mayor Ron Norick was the perfect person to lead our community out of the chaos of April 19, 1995. Ron is a person of strong character, he is universally respected, and he possesses the innate leadership ability to inspire and motivate others in the midst of horrific circumstances. Phillip Thompson, whose mother, Virginia Thompson, died in the bombing and whose body was not recovered until after the Murrah Building was imploded, said: "Ron Norick was incredible. He was a magnificent leader who would call me and give me this great sense of calm." Ron Norick led us during our city's darkest hours in a manner few could have achieved. Very simply, the importance of Ron Norick's leadership and support following the bombing and throughout the memorialization process cannot be overstated.

I am grateful for the understanding and tolerance of my partners at Crowe & Dunlevy for losing about half of my productivity for six years.

To all of the victims' family members, survivors, and first responders who stuck with the memorialization process when it would have been so easy to withdraw and who guided our efforts through the planning, creation, and dedication of the Memorial and Museum, I offer my heartfelt gratitude.

There are so many victims' family members, survivors, first responders, and volunteers whose contributions were so valuable. The list that follows is not exhaustive. Throughout the memorial process we were blessed to have people with the needed expertise step forward at the right time. Rowland Denman, with his huge heartfelt, selfless compassion, contributed in so many important ways, including volunteer service as the initial Executive Director; Phyllis Stough carried the early administrative burdens during an extended period when we could not afford staff; Bruce Bockus helped guide the construction planning; Frank Hill also assisted in construction planning and provided an important second set of legal eyes; Jeanette Gamba, Clark Bailey, and Sam Armstrong Lopez kept us on track and consistent in our communications with the public and all constituents; Tom McDaniel made significant contributions in many areas, including government relations; Linda Lambert's financial management kept our process transparent and beyond reproach; Kay Goebel, Cheryl Vaught, Ray Bitsche, Tim O'Connor, Kim Jones-Shelton and others helped so many victims' family members and survivors in the healing process; Jimmy Goodman provided great sensitivity and also served admirably as Co-Chair of the Memorial Ideas Input Committee; Polly Nichols stepped forward in many important ways, including Co-Chairing the Memorial Ideas Input Committee, Co-Chairing the Capital Campaign, and serving on the Design Evaluation Panel; Jackie Jones and Beth Tolbert carefully guided us through the international design competition from which we discovered an incredible Memorial design; Phillip Thompson,

Kathleen Treanor, and Toby Thompson, led the emotion-ridden victims' families and survivors meetings rather than just focusing on their own losses; Kathleen also provided a monthly newsletter for victims' families and survivors during the critical early stages of the memorialization process; Richard Williams and Earnestine Clark led an extended and complicated effort to define "survivor" and also contributed greatly to the creation of a consensus-based ten-chapter storyline for the Museum; Susan Winchester provided valuable guidance throughout the Oklahoma legislative process; Bill Bell also provided assistance with the legislative process; Lee Allan Smith came to the front as he always does on community projects and needs to assist with fundraising planning and events; Beth Shortt served so effectively as the facilitator for the Mission Statement Drafting Committee and the Survivor Definition Committee; Sue Hale and Gary Marrs provided valuable contributions as we rewrote the narrative and approved exhibits for the Museum; Hardy Watkins provided exceptional assistance in the construction of the Memorial and Museum and as the scrivener for the narrative within the Museum; Dr. Bob Long of St. Luke's United

Methodist Church provided meeting space for all of our early meetings; Dr. Bob Blackburn and his staff at the Oklahoma Historical Society; Anita Arnold, Tom Toperzer, and Deb Ferrell-Lynn, provided valuable archival guidance; Richard Williams, Priscilla Salyers, Phillip Thompson, Kathleen Treanor, John Cole, Cheryl Vaught, Jimmy Goodman, Sydney Dobson, John Kennedy, Tim O'Connor, and Kim Jones-Shelton produced a remarkable Memorial Mission Statement; Richard Williams, Toby Thompson, John Cole, Tom Hall, Dr. Paul Heath, Jeannine Gist, Calvin Moser, Cheryl Scroggins, Phillip Thompson, Bud Welch, Kimberly Ritchie, Ron Norick, Luke Corbett, and Dave Lopez provided invaluable participation in the selection of the design of the Memorial; Marty Grubbs, George Skramstad, and others from Crossings Community Church, and Dr. Kenneth Kilgore and the Ambassadors' Concert Choir provided music at many of the anniversary ceremonies; and last, but not least, one of the unsung champions of our memorialization process was my very capable assistant of many years, Mary Thomas, who made enormous contributions to our efforts over a six year period.

Those of us who represented the "face" of the memorial effort received too much credit, because the Oklahoma City National Memorial & Museum would not have been created in such an unprecedented manner without a tremendous number of caring and capable participants and a very devoted and talented staff. I have never witnessed a more selfless and heart wrenching effort than that carried out by the participants and staff who made the creation of the Memorial and Museum a labor of love. Their efforts truly epitomized the "Oklahoma Standard" of neighbor helping neighbor in time of need. It was my great honor and privilege to be a part of that endeavor.

Special thanks to Gini Moore Campbell, Mike Brake, and Brent Johnson, who provided their valuable editing skills; to Oklahoma Hall of Fame Publishing for bringing this project to reality; and to Joanna Butterworth, Mary Ann Eckstein, Lauren Long, Dustin Potter, and Helen Stiefmiller, members of our extraordinary Memorial and Museum staff, who provided photos and thoughtful guidance.

Bob Johnson

LOOKING BACK
THINKING
FORWARD

OKLAHOMA CITY
NATIONAL MEMORIAL & MUSEUM

The story within these pages is of an unexpected journey that began on 9:02 a.m. on April 19, 1995, when a massive bomb ripped apart the Alfred P. Murrah Federal Building in Oklahoma City, took 168 innocent lives, including 19 children, and changed our lives forever. It is a story of a journey of violence turning to hope as the world witnessed a response characterized by an unprecedented melding of courage, compassion, selflessness, and unity, which response became known around the world as the "Oklahoma Standard." And, it is a story of a journey of a wounded and shocked community that dared to be different in its approach to memorializing the losses suffered, the lessons learned, and the hope that arose from chaos.

Bob Johnson and Kari Watkins

CHAPTER 1

An American Tragedy—
9:02 a.m., April 19, 1995

Looking Back

BY BOB JOHNSON

The Myriad Botanical Gardens, located in downtown Oklahoma City at 301 West Reno Ave., in 1995. *Courtesy City of Oklahoma City.*

Many in downtown Oklahoma City had just returned to their offices following the annual Mayor's Prayer Breakfast. For federal employees, citizens seeking services from federal agencies, children in America's Kids Day Care, and others in the Alfred P. Murrah Federal Building at 200 Northwest 5th Street, it was a normal morning. The building was full of activity, the same activity experienced in other federal buildings across the United States.

April 19, 1995, began like any other beautiful spring day in Oklahoma. People were driving to work, dropping children off at school, and going about their daily routines. That Wednesday morning did not seem anything but ordinary. The "ordinary" for Oklahomans included awareness of the terrorism threat in the dark corners of the world, but never was any thought given to the possibility of the unthinkable ... terrorism in the Heartland of America.

An aerial view of downtown Oklahoma City from the early 1990's. *Courtesy Ace Aerial Photography.*

The children of America's Kids Day Care celebrated Easter just days before the bombing of the Alfred P. Murrah Federal Building. *Courtesy HUD Employee Linda Florence.*

The front page of *The Daily Oklahoman* on April 20,1995. *Courtesy Oklahoma Publishing Company.*

At 9:02 a.m. on April 19, 1995, the senses of innocence and security of every Oklahoman were forever shattered when a massive bomb exploded in front of and ripped apart the nine-story Alfred P. Murrah Federal Building. At that moment, terrorism became a clear and present danger for everyone in America.

Those who sought terror to divide us instead awakened us to the reality that Americans could no longer view terrorism from a safe and comfortable distance. The bomb exploded in Oklahoma City, but there were concentric rings of impact radiating out across the nation. While the severity of the losses varied, all Americans were diminished... all were changed forever.

The memories of epic events often never leave us. Like any violent atrocity, the Oklahoma City bombing was a watershed moment that caused everyone to remember where they were and what they were doing on April 19, 1995. As the explosion was heard, many believed it was a gas leak explosion. Never could we have imagined that a massive bomb had been detonated. Oklahomans soon watched in shock at the televised video streaming from the local news helicopter that happened to be a few minutes from the Alfred P. Murrah Federal Building at the time of the explosion.

In one instant, the worst terrorist attack on American soil to date had an overwhelming and devastating impact on our city, state, nation, and lives. By its very nature—an attack on the American government and our public servants—the bombing was a violent assault on each American. Soon after the bombing, a cartoon appeared in a newspaper depicting two individuals standing in front of the remains of the Alfred P. Murrah Federal Building. One said to the other, "How many people were hurt here?" The other person responded: "263 Million Americans." The Oklahoma City bombing was, indeed, an American tragedy.

A FEW FACTS:

- •168 INNOCENT PEOPLE WERE KILLED, INCLUDING 19 SMALL CHILDREN

- •680 OTHERS WERE INJURED

- •7,000 PEOPLE WERE LEFT WITHOUT A WORKPLACE

- •200 CHILDREN LOST AT LEAST ONE PARENT

- •7 CHILDREN LOST THEIR ONLY REMAINING PARENT

- •MORE THAN 300 BUILDINGS WITHIN AN 80-BLOCK AREA WERE DAMAGED OR DESTROYED

- •86 VEHICLES WERE BURNED OR DESTROYED

- •THE EXPLOSION WAS FELT AS FAR AWAY AS 50 MILES FROM THE ALFRED P. MURRAH FEDERAL BUILDING

Co-workers and volunteers carry an injured survivor to one of the multiple triage locations. *Courtesy KOCO-TV.*

In the face of their own shock and disorientation, the initial rescue effort was led by co-workers and volunteers who assisted the living and comforted the dying. No matter what their profession, race, religious preference, or education, volunteers worked side by side with the professional first responders who arrived during that first hour.

One of those heroic volunteers was Raymond Washburn. He operated the snack shop in the Murrah Federal Building and was pinned under a pile of rubble when he heard his employee, Kim Wallace, crying. Washburn, who had been blind since childhood, managed to free himself and, relying on his other strong senses, guided Wallace to safety.

Within minutes of the blast, a rescue and recovery effort led by Oklahoma City Mayor Ron Norick, Oklahoma City Fire Chief Gary Marrs, and Oklahoma City Police Chief Sam Gonzales was put in place. More than 12,000 volunteers and first responders participated in the effort. Such rescue and recovery efforts was unlike any we had seen in America. The Federal Emergency Management Agency (FEMA) arrived in Oklahoma City within four hours of the bombing. It immediately activated 11 of its Urban Search and Rescue (USAR) Task Forces that consisted of 665 first responders. The FEMA Task Forces came from Phoenix, Arizona; Dade County, Florida; Sacramento, Los Angeles, Menlo Park, and Orange County, California; Montgomery County, Maryland; New York City, New York; Fairfax County and Virginia Beach, Virginia; and Puget Sound, Washington. As the world watched, the courageous and selfless efforts of the first responders and volunteers gave hope to all.

With the ability to meld two distinctly different ways of handling the scene at the Murrah Federal Building, former Oklahoma City Fire Chief Gary Marrs successfully coordinated a rescue and recovery operation within a very extensive federal

Oklahoma City Fire Chief Gary Marrs, Mayor Ron Norick, and Police Chief Sam Gonzales address the media following the bombing of the Alfred P. Murrah Federal Building. *Courtesy City of Oklahoma City.*

Shortly after the bombing, the words "We Will Never Forget" were written on the window of an Oklahoma City police car by Oklahoma City Police Department Lt. John Clark. *Courtesy City of Oklahoma City.*

crime investigation. Chief Marrs will tell you that at the heart of the coordinated effort was the fact that he, Oklahoma City Police Chief Sam Gonzales, and Oklahoma City Federal Bureau of Investigation (FBI) Agent In-Charge Bob Ricks knew and trusted each other. And, Mayor Ron Norick supported them anyway he could. Ricks assured Chief Marrs that while the investigation was important, it would not interfere in any way with the rescue effort. FEMA Director James Lee Witt also made it clear to the USAR teams that Chief Marrs was in charge, an unprecedented nod to local officials at a time of national interest that, to my knowledge, has not been repeated.

Almost immediately after the bombing Oklahomans resolved that the probability of recurrence could be reduced if the world never forgot the senseless losses suffered in Oklahoma City and only if Americans remain continually vigilant in preserving our free society.

The Memorial Slab at the Alfred P. Murrah Federal Building on the last day of the 16-day rescue and recovery effort. *Courtesy City of Oklahoma City.*

13

On May 5, 1995, a ceremony was held at the Memorial Slab to mark the end of the recovery effort and honor rescue and recovery personnel. *Courtesy Oklahoma Publishing Company.*

14

During the 16 days of around-the-clock rescue and recovery efforts, a spontaneous memorial developed at the base of a large vertical concrete slab at the Murrah Federal Building. A member of one of the FEMA teams painted "Bless the Children and the Innocent" on what became known as the "Memorial Slab." Initially, at the base of the Memorial Slab first responders left photos, coffee mugs, and other objects recovered in the building during their shifts. Then, first responders began leaving flowers, flags, and personal items to reflect respect for the victims.

It was at the Memorial Slab that the first responders gathered before entering the building and again as they ended their shifts. It was this first impromptu memorial that suggested that there should be a permanent memorial created to honor the memory of those who were killed, those who survived, the first responders, and all who were changed forever by the horrific tragedy. On May 5th, the day after the recovery effort ended for safety reasons, a very solemn ceremony involving all of the rescue and recovery personnel was held at the Memorial Slab to mark the conclusion of their heroic and courageous efforts.

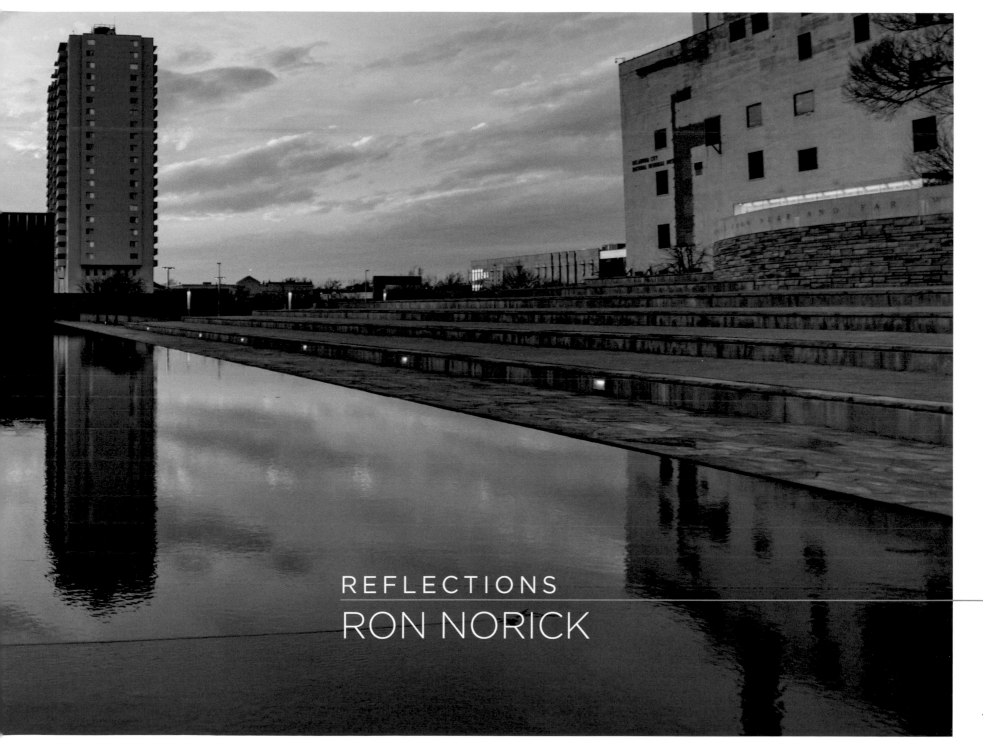

REFLECTIONS
RON NORICK

REFLECTIONS ON THE BOMBING, THE RESCUE AND RECOVERY EFFORT AND THE OKLAHOMA CITY NATIONAL MEMORIAL & MUSEUM

Ron Norick
MAYOR OF THE CITY OF OKLAHOMA CITY, 1987-1998

I will never forget April 19, 1995. What began as a beautiful spring day turned into the most tragic day imaginable for all of us who call Oklahoma home. As Mayor, I had just concluded the annual Mayor's Prayer Breakfast located a short distance from the Murrah Federal Building and was headed to my office when a cowardly act of terrorism shook the soul of our City and Nation. I have never wavered from my belief that the people of the United States are caring and warm citizens when our country is in need. The outpouring of support and love in the wake of the bombing from every State in our Union was overwhelming. It was not difficult for me to see that we are not just Republicans or Democrats, we are Americans first.

My good friend Fire Chief Gary Marrs led the effort to recover the 168 innocent victims from tons of concrete and steel rubble where the Murrah Federal Building previously stood. I will never forget the compassion and loving care that each first responder showed during the rescue and recovery effort. Chief Marrs' leadership went beyond the call to duty and embodied Dwight D. Eisenhower's vision of leadership, the art of getting others to do something you want done because they want to do it. Not only did April 19, 1995, change my life, it changed the lives of every citizen, policemen, fireman, and

thousands of volunteers. It taught us that love is more powerful than hate, and when our City cries, the Nation cries with us.

The Oklahoma City National Memorial & Museum is the work of hundreds of volunteers who devoted countless hours to preserve the tragic events of April 19, 1995, and the days that followed. There are a few very special people who went far beyond what was asked of them to make the Memorial and Museum what they are today: Bob Johnson, Karen Luke, Kari Watkins, and Phillip Thompson. I will never forget their compassion, love, and thoughtfulness during the process of building the Memorial and Museum. Because of them and the millions of citizens and well-wishers who have helped our City, State, and Nation to heal, we will never forget.

CHAPTER 2

The Oklahoma Standard

The losses suffered from the bombing of the Alfred P. Murrah Federal Building were immense and the collective despair was evident. However, something unexpected also emerged in Oklahoma on April 19, 1995, and in the days that followed. The response of Oklahomans proved they would not be defeated by the forces that sought to divide them. Their spirit, hope, and determination would not be stilled. Rather, Oklahomans reminded the world that they are a courageous, resilient people capable of great compassion and selflessness.

In many parts of the world, people have stayed away from the epicenter of tragedy. Oklahomans reacted differently, they ran towards the tragedy to help in any way possible. It became apparent that no heart in Oklahoma was untouched by the attack. In the aftermath of the bombing, Oklahomans were all linked together in compassion, all linked together as neighbors helping neighbors. Immediately following

Almost immediately following the bombing, a public plea for blood donations was made. People from all over central Oklahoma answered the plea. The lines were long, and the wait for many was several hours. *Courtesy Oklahoma Blood Institute.*

the bombing there were endless lines of volunteers to help.

The most frequent comments heard after the bombing were "I want to do something!" and "What can I do?" Because the public demand to help in some manner was so great, Oklahoma City's daily newspaper, *The Daily Oklahoman,* published a daily list of ways to help. There was no hesitancy to step forward to help, regardless of the degree of assistance needed.

The Oklahoma City medical community responded in a manner that merited the American Medical Association's highest award—the AMA Medal of Valor.

Announcements regarding what was needed at the Murrah Federal Building site and the public's response to those needs continued for days. Examples of the tremendous generosity and caring of Oklahomans was the rapid response by citizens who answered the call.

One man drove to the site with his family and offered his steel toe work boots to the first responders. A woman brought to the site several hundred sandwiches she and her neighbors had made. A police captain working the disaster perimeter received a package from a little girl, which contained candy, $1.15, and a note thanking him for his help.

The American Medical Association's (AMA) Medal of Valor was presented to the physicians of the Oklahoma County Medical Society for their heroic deeds performed during the aftermath of the bombing. Inscribed on the solid gold medallion is: "The bravest are surely those who have the clearest vision of what is before them, glory and danger alike, and yet notwithstanding go out to meet it." This was only the fifth time the AMA had given the medal. Dr. John Bozalis, president of the Oklahoma County Medical Society, accepted the award on behalf of the Society. In his acceptance remarks, he was quick to add that the doctors involved in response to the bombing came from all over the State of Oklahoma.

Bravery, as defined on the AMA Medallion, was clearly reflected by the actions of one of the victims. Rebecca Anderson, a nurse enjoying a day off work at home with her husband, rushed to the site when she saw the first images of the bombing on television. Anderson helped two people out of the building before re-entering and receiving a fatal head injury from falling debris. *Newsweek* Magazine named her one of its five heroes and heroines in 1995.

A grief counselor emerged from ten hours of

"Our lives are not determined by what happens to us, but by how we react to what happens, not by what life brings us, but by the attitude we bring to life."

WADE BOGGS, THIRD BASEMAN
BOSTON RED SOX AND NEW YORK YANKEES

Offers of help and support for Oklahoma City came from all areas of the United States. Billboard advertisements were purchased to convey messages of support and compassion. Courtesy Stephanie Rauch.

sitting with grieving families to find that he had left a light on in his car and the battery was drained. A couple approached him and offered to bring their car around to give him a jump-start. The counselor recognized the man, who less than an hour earlier learned the bodies of his two small children had been found. The man pulled the photo of his children from his chest pocket and said to the counselor, "We're all in this together."

The world not only watched in shock as the death toll continued to rise, including 19 innocent children, but people around the world also witnessed with amazement an incredible altruistic public response from Oklahomans of all walks of life.

People from all over the world sent cards, donations, and offers to help. President Bill Clinton received messages of compassion, including those from Queen Elizabeth II of the United Kingdom, Yasser Arafat of the Palestine Liberation Organization, and Narasimha Rao of India. Condolences also came from Russia, Canada, Australia, the United Nations, and the European Union, among countless other nations and international organizations.

Several countries offered to assist in the rescue efforts and investigation. France offered a special rescue unit and Israeli Prime Minister Yitzhak Rabin offered to send agents with anti-terrorist expertise to help in the investigation. President

Clinton declined Israel's offer, believing that to accept it would increase anti-Muslim sentiments and endanger Muslim-Americans.

In the moments, days, and weeks that followed the bombing, the character of Oklahomans was revealed to the world. Many have said they had never witnessed such a noble blending of resilience, courage, love, and compassion. Visiting first responders and journalists called it the "Oklahoma Standard." This generous spirit of neighbor helping neighbor has been a part of Oklahoma's DNA since its founding in 1907. *The Daily Oklahoman* published the following editorial in June 1913:

"The people of Oklahoma can be depended upon to answer all signals from those who need aid. To think of those who have met with misfortune shows the real Oklahoma spirit."

During the memorialization process the question was often asked, "Did the Oklahoma City bombing change Oklahomans?" The consistent answer was the bombing did not change Oklahomans, but simply revealed to the world the character of Oklahomans. The public response to the bombing revealed the "neighbor helping neighbor" compassion that is at the very core of our heritage. In the soul of every Oklahoma volunteer in April 1995 was the simple inability to abide by human suffering in silence, the inability to stand by without giving solace, and the inability to do nothing when doing something could make a difference.

"Nobody made a greater mistake than he who did nothing because he could do only a little."

EDMUND BURKE,
IRISH STATEMAN, AUTHOR AND PHILOSOPHER

During the days following the bombing, the world was reminded that no small act of kindness is ever wasted.

As a sign of support and compassion for all impacted by the bombing of the Alfred P. Murrah Federal Building, many people wore ribbons, most of which were purple for courage, yellow for hope, blue for the State of Oklahoma, and white for innocence. *Courtesy Ackerman McQueen.*

BLESS YOU, AMERICA.

PURPLE:
Courage

WHITE:
Innocence

BLUE:
Statehood
(Our Flag)

YELLOW:
Hope

FOR COMPASSION
ON A NATIONAL SCALE –
A VAST, SHINING OUTPOURING,
UNPRECEDENTED IN ITS DEPTH,
AND SCOPE, AND NEED.

FOR COUNTLESS, TIRELESS HOURS.
FOR WORDS AND TEARS AND PRAYERS RECEIVED
FROM STATES UNITED BY GRIEF, AND A BELIEF IN GOODNESS.

AND FOR RECOGNIZING THE STRENGTH OKLAHOMANS HOLD –
SEEING THE COURAGE AND CARING THAT LIVES HERE,
THAT LIVES *ON.*

Governor Frank Keating

Oklahoma City Mayor Ron Norick

From The People Of
OKLAHOMA

1995

NBC's Tom Brokaw said, "Being from the Plains states, Oklahoma City citizens responded just the way I expected they would." Dan McGraw, from *U.S. News & World Report,* said, "I never thought too much about the place, but after seeing hundreds of people standing for hours to give blood, I quickly changed my mind about Oklahoma City." A Dallas TV reporter said that she had never made a personal comment before in a news story, and then she paused and said, "But these Oklahoma people are wonderful!" Two television crews, one from Japan and the other from France, said they had covered stories all over the world, but had never seen anything like the generosity of Oklahomans.

In a sermon on April 23, 1995, an out-of-state minister, the Reverend James W. Law, said:

"I envy you Oklahomans. There is a part of me that is terribly, terribly humbled by you, because you have shown the world how to love, you have shown the world how to take

26

care of each other. We have seen the best that humankind can offer come to the fore. Not one of us has been left untouched by the courage of the firefighters, the policemen, and the rescue workers. Not one of us has been left untouched by the dedication and commitment of the medical personnel and all the volunteers who have given of themselves so readily and instinctively. The world has seen the best humanity has to offer. The world has seen the best through you."

FBI Director James Comey, at the commemoration services for the 20th Anniversary of the bombing, stated:

"In the moments that followed the bombing, the people of Oklahoma City did something that the rest of the world watching from afar found hard to fathom. The people of Oklahoma City ran toward darkness, pain, anger, and destruction, because on that day those most affected were considered to be neighbors and family. On that day, the people of Oklahoma City were unbending and fearless in the face of terrible hatred. In the midst of evil the people of Oklahoma City understood that courage is stronger than fear, love is stronger than hatred, and hope is stronger than grief. That is the Oklahoma Standard."

In addition to the assistance offered in the rescue and recovery effort, compassion by the Oklahoma City community was evidenced in many other ways during the aftermath. For many days following the bombing, almost all cars in the metropolitan Oklahoma City area were driven with their headlights on during daylight as a poignant gesture of unity, compassion, and respect for those who lost loved ones, for the survivors, and for all whose lives were impacted by the tragedy.

Regrettably, in today's society any mass calamitous event is too often accompanied

The Myriad Convention Center served as the headquarters for the rescue and recovery teams. *Courtesy Oklahoma Restaurant Association.*

by looting and associated crimes. As further evidence of the compassion of the entire Oklahoma City community, there was no looting of the hundreds of damaged and destroyed buildings. A major bank in downtown Oklahoma City had to evacuate after the bombing, leaving money out at teller windows unsecured. Upon return to the building five hours later, the money was counted and not one dollar was missing. Not only was there an absence of looting, the general crime rate in Oklahoma City dropped dramatically following the bombing.

April 19th was the second day of the Mid-Southwest Foodservice Convention and Exposition sponsored by the Oklahoma Restaurant Association. The event was located in the Myriad Convention Center, five blocks south of the Murrah Federal Building site. The Oklahoma Restaurant Association and exhibitors quickly converted the event into a 24-hour service operation to house and feed all emergency response workers during the 16-day rescue and recovery effort.

In regard to the headquarters for the rescue and recovery teams, Oklahoma City Fire Chief Gary Marrs said:

"There was not anything the members of the FEMA search and rescue teams wanted that wasn't available. If they broke glasses or lost contact lenses, there were optometrists there in a booth to replace their glasses or contact lenses. There were physical therapists there to give daily massages if they needed them after they came off their shifts. There was a room set up that would rival any Walgreens and everything was free. If they needed T-shirts, underwear, skin lotion, whatever it might be, it was there for them. When a crew left the sleeping area, volunteers would make their beds, pick up their dirty clothes and launder and fold them before they returned from their shift.

"The community came out like you wouldn't believe. The first responders will tell you they never paid for anything in the city. If a restaurant found out they were part of the rescue teams, they never paid for their meals. It was just a very heartening experience."

As rescue and recovery workers came off their shifts and returned to the Myriad Convention Center, there were roses on their beds and messages or drawings from children to lift their spirits. Donated clothing, food, and supplies were available on a 24-hour basis. Volunteer services also included free medical care, free telephone calls home, and free mail and parcel delivery service.

One of the first responders commented at the time of his departure from Oklahoma City that he left his home on April 19th in such a hurry he had no time to go the bank for cash. He had come to

The Myriad Convention Center became a haven for first responders. *Courtesy Oklahoma Restaurant Association.*

Oklahoma City with $1.00 in his wallet and he was departing Oklahoma City with that same dollar. He asked Governor Keating to autograph it for him.

Dennis Compton, a member of one of the FEMA Teams, said:

"We went to Oklahoma City to assist with a horrible situation that centered around death and destruction, but we went home with a life lesson on how a community should react to adversity."

Part of the referenced Oklahoma Standard originated with the feeling of the first responders that they had never been to a place where they were so appreciated and revered.

Oklahoma City churches were among the leaders in providing aid, food, shelter, prayer, and counseling. Many remained open around the clock. Dr. Bob Long, senior pastor of St. Luke's United Methodist Church, immediately opened the facilities at St. Luke's as an American Red Cross shelter. There, hundreds of people were fed and housed for several weeks after the bombing. Reverend Don Alexander, senior pastor of the First Christian Church, established a compassion center for families and counselors to await word as to the recovery of missing loved ones. Many other churches across the metropolitan area sprang into action with prayers and offers of assistance.

Local companies launched initiatives to assist those in need. The Guardian Angel Fund was established by Crowe & Dunlevy for the purpose of providing assistance to the family of Sonja Lynn Sanders. Sanders, killed in the bombing, was an employee of the Federal Employees Credit Union housed in the Murrah Federal Building. She was survived by her husband, Mike, and two daughters—two-year-old Savanna and three-year-old Brooklynn.

CHAPTER 3

A Nation Mourns

Late on the evening of April 19th, Oklahoma's First Lady Cathy Keating met with five other women at the Governor's Mansion to commence the planning of a memorial service. Incredibly, the Oklahoma City Bombing Memorial Prayer Service was held just four days after the bombing on Sunday, April 23, 1995, at the Oklahoma State Fairgrounds in Oklahoma City. Several thousand people in attendance, and many millions from around the world in the television audience, witnessed a mixture of tears, sympathy, compassion, and inspiration as President Bill Clinton, Governor Frank Keating, First Lady Cathy Keating, Mayor Ron Norick, and Reverend Billy Graham made their respective remarks.

The memorial service was organized as a day of mourning and reflection not only for the families of those who died or were missing and the survivors, but also for all people throughout the world whose hearts had been wounded by the tragedy. First

Thousands waited in line to attend the April 23, 1995, Oklahoma City Bombing Memorial Prayer Service in the Jim Norick Arena at the Oklahoma State Fairgrounds in Oklahoma City. *Courtesy Oklahoma Publishing Company.*

Lady Keating noted that this was an occasion to come together for prayer and the beginning of healing. She acknowledged the deep and raw wounds of the families of lost loved ones and the survivors who suffered the horror of the attack. She also praised the first responders who both day and night, often in difficult weather conditions, had worked and were continuing to work tirelessly with courage to find, save, and protect those who had not yet been found. First Lady Keating also underscored the remarkable outpouring of love and compassion from all sectors of Oklahoma, and the world. In closing, she said it was a terrible crime to steal a child's trust in the goodness of humanity and she emphasized the importance of teaching our children that evil is not the norm.

First Lady Keating's efforts in organizing and coordinating the memorial service were timely, respectful, and sensitive. They struck a tone of sincere compassion and served notice to all who were hurting that they were being held in the hearts of Americans and people around the world.

Governor Keating said the unspeakable evil of April 19th shocked America and sickened the world. He stated that never in the history of our country had Americans witnessed such senseless barbarism. He noted that there was something special about Oklahoma. Oklahomans had always known that, and now the world knew. Governor

Keating said the criminals responsible for the bombing misjudged the response of Oklahomans. He said rather than being intimidated by their terror, we stood before the world and before God with hands and hearts linked in solidarity and heartfelt love.

During his remarks, President Clinton said:

"If anyone thinks that Americans are mostly mean and selfish, they should come to Oklahoma. If anyone thinks Americans have lost their capacity for love, caring, and courage, they should come to Oklahoma.

"Let us let our children know we will stand against the forces of fear. When there is talk of hatred, let us stand up and talk against it. When there is talk of violence, let us stand up and talk against it. In the face of death, let us honor life."

President Clinton also stated Oklahomans had lost too much. He added that Oklahoma had not

Dr. Billy Graham shared his thoughts about Oklahomans coming together in the aftermath of the bombing of the Alfred P. Murrah Federal Building in downtown Oklahoma City. *Courtesy Billy Graham Evangelical Association.*

lost America and that America would stand with Oklahoma for as many tomorrows as it took.

Mayor Norick epitomized a special calm courage during the hours and days that followed the tragedy. He expressed gratitude to the many citizens who responded by donations of their property, their time, and their blood. He commended the extraordinary effort that citizens had made to establish the headquarters for the rescue and recovery teams and the volunteers who stepped forward to address their every need. He stated, "In time of crisis, I know of no other country, state, or city that takes care of their citizens like we do."

Reverend Billy Graham spoke of the tears of people across America mingling with those of Oklahomans. He stated that words could not express the horror, shock, and revulsion Americans felt over what took place in Oklahoma City. He said that the blast ripped at the heart of America and that the senseless tragedy ran against the grain of every standard, belief, and custom we hold as a civilized society.

Dr. Graham said, "I say to those who masterminded this cruel plot and to those who carried it out, the spirit of this city and this nation will not be defeated."

Dr. Graham's statement later was incorporated into the "Promontory Wall" that surrounds the iconic "Survivor Tree" on the grounds of the Oklahoma City National Memorial & Museum. He acknowledged that the wounds of the bombing were deep, but that it was very apparent that the courage, faith, and determination of the people of Oklahoma City were even deeper. He said a tragedy like ours could tear a city apart, but instead it united us like we had never before been united. He noted that the lessons of the bombing included a lesson of a community coming together to offer an example to the world not before witnessed and a lesson of cooperation of officials at every level of government as an example not seen before. He said the tragedy gave the world a lesson in comfort and compassion evidenced by the outpouring of support and help offered from throughout the United States and the world and that we have been reminded that a cruel event like the bombing demonstrates that the depth of human evil also brings out the best of us, the best of the human spirit, sympathy, compassion, and sacrifice.

Reverend Graham concluded by saying, "Oklahoma City has taught the world that there is hope, because it is readily apparent that this City and State will never give up."

President Bill Clinton spoke at the April 23, 1995, Oklahoma City Bombing Memorial Prayer Service.

CHAPTER 4

The Important Role of the Media

Reflective of the tragedy's impact, within hours of the bombing media from around the world descended on Oklahoma City. In addition to national and international media outlets, many television, radio, and newspaper crews from local markets across the nation were present to communicate the story to communities across America. Some of those present in Oklahoma City were ABC, Associated Press Bureau, BBC, Canadian Broadcast Network, CBN, CBS, Chinese TV Network, CNN, Crain Communications of Chicago, El Pais Service (Spain), Federal Times, FOX Network, *Good Morning America, Hard Copy, Investors Business Daily*, Japanese News Network, Le Monde (France), *London Daily Express, London Sunday Times, London Daily News, McNeil Lehrer News*, NBC, News 4 New York, News Limited of Australia, NHK Japanese Television, U.S. Bureau, Swedish News Service, *TIME* Magazine, *U.S. News & World Report, USA Today, The New York Times,*

The Wall Street Journal, The Washington Post, White House Press, and Worldwide Television News.

Mayor Norick and Chief Marrs laid out a very structured plan as to the times of the daily press briefings with city, state, and federal officials and the allocation of responsibility for reporting on various areas of public interest during such briefings. The media knew that if a question could be answered it would be answered truthfully and if a question could not be answered they would be told why. As a result, the media responded with respect for the sensitive information that could not be disclosed and handled interviews and reporting of the bombing and the aftermath with fairness and sensitivity.

The local media provided around-the-clock coverage without commercial breaks. In addition, they served a vital role in coordinating the public support of the rescue and recovery effort with frequent public announcements of needed supplies, equipment, and facilities.

And, the media played an important role in the process by which the Oklahoma City National Memorial & Museum was created. The memorialization process was transparent and proactive in reporting to the media. The only meetings that were closed to the media were those of victims' families and survivors to ensure their comfort in sharing their feelings and concerns. The media responded with fair, respectful, and accurate reporting on the planning and creation of the Memorial and Museum. The Memorial Task Force included the following media representatives: Clayton I. Bennett, Oklahoma Publishing Company; Sue Hale, *The Daily Oklahoman*; Dick Hefton, Oklahoma County Newspapers Inc.; Lawrence Herbster, KOCO-TV; Ray Hibbard, *Edmond Life & Leisure*; Kirk Jewell, *The Oklahoman*; Bill Katsafanas, KFOR-TV; Ed Livermore, *Edmond Evening Sun*; Bob Lorton, *Tulsa World*; Jim Miller, *Norman Transcript*; John Perry, *The Daily Oklahoman*; Russell Perry, *The Black Chronicle* Newspaper; and Joyce Reed, KWTV.

The media response to the bombing is a significant part of the story told in the Oklahoma City National Memorial Museum.

Facing page: The Oklahoma City Police Department designated the area at NW 7th Street and Harvey Avenue, two blocks from the Alfred P. Murrah Federal Building, for all media operations. Quickly named "Satellite City", it hosted over 300 news agencies from all over the world for more than a month. *Courtesy City of Oklahoma City.*

CHAPTER 5

Memorial
Planning

On Monday, April 24th, five days after the bombing, I attended an American Red Cross Board of Directors meeting. After the meeting I made a comment to another board member that I had heard rumors of various memorials being planned at various locations in our city. I was hopeful that Governor Keating and Mayor Norick would consolidate memorial efforts. That statement was made without intent of becoming involved personally in the memorial planning effort. However, the board member relayed my comment to First Lady Keating.

The next day I received a call from First Lady Keating. She said the Governor's office was being overwhelmed by suggestions for a memorial and by receipt of items to be archived for possible inclusion in any memorial created. She asked if I would take responsibility for these items and the planning of a memorial. I committed to organize a memorial-planning group. I also said

I would visit with Mayor Norick as I believed he should be involved in credentialing the memorial planning organization. I did not realize then that the April 25th call from First Lady Keating was the commencement of my six-year memorial journey.

I discussed with Mayor Norick the creation of a task force to plan an appropriate memorial and agreed to develop an organizational plan and a list of proposed participants for his consideration. The next day I called two trusted and respected friends, Karen Luke and Tom McDaniel, and asked them to help formulate a plan for the creation of a memorial. Karen Luke is a respected community volunteer who has a keen sense of the pulse of Oklahoma City. Ultimately, I asked Mayor Norick to designate Karen Luke as the Vice Chairman of the Memorial Task Force. I was confident she would bring great warmth and sensitivity to the memorialization process. At the time, Tom McDaniel was Vice Chairman of Kerr-McGee

Corporation. Tom McDaniel is intelligent and thoughtful; his judgment is consistently balanced. I knew he had enormous capacity to cover many varied tasks within the envisioned memorialization process, including the critical matter of government relations.

After meeting with Karen Luke and Tom McDaniel, the Memorial Organizing Group expanded to include Bill Johnstone, a respected community volunteer and banker; Jackie Jones, Executive Director of Arts Council Oklahoma City; Cheryl Vaught, an attorney with wide and diverse experience as a community volunteer; Tim O'Connor, Director of Catholic Charities of Oklahoma City; and Dr. Bill Thurman, President of the Oklahoma Medical Research Foundation and Chairman of the Oklahoma City Chamber of Commerce. Dr. Thurman also was among the first medical personnel on the scene after the blast.

Although a memorial plan had yet to be completed to present to Mayor Norick, preliminary information about a memorial planning process was included in an article in *The Daily Oklahoman* on May 20th. The article announced, "the committee will be 'sizeable' and represent as many segments of the community as possible" and "special consideration will be given to the feelings of bombing survivors and families of victims." Also announced was the establishment of the Murrah Federal Building Memorial Fund at the Oklahoma City Community Foundation.

On May 22nd, Karen Luke and I were escorted inside the perimeter security to the base of the Murrah Federal Building. As we stood at the base of the Memorial Slab and gazed at the remains of the building, the thought of someone being so calloused as to park a truck containing a bomb immediately in front of the America's Kids Day Care section of the building was unfathomable. We were overwhelmed with an emotional and compelling need to help those who had suffered and survived, the families of lost loved ones and all who had otherwise been impacted by the bombing. The depth of that commitment was important and would be tested several times as challenges were encountered during the memorial planning process.

The following day, in order to facilitate the recovery of the bodies of two known victims, the remainder of the Murrah Federal Building was imploded. A mere 1,500 pounds of explosives, compared to the estimated 4,800 pounds of ammonium nitrate and fuel oil that were ignited on April 19th, brought the rest of the building down.

On Memorial Day, May 29th, the bodies of the two known victims and one additional victim were found and returned to their families. One of those victims was Virginia Thompson, an employee of the Federal Employees Credit Union. Her son, Phillip Thompson, became co-chairman of the Victims' Families and Survivors Liaison Committee

of the Memorial Task Force and his contributions were among the most important.

It was fortuitous that a Symposium on Commemoration had been scheduled by the National Assembly of Local Arts Agencies in San Jose, California for June 8th through the 10th. Arts Council Oklahoma City Executive Director Jackie Jones was instrumental in arranging for a delegation from Oklahoma City to attend. The delegation included Jones, Linda Lambert, Jimmy and Debby Goodman, Toby Thompson, Sunni Mercer, Deborah Dalton, Jerry Steiver, John Kennedy, and me. Upon arrival in San Jose, we were received with great compassion. The focus of the symposium turned to helping us understand the mistakes made and the lessons learned in other memorial efforts. The information obtained and contacts established proved invaluable.

After returning from the symposium, our eight-person Memorial Organizing Group began evaluating the approaches taken in creating other memorials. Additional insight was gained from Michael Berenbaum, Project Director of the United States Holocaust Memorial Museum in Washington, D.C., who called to offer his support in any way needed.

We concluded that memorialization processes were controversial for two reasons. First, typically they are closed exclusive processes void of public participation. Second, they are frequently subjected to political intervention.

From our study of other memorials, we concluded that no memorial had ever been created so soon when raw emotions integral to the healing and grieving process were so elevated. For example, 26 years elapsed between the assassination of President John F. Kennedy and the opening of The Sixth Floor Museum in Dallas, Texas. Memorial processes are further complicated by the necessity of walking a fine line between something we do

not want to remember and the positive memories. In short, we learned memorialization processes are fraught with emotional traps and there was no precedent or road map for memorializing a tragedy so soon after its occurrence.

Based on our evaluation, it was determined that ours would be a very open, inclusive, public participatory memorial process oriented toward consensus-based decisions ... made by a very large, diverse task force ... representing a true cross-section of our community.

On June 15, 1995, the final details of a proposed memorial planning process and organization were presented to Mayor Norick. Pursuant to our recommendations, Mayor Norick created the Memorial Task Force by appointment letters sent 13 days later. The initial appointments totaled 322. Subsequent appointments increased the Memorial Task Force membership to 350.

Like the selfless public support of the rescue and

recovery effort, the Memorial Task Force was made up of people from all walks of life, races, religions, and geographical sectors. The 34 constituencies represented on the Task Force were:

1. Victims' Families
2. Survivors
3. First Responders, including representatives of the 11 FEMA Rescue Teams
4. Architects
5. Business/Financial
6. Legal/Judiciary
7. Children's Advocacy
8. City of Oklahoma City Government
9. Clergy/Church Community
10. Community Volunteers
11. Downtown Building Owners
12. Education
13. Elderly
14. Ethnic Community Groups
15. Federal Employees
16. General Contractors
17. General Relief Providers
18. Historical Preservation
19. Judge Alfred P. Murrah Family Representative
20. Local and State Chambers of Commerce
21. Media/Print
22. Media/Radio-Television
23. Medical Community
24. Mental Health
25. Military
26. Oklahoma City Beautiful
27. Oklahoma City Community Foundation
28. Oklahoma City Firefighters
29. Oklahoma City Police
30. Oklahoma County Government
31. Other Oklahoma Communities
32. Professional Engineers
33. State of Oklahoma Government
34. United Way

The Memorial Task Force represented a diverse cross-section of our community and beyond. Literally, the Oklahoma City National Memorial & Museum was created for the people and by the people. The Task Force consisted of a 181-member Advisory Committee, a 30-member Coordinating Committee, and 10 subcommittees.

An acquaintance told me the proposed Task Force was far too large and the inclusiveness was unneeded, but our eight-person Memorial Organizing Group firmly believed representation from a cross-section of our community would be critical to building a community wide consensus and wide spectrum of public ownership of the resulting memorial.

In volunteering to chair the memorialization process I believed we could create a memorial that would forever preserve the inspiring contrast between the brutality of the bombing and the tenderness and selflessness of the public response.

Most important, I believed the memorial process could be conducted in a manner that would be cathartic for a wounded and shocked community and, possibly, be more important than the memorial itself.

After the appointment of the Memorial Task Force by Mayor Norick, but before the Orientation Meeting occurred, a local television reporter apprised us of a petition that had been circulated to some of the victims' family members by a person who signed the petition as the President of World Charities Fund. Although no other signatures appeared on the copy of the petition, it stated it had been adopted by the families of the victims of the bombing and that the decision as to what should happen to the Alfred P. Murrah Federal Building site should rest solely with the victims' families. In addition, it stated that the site should be made into a park with a monument or monuments to be designated by the victims' families.

We responded that the feelings and opinions of the victims' families and survivors regarding the values, themes, and messages to be reflected by the memorial should carry great weight in the planning process to make certain that the memorial is appropriate, non-exclusionary, and sensitive to their feelings. We also believed we had the obligation to listen to the input of all citizens whose hearts were impacted by the bombing and stated that until we had extensive input as to what should be reflected by the memorial, it would be inappropriate to focus on its physical design.

A few days later, a few victims' family members held a news conference in which they expressed their concerns about not being solely responsible for planning a memorial. However, after many one-on-one meetings and their involvement in the memorialization process, those individuals became vital contributors to the planning and creation of the Memorial and Museum.

The Orientation Meeting of the Memorial Task Force was held at St. Luke's United Methodist Church on July 26, 1995. At that meeting, the organizational structure of the Task Force and the scope of each of the committees and subcommittees was set forth. The most important message offered that day was the following:

"We must be realistic regarding the fulfillment of our expectations as to the end result of this process, that is, the completed Memorial. Any symbolic component of the Memorial will be an art form, and opinions as to its perfection will vary; however, we firmly believe the meaning of the Memorial developed through our process of memorialization will be more important than the end physical result. If the process is conducted in an open, caring, public participatory, non-political and non-commercial manner, as it must be, we believe we will form a strong consensus as to the objectives and meaning of the Memorial. Hence, the results of the memorialization process will interpret whatever the physical form may be. Most importantly, if we administer the Memorialization Process appropriately, it will not only be a planning process, but it will be a major component of the healing process."

Another important step was taken that day. We began the meeting with a moment of silence to remember those who were killed, those who survived, and all who were changed forever by the bombing. The custom of beginning Memorial meetings in that same solemn, reflective manner continues to this day.

During the first eight months, the Memorial Task Force functioned without any outside funding and without any paid employees. It is remarkable that, to my knowledge, no member of the Task Force requested reimbursement for personal

expenses incurred. Clearly, the memorial planning effort was a labor of love for all involved and it continued to be such through the completion and dedication of the Memorial and Museum.

Going into a memorialization process on the heels of an event that involved extreme malice was a daunting task. The Task Force expected a diverse array of emotions would need to be resolved to the greatest extent possible before focusing on the physical design of the memorial, but the level of raw emotions at the first meeting with victims' family members and survivors caught everyone by surprise. The room was awash with animosity. After Mayor Norick introduced the leadership of the Memorial Task Force, a few victims' family members stated that volunteers should not be involved in memorializing losses that could only be understood by those who had suffered most from the tragedy. That evening all victims' family members and survivors were assured they would have the opportunity to be involved in all aspects of the memorial planning process. However, widespread distrust and disbelief were evident.

Many of the volunteers felt very much outside our respective comfort zones as we moved from that rocky beginning, but we believed trust could be established if the process was approached with patience.

"The greatest rewards in life come from living outside and beyond one's self."

JUDGE ALFRED P. MURRAH

Very soon after the bombing, the offices of Governor Keating and Mayor Norick received numerous unsolicited memorial design ideas. Unsolicited designs continued coming to us after the Memorial Task Force was created. Some of those suggested designs came from recognized artists such as Felix de Weldon, the sculptor who designed 33 monuments in the Washington, D.C. area, including the U.S. Marine Corps Iwo Jima Memorial. In his letter to Mayor Norick, de Weldon stated that he was "inspired by the reaction of the citizens of Oklahoma and decent citizens across our nation" and "not since 1945 when I saw the photograph of our Marines raising the flag atop Mount Suribachi on a tiny island known as Iwo Jima, have I been this inspired to create a lasting tribute to the spirit of a united people ...."

A representative of Glenna Goodacre, who designed the Vietnam Women's Memorial, informed us that Goodacre would bring "sensitivity of catharsis and healing" to her work on a memorial. We also received a design concept from Edwina Sandys, a British sculptress who is Winston Churchill's granddaughter and whose monumental sculptures have been installed in several United Nations centers around the world.

"De gustibus non es disputandum" is a Latin phrase meaning, essentially, there's no accounting for taste. Any project involving design elements normally draws as many mixed subjective opinions and levels of appreciation as people have mixed tastes. Those opinions are exacerbated when the art form is a memorial relating to tragedy. We believed at the beginning of the memorial planning process, and firmly believe today, that the only means of creating a widespread sense of appreciation and ownership of a memorial design was to first create a strong consensus on what the memorial was intended to portray and communicate. Hence, the focus during the early months of the memorialization process was not on the physical form of the memorial, but, rather, on what the objectives of the memorial should be.

There were efforts by some people to lobby victims' family members and survivors for support of their respective design ideas, including some who misrepresented themselves as victims' family members and gained entrance to the meetings of the victims' families and survivors that were closed to the public and media. Fortunately, we were able to handle those situations with diplomacy.

The Fence

Soon after the implosion of the Murrah Federal Building, the recovery of the bodies of the remaining three victims, and the removal of the building debris, an ordinary chain link fence was installed as a security fence. That fence became much more than a barrier; it became a memorial destination for people from all corners of the world. Whether a visit to the site was made during the day or night, there always were people gathered at "The Fence."

The sentiment of visitors left on The Fence was evidenced by teddy bears, key chains, T-shirts, license plates, and anything on which words from the hearts of visitors could be written. The items and messages reminded us that the world had not forgotten our tragedy, and it was that sentiment that provided great comfort to the victims' families, survivors, first responders, and all who had been impacted by the bombing.

One of the many blessings realized during the memorialization process occurred at one of the many town hall meetings held to solicit input from the public-at-large regarding what a visitor to the completed memorial should feel, learn, experience, and encounter. One of those meetings was held in Guthrie, Oklahoma, and attended by a remarkably talented and selfless lady named Jane Thomas. At the end of that meeting, Jane volunteered to serve on the Archives Committee. She not only assisted; she became a full-time volunteer archivist. Her dedication was evidenced by the fact that there were many nights when she slept in the

The Fence, as it appeared in 1996, secured the Alfred P. Murrah Federal Building footprint.

warehouse where the archives collection was processed, catalogued, and stored. After the Memorial Foundation was able to hire paid staff in 1996, Thomas became the Foundation's Archivist, a position in which she served in an admirable

The Oklahoma City National Memorial and Museum's first archivist, Jane Thomas, collected thousands of artifacts from The Fence. *Courtesy Oklahoma Publishing Company.*

54

manner for many years. Through her efforts, the assistance of Dr. Bob Blackburn and the staff at the Oklahoma Historical Society, and the many volunteers, thousands of teddy bears, quilts, cards, letters, posters, banners, videos, songs, poems, and numerous other items representing an outpouring of sympathy were removed from The Fence, preserved, and catalogued. Many of the items have since been sent to victims' families, survivors, and people around the world whose lives were in need of comfort and hope.

Victims' Families and Survivors Meetings

Hearkening back to First Lady Cathy Keating's remarks at the April 23, 1995, Memorial Prayer Service, as we developed the process by which we would plan an appropriate Memorial we underscored the need for conducting the process in a manner that included the fostering of healing as the top

priority. The Task Force recognized that everyone has a different path to recovery and volunteers who participated in the process worked incessantly to promote healing of all who were impacted by that tragic day. We acknowledged the validity of the anger of the victims' family members and survivors, and we stressed to them our commitment to listen and to help prevent anger from turning into hate.

A Victims' Families and Survivors Liaison Committee was created and co-chaired by Phillip Thompson, whose mother Virginia was killed in the Murrah Federal Building; Toby Thompson, whose brother Michael Thompson was killed in the blast; Kathleen Treanor, whose four-year old daughter Ashley Eckles and mother-in-law and father-in-law, LaRue and Luther Treanor, died in the bombing; and volunteers Ray Bitsche, Kay Goebel, Tim O'Connor, Kim Jones-Shelton, and Cheryl Vaught. By written survey, Internet survey, and frequent meetings, we asked "What

Oklahoma City Memorial Foundation Chairman Bob Johnson and Barbara Kerrick listen during a round table discussion with victims' families and survivors in the beginning of the memorialization process. *Courtesy Oklahoma Publishing Company.*

should a visitor to the completed memorial feel, learn, encounter, and experience?" Most of each meeting focused on small round table discussions, with each small group consisting of a mixture of victims' family members, survivors, and volunteers. As previously stated, our thesis was to defer any focus on the physical design of the memorial until we developed a strong consensus on the memorial's objectives and messages.

During the listening process with the victims' families and survivors, a mother who lost her daughter in the bombing argued that we should not use the word "hope" in our Mission Statement. She said, "there will never be hope." Later in the memorial process she said, "Thank you for allowing me to help in this process. The process alone has given me hope."

Survivor Richard Williams said, "One of the things I have remembered the most over the years was the willingness of the community leaders to listen. They did not tell us what we should feel, when we should get over it, or when the healing process should end. They allowed us to be part of the process, and they listened to what we said. They said everyone had a voice. A consensus carried us through the process, because they were willing to listen."

After eight months of meetings, round table discussions, and many one-on-one conversations, a Final Report on the proposed objectives of the Memorial was adopted by a unanimous vote of the Victims' Families and Survivors Committee. The most significant aspect of the consensus evidenced by such unanimity was the healing that had progressed during the period.

The Final Report of the Victims' Families and Survivors Committee regarding the proposed objectives of the Memorial stated: "We began with a lot of anger and distrust, but we have progressed to working as a family unit."

Phillip Thompson said, "Through the Memorial Process, chaos was transformed into hope and unity."

The validation of the Task Force's efforts to promote healing was fully realized years later when I had lunch with one of the survivors who had been trapped in the Murrah Federal Building for several hours. After being rescued he went back into the building to assist in the rescue operation and witnessed many horrific images. As a result of his experience, he, along with many other survivors, had grave difficulty coping with post-traumatic stress. During our lunch he told me he would not be alive if we had not engaged him in the memorialization process.

Input from the General Public

Apart from the input of the victims' families and survivors, the Memorial Ideas Input Committee, led by Jimmy Goodman, Polly Nichols, and Sydney Dobson, sought from the public-at-large what the memorial objectives should be. Just as was the case with the victims' families and survivors, the question posed was, "What should a visitor to the completed memorial feel, learn, encounter, and experience?" Such effort was made through a distributed written survey, a survey on the Internet, small focus group discussions, and town hall meetings conducted in many locations and communities.

At the first meeting of the Memorial Ideas Input Committee one of the victim's family members vented anger about volunteers being involved in the memorial planning and the solicitation of input from the public-at-large. She believed that someone who had not experienced the murder of a family member could not possibly comprehend the pain. Understandably, such raw emotions caused a few volunteers to withdraw from the Memorial Task Force during the early stages of the process.

Beverly Rankin, a survivor and volunteer at the Oklahoma City National Memorial & Museum, was one of the many individuals who made the Memorial and Museum a reality.

At the conclusion of the eight-month effort of the Memorial Ideas Input Committee, a Final Report on the public-at-large input on the objectives of the memorial was submitted for review in preparation of a mission statement. The survey results of the public-at-large mirrored almost identically the survey results from the victims' families and survivors.

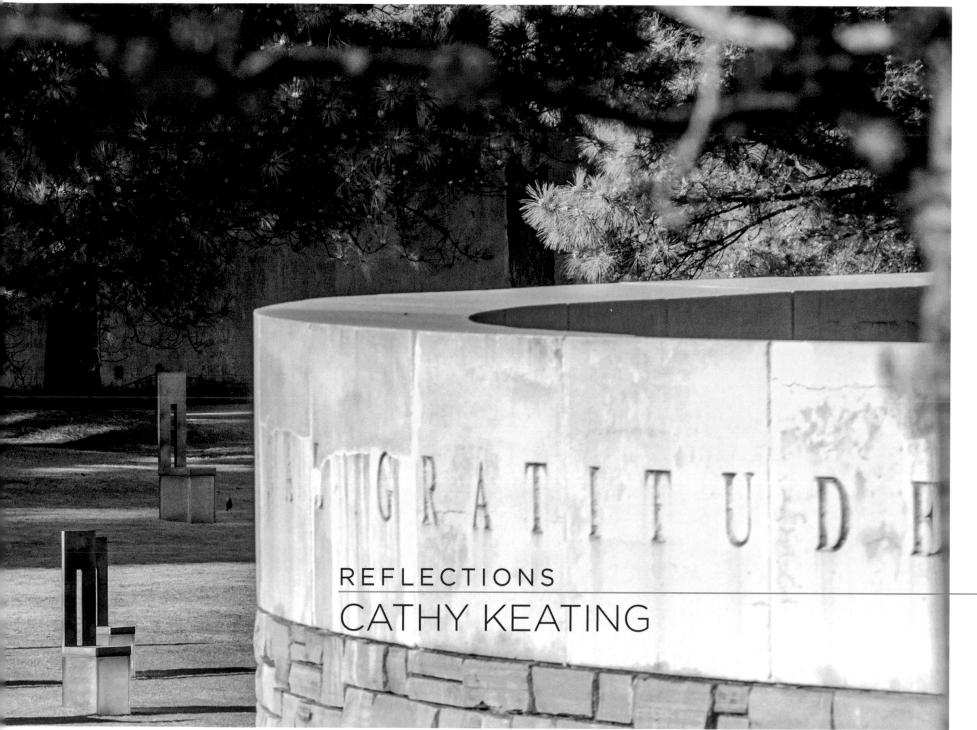

REFLECTIONS
CATHY KEATING

REFLECTIONS ON MEMORIAL PLANNING

Cathy Keating
FIRST LADY OF OKLAHOMA, 1995-2003

Looking back, a fateful phone call to a "yet unmet" community leader, Bob Johnson, proved to be inordinately valuable to the success of the Memorial and Museum. There simply are not enough words to illustrate his extraordinary leadership throughout creation of The Oklahoma City National Memorial & Museum. Early on he formed a strong working partnership with Kari Watkins, whose leadership, vision, and passion have also been beyond measure. Together their efforts have been instrumental in navigating the unchartered waters of building a Memorial and Museum on the heels of a tragedy all the while "Thinking Forward." With hundreds of people's help they have ensured that the messages of the Oklahoma City National Memorial & Museum will have relevance for generations to come. Thank You!

REFLECTIONS
PHILLIP THOMPSON

REFLECTIONS ON THE EXPERIENCE
OF VICTIMS' FAMILY MEMBERS

Phillip Thompson
CO-CHAIRMAN OF THE VICTIMS' FAMILIES AND
SURVIVORS LIAISON COMMITTEE OF THE MEMORIAL TASK FORCE

Early the morning of May 23, 1995, our family stood with Oklahoma City Mayor Ron Norick in an open window across the street and high above the bombed-out shell of the Alfred P. Murrah Federal Building. With loud detonation, the building imploded into a large pile of concrete and debris. It was a startling and violent reminder of the impact of the bombing. As we were about to depart, we asked "What now?" For three of the victims' families, we would have to continue to wait. It would be another six days of digging before the bodies of Christy Rosas, Alvin Justes, and Virginia Thompson, our mother, would be recovered.

Family members were facing sorrow and loss by lives cut short through an act of cowardice and cruelty. The disregard for human life added to overwhelming feeling of confusion, distrust, injustice, and helplessness. The Memorial Task Force Victims' Families and Survivors Liaison Committee meetings gave us an opportunity to share our thoughts and feelings. I am still humbled by the courage of the hundreds of victims' family members to participate in this challenging process, while dealing with their very personal grief and pain. The open and collaborative memorial process gave us hope. Hope is very powerful when you are hurting.

We will be forever grateful to the countless community, state, and national leaders. Without their compassionate leadership, the Oklahoma City National Memorial & Museum would have never been built. We are also eternally grateful to the women and men who continue to manage, maintain and advocate for the Memorial and the Museum. Their work ensures the victims' and survivors' stories will continue to be told. We will "Never Forget!"

CHAPTER 6

Design Selection Methodolgy

Before proceeding to develop a mission statement, the fulfillment of which would guide the Memorial design selection, a methodology was developed by which such design would be discovered. In the first meeting with victims' families and survivors they were promised they would have an opportunity to be involved in all aspects of the memorial process, including physical design selection.

In November, 1995, Paul Spreiregen, the design competition advisor for the Vietnam Veterans Memorial in Washington, D.C., was contacted. The Task Force leadership believed he would enhance the credibility of the process in the international design community. When I met with him in Washington, D.C., I explained that the design selection would be unlike any he had likely experienced as those closest to the tragedy would be involved in design selection. He believed he could work within our process structure.

However, he emphasized that in order to solicit design proposals from the very best national and international designers it would be important to balance the commitment to family members and survivors with a selection committee whose members were, at least in significant part, highly respected design professionals.

In a November 30, 1995, letter to Spreiregen, authorizing him to proceed with the preparation of a design competition operational plan, we stated:

"As we discussed in Washington . . . one of the early issues to be visited should be the structure and composition of the evaluation panel and selection committee. In particular, we believe it is critical that we assure the representation of the victims' families and survivors in such selection process."

In a later telephone conversation, we reiterated the foregoing, and he replied that he understood our need and that the desired representation would be a part of the plan presented to us.

Because of the efforts to emphasize the importance of community participation in every stage of the design selection process, the Task Force leadership was surprised by a telephone conversation on January 9, 1996, in which Spreiregen advised the Design Solicitation Committee that the design selection should be made by an all-professional jury. Following Spreiregen's arrival in Oklahoma City on the following day, Bill Cleary, Rowland Denman, Jimmy Goodman, and I met with him. After several hours, a resolution was agreed upon and approved by the Task Force Coordinating Committee at a meeting later that afternoon. The resolution provided that:

> Because the response to the bombing reflected that the tragedy had touched hearts worldwide, the design would be selected by an open

international design competition rather than a national competition as Mr. Spreiregen recommended. Secondly, we decided that the design selection process should have two phases.

Phase One would consist of a nine-member Evaluation Panel that would be charged with selecting five finalist designs. Such Evaluation Panel would be comprised of six internationally respected design professionals and three representatives of victims' families and survivors. All members of the Evaluation Panel would be appointed by the Mayor of Oklahoma City after receipt of a recommendation from the Memorial Task Force.

Phase Two would consist of a fifteen-member Selection Committee that would be charged with selecting the Memorial design from the five finalist designs after such designs were refined and three-dimensional models were submitted. Such Selection Committee would be comprised of eight representatives of victims' families and survivors, four internationally respected design professionals, and three community leaders. All members of the Selection Committee would be appointed by the Mayor of Oklahoma City after receipt of a recommendation from the Memorial Task Force.

Following receipt of the refined finalist designs and three-dimensional models, the Evaluation Panel would review such designs to assure the Selection Committee that the integrity of the original designs had been maintained, and the victims' families and survivors would be invited to view such designs and leave comment cards on each of the finalist designs.

Upon completion of the review of the completed designs by the Evaluation Panel and victims' families and survivors, the Selection Committee would convene and select the design for the Memorial.

That evening, Spreiregen attended a victims' families and survivors meeting for the purpose of presenting the design selection process. After the meeting, and witnessing the outpouring of strong emotions, he stated he had further reflected on the compromise approach and believed only an all-professional jury making the selection would be manageable. He also stated that if the Task Force proceeded as planned with victims' family members and survivors involved in the design selection, we would not have credibility with the design community and very few designs would be received. At a meeting before his departure we told him that, although we respected his opinion and believed in his capability, his philosophy did not match our process. Spreiregen was surprised that we would not negotiate the difference in beliefs. We responded that the Task Force simply would not negotiate issues that would impugn the integrity of our memorialization process.

Within a week of Spreiregen's return to Washington, D.C., the Task Force received a letter in which he stated that he would be agreeable to committing to the design selection process developed on January 10. However, in our opinion, his comments in that letter and his previous statements that such design selection structure was not manageable reflected that it would be very difficult for him to fully support our selection process.

On January 18, a letter of response to Spreiregen stated:

"When the Task Force was appointed by Mayor Norick, we stated that the hallmarks of our memorialization process would be listening and public participation. We also stated that the healing effect and community ownership of the memorial developed with thorough and meaningful participation by those directly affected was equally as important as the end physical result. Such

philosophy is set forth in the July 26, 1995 Minutes of the Orientation Meeting of the Task Force, a copy of which was given to you during our November 16 meeting in Washington. I also attempted during such meeting to stress that the design selection process must be consistent with such thesis, i.e. every aspect of such process must be inclusive of public participation.

"After considerable thought and painful deliberations, we have concluded that while you have an admirable reputation as a design competition adviser, we do not universally share the same philosophical approach to the design selection process as it relates to community involvement. This decision has been a very difficult one for all concerned, particularly in view of the acknowledged fact that none of us can say with certainty that our judgment is always correct. We are simply attempting to exercise our best collective judgment to fulfill our fiduciary obligations to the public we are serving."

Spreiregen acknowledged the detailed explanation of our views and our obligations to victims' families and survivors. He suggested that in lieu of an open competition we should have an invited competition consisting of six design firms to develop schematic designs, one of which firms would be selected to develop the physical design of the memorial. He stated, "I'm afraid I see a rather unhappy course for the effort if you do an open competition."

When it was announced at the next meeting of victims' family members and survivors that we would be seeking a different design competition advisor in order to uphold the commitment to involve them in design selection, they responded with a standing ovation. That evening, six months

into the memorial process, was a defining moment when widespread trust was first established.

Phillip Thompson, co-chair of the Victims' Families and Survivors Liaison Committee, said, "Prior to that evening, Bob had some trust among the families and survivors, but he was viewed as part of the City establishment. On the evening of his announcement about dismissing Spreiregen, it was a defining moment in gathering the commitment from the families and survivors that Bob was our leader."

Trust must be earned, and it does not happen quickly in circumstances involving elevated raw emotions. Patience, effective listening, remaining consistent with our original July 26, 1995, memorialization plan, and keeping our word at every step of the planning process ultimately established trust.

CHAPTER 7

Memorial
Mission
Statement

Following the conclusion of a very intensive, deliberate, and inclusive listening process to gather input on the objectives of the Memorial from victims' families, survivors, first responders, and the general public, a 13-member Mission Statement Drafting Committee was appointed. The members were Beth Shortt, executive director of Leadership Oklahoma City who served as facilitator; Yvonne Maloan, Association of Central Oklahoma Governments who served as recorder; survivors Richard Williams and Priscilla Salyers; victim's family members and co-chairs of Victims' Families and Survivors Liaison Committee Phillip Thompson and Kathleen Treanor; victim's family member John Cole; Cheryl Vaught, attorney and co-chair of Victims' Families and Survivors Liaison Committee; Jimmy Goodman, attorney and co-chair of Memorial Ideas Input Committee; Sydney Dobson, executive director, Oklahoma City Beautiful and co-chair of Memorial Ideas Input

Committee; John Kennedy, real estate investor and member of Memorial Ideas Input Committee; Tim O'Connor, executive director, Catholic Charities of Oklahoma City and co-chair of Victims' Families and Survivors Liaison Committee; and Kim Jones-Shelton, co-chair of Victims' Families and Survivors Liaison Committee.

The basic charge to the Drafting Committee was to carefully craft a mission statement that would propel the design selection process to fulfill the consensus memorial objectives reflected in the Victims' Families and Survivors and Public-at-Large Final Reports.

An initial draft of the Mission Statement was presented to the Victims' Families and Survivors group for comments. Next, the large diverse Advisory Committee of the Memorial Task Force gathered on March 12, 1996, for a presentation of the initial draft. At such meetings the members of the Mission Statement Drafting Committee presented their respective views of the draft. After the Drafting Committee presentation, those in attendance broke out into round table discussion groups. A recorder at each table presented all comments and suggestions to the Drafting Committee for consideration.

On March 25, 1996, the second draft of the Mission Statement was presented to the Victims' Families and Survivors group. This group of shocked and grieving individuals, who had struggled mightily during the earlier memorial meetings, approved the Mission Statement without any dissenting votes. That moment reaffirmed that healing had occurred to some degree and that trust had been established. Unity came with extreme difficulty, but it arrived.

The following day the second draft was presented to the large diverse Advisory Committee of the Memorial Task Force in a meeting at St. Luke's United Methodist Church.

The Mission Statement Drafting Committee once again presented the draft, followed by each member describing the committee's discussion of all comments and questions that had been posed by members of the Victims' Families and Survivors group and the Advisory Committee of the Memorial Task Force. Everyone in the large crowded room listened intently. No questions or comments were made. After a few moments of silence, a motion was made to approve the revised draft of the Mission Statement as presented.

At that meeting, eight months to the date of the Orientation Meeting of the Memorial Task Force, the most important milestone of the memorialization process occurred when the Mission Statement, containing the objectives of the Memorial, was approved by unanimous vote of the large, diverse Advisory Committee of the Memorial Task Force. When that motion was approved without any dissenting vote, a groundswell of emotions filled the room with an incredible sense of unity. It was at that moment that everyone knew an appropriate memorial could be created that would be supported by a community-wide sense of ownership.

The carefully crafted preamble of the Mission Statement can be found on the exterior of the "Gates of Time" at the Oklahoma City National Memorial & Museum. It reads:

We come here to remember.

Those who were killed, those who survived and those changed forever.

May all who leave here know the impact of violence.

May this memorial offer comfort, strength, peace, hope and serenity.

It should be noted that the second line of the preamble was intended by the Mission Statement Drafting Committee to be as inclusive as the

memorialization process had been. It also is important to note that the Mission Statement recites that: "a solid effort was made to avoid addressing what the Memorial should look like, feeling deeply that talented designers were better qualified to suggest meaningful ways to evoke feelings and create memorable experiences."

The Mission Statement continues to be our cornerstone document. When unsure about a particular issue, the proper resolution always can be found in our Mission Statement.

Presentation of the Memorial Mission Statement to President Bill Clinton on April 5, 1996, in Oklahoma City. *Courtesy the White House.*

CHAPTER 8

Survivor Tree

When the bomb exploded on April 19, 1995, it engulfed in flames many of the vehicles in the parking lot located north and across the street from the Murrah Federal Building. Located in that parking lot, in the midst of the burning vehicles, was a 70+ year-old American Elm. Its bark, limbs, and leaves were singed by the blast, but it did not wither. Further damage occurred when some of the tree's limbs were broken by investigators removing evidence from the tree.

Miraculously, the tree survived. This American Elm, known as the "Survivor Tree," has become an iconic symbol of the Oklahoma City National Memorial & Museum. Reflective of the community's reaction to the bombing, it bent but did not break. It remains a symbol of strength, resilience, and hope for humankind.

At the request of the victims' families and survivors, the Advisory Committee of the Memorial Task Force adopted a resolution on

The Survivor Tree, in the parking lot to the north of the Alfred P. Murrah Federal Building, as it looked on April 19, 1995— burnt and filled with debris. *Courtesy City of Oklahoma City.*

January 16, 1996, requiring one of the components of the Memorial to be the Survivor Tree.

Soon after the resolution was adopted, Mark Bays, an urban forester with the Oklahoma Department of Agriculture, Food and Forestry, was contacted to help preserve the tree. He developed a plan, took it on as his personal project, and has continued oversight and care of the tree along with the Memorial Foundation's facilities staff. Owners of landscape nurseries, arborists, urban foresters, and expert horticulturists from across our state and nation also have come together to preserve this iconic piece of history.

Each year, the Memorial's grounds crew collects seeds from the Survivor Tree for planting. Today, thousands of Survivor Tree are growing all over the United States, including one on the White House lawn in Washington, D.C.

Sarah Ferguson, Duchess of York, visited the site during construction of the Memorial. With her hand on the Survivor Tree, she looked up and said, "This symbolizes so much. I've never been more honored than being here today and to be standing by this tree. Oklahoma is giving such an example to the world."

The Mission Statement required that the Memorial should "speak of the spirituality of the community and the nation that was so evident in the wake of the attack." Accordingly, the message to visitors on the interior of the Survivor Tree promontory wall reads: "The spirit of this city and this nation will not be defeated. Our deeply rooted faith sustains us."

Just as this deeply rooted tree survived, the deeply rooted faith grounded in many religions sustained us during the aftermath of the bombing.

Today the iconic Survivor Tree is one of the prominent features of the Oklahoma City National Memorial & Museum.

CHAPTER 9

Avoiding Political & Non-Political Controversy

Memorialization processes often become controversial due to political intervention. However, through the efforts of Tom McDaniel, Zach Taylor, Bud Welch, whose daughter Julie Marie Welch was killed in the bombing, and other members of the Government Liaison Committee, the memorial process was depoliticized in 1996 by negotiating and signing an unprecedented Intergovernmental Letter of Understanding.

The Intergovernmental Letter of Understanding, dated October 28, 1996, was endorsed by President Bill Clinton and signed by federal, state, county, and city executive and legislative leaders.

In his endorsement, President Clinton stated:

"It has been almost two years since the bombing of the Alfred P. Murrah Federal Building in Oklahoma City, but the memory of that terrible day is still fresh in the minds and hearts of all Americans.

"We learned a lot about ourselves that day. We recognized that we are a family, that a cowardly terrorist attack on one American is an attack on us all. We were reminded that despite our differences in outlook, background and politics, Americans still unite to help one another when tragedy strikes. And in the wake of that tragedy, we realized anew that the human spirit, blessed by hope and strengthened by determination, can rise above any adversity.

"Now we have an opportunity to unite again around citizens of Oklahoma City. I ask all Americans to join me in supporting the effort to establish a memorial on the site of the bombing. Together, let us transform that scarred square of earth into a fitting tribute to those who died, to those who survived, and to those whose lives have been changed forever by this devastating event. By honoring them, we can help to bring healing and create hope for a brighter, more secure future."

The unprecedented signing of the Intergovernmental Letter of Understanding depoliticized the memorial process and assured cooperation of the City, State and Federal governments. *Courtesy City of Oklahoma City.*

The signatories to the Intergovernmental Letter of Understanding were:

Bob Johnson, Chairman of the Oklahoma City Memorial Foundation

Karen L. Luke, Vice Chairman of the Memorial Task Force

Ronald J. Norick, Mayor of The City of Oklahoma City

Frosty Peak, Councilmember, Ward One, The City of Oklahoma City Council

Mark Schwartz, Councilmember, Ward Two, The City of Oklahoma City Council

Jack W. Cornett, Councilmember, Ward Three, The City of Oklahoma City Council

Frances Lowrey, Councilmember, Ward Four, The City of Oklahoma City Council

Jerry W. Foshee, Councilmember, Ward Five, The City of Oklahoma City Council

Ann Simank, Councilmember, Ward Six, The City of Oklahoma City Council

Willa D. Johnson, Councilmember, Ward Seven, The City of Oklahoma City Council

Guy H. Liebmann, Councilmember, Ward Eight, The City of Oklahoma City Council

Zach D. Taylor, Executive Director, Association of Central Oklahoma Governments

Stuart E. Earnest, Sr., Commissioner, District Three, Oklahoma County

Frank Keating, Governor of the State of Oklahoma

Mary Fallin, Lieutenant Governor of the State of Oklahoma

Keith Leftwich, President Pro Tempore of the Oklahoma Senate

Debbie Blackburn, Oklahoma House of Representatives

Don Nickles, United States Senator from the State of Oklahoma

James Inhofe, United States Senator from the State of Oklahoma

Steve Largent, United States Representative from the State of Oklahoma

Tom Coburn, United States Representative from the State of Oklahoma

Bill Brewster, United States Representative from the State of Oklahoma

J.C. Watts, United States Representative from the State of Oklahoma

Ernest Istook, United States Representative from the State of Oklahoma

Frank Lucas, United States Representative from the State of Oklahoma

Leighton Waters, Acting Regional Administrator, U.S. Government–General Services Administration

Buddy Young, Regional Director, U.S. Government–Federal Emergency Management Agency

All signatories, on behalf of themselves and their organizations, recognized that all planning activities relating to the Memorial would be conducted by the Oklahoma City Memorial Foundation, and agreed to:

1. Remain faithful to the ideal that the development of the Memorial shall be respectful, non-political and timely.

2. Recognize, respect and support the autonomy of the Task Force and the Foundation as non-profit, non-political organizations dedicated to creating and overseeing a Memorial development process that is sensitive, inclusive, collaborative, thorough and productive.

3. Recognize and respect the special role the local community has as the site of the 1995 bombing and as the home of the Memorial. While the crime has national and international implications, victims' families, survivors

and residents of Central Oklahoma bore the brunt of the impact and rightly shall play a leadership role in planning and establishing a lasting Memorial.

4. Recognize that among the range of opinions, ideas and priorities expressed in the information-gathering phase of the Memorial development process, those expressed by victims' families and survivors shall be given the greatest weight and highest degree of respect.

5. Recognize and abide by the Task Force Mission Statement adopted by the Advisory Committee of the Task Force on March 26, 1996.

6. Recognize as being final the design selection made pursuant to the design selection methodology adopted by the Task Force and an International Design Competition administered by the Task Force.

7. Recognize, respect and facilitate a Memorial development timeline to be outlined by the Task Force.

8. Recognize the importance of working together to accommodate the Memorial design selected pursuant to the International Design Competition. For instance, should the selected design call for using a portion of the Murrah Building site, its plaza and/or acquiring a parcel of land near the site of the former Murrah Building, all participants agree to cooperate in making such efforts possible.

9. Recognize the importance of administering and maintaining the Memorial and surrounding sites with dignity and honor befitting the memories of those killed or injured in the blast. Signatories of this Letter of Understanding agree to cooperate with one another to ensure that such ongoing administration and maintenance of the Memorial is consistent, efficient and respectful.

10. Recognize that governmental and private financial assistance may be required to support the planning, design, construction and operation of the Memorial.

11. Recognize the work of the Task Force and Foundation as a unified effort to establish one Memorial commemorating the April 19, 1995, bombing and commit not to develop or take part in developing competing Memorial proposals without the prior written consent of the Foundation.

12. Pursue Congressional Authorization for the completed Memorial Complex to be designated a National Monument to be operated and maintained by the National Park Service.

In addition to the mutual commitments, each of the signatories made certain specific commitments. All signatories honored the Intergovernmental Letter of Understanding. As a result, there was no encounter of any politically-based controversy.

The execution of the Intergovernmental Letter of Understanding sent yet another message that the terrorists failed to divide us. It reinforced that we were united in one vision to create a memorial that would attest to their failure.

A concerted effort also was made to avoid non-political controversy by being inclusive. People were not only allowed to talk; they were assured they were being heard. The necessary patience was exercised to develop trust and build a consensus on every major decision.

The September 25, 1998, edition of *The Wall Street Journal* contained an article that focused on controversy caused by commemoration. In the article, the Oklahoma City National Memorial was cited as the single exception to the general rule that the creation of a memorial breeds controversy. In his book *The Unfinished Bombing: Oklahoma City in American Memory,* Edward T. Linenthal said the Memorial was the exception because "The decision process was intentionally part of the therapeutic process." The Task Force Leadership also believed the Memorial became the exception because the same kindness that characterized the public response to the bombing became an integral part of the memorialization process.

"Kindness is the language the blind can see and the deaf can hear."

MARK TWAIN

CHAPTER 10

Assembling the Memorial and Museum Site

Before we could proceed with selection of a design of the Memorial, we first had to assemble the memorial site, which was defined in the Mission Statement as consisting of the Murrah Federal Building block, the south half of the Journal Record Building block, including the Oklahoma Water Resources Building, the Athenian Building, five other parcels, and the segment of Fifth Street located between such two blocks.

Thanks to the efforts and the support of Mayor Norick and the Oklahoma City Council, the south half of the Journal Record Building block (consisting of seven different properties) was acquired by the Memorial Foundation. The City of Oklahoma City also assisted in vacating the alley between the south half of the Journal Record Building block and the Journal Record Building.

The Memorial Foundation also worked with the City of Oklahoma City to arrange for the purchase of the Journal Record Building by the Oklahoma

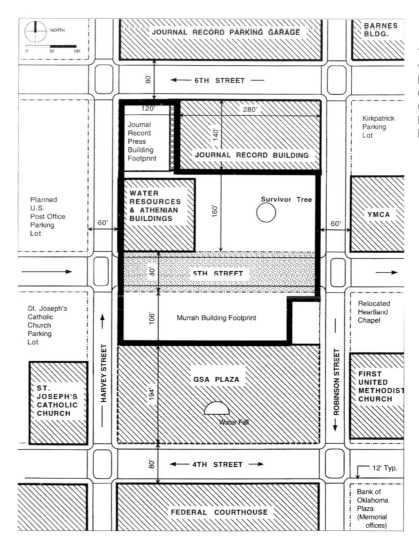

The site that would become home to the Oklahoma City National Memorial & Museum.

91

City Industrial and Cultural Facilities Trust, and, in turn, a portion of the building was purchased by the Memorial Foundation for the Museum. Lots west of the Journal Record Building were purchased for the "Children's Area" of the Memorial. A parcel on the east side of the Journal Record Building also was purchased by the Memorial Foundation for the designated area for anyone desiring to exercise their First Amendment freedom of speech rights. The Memorial Foundation is grateful to Dan Hogan and his family, who owned the Journal Record Building at the time of the bombing, the City of Oklahoma City, and the Trustees of the Oklahoma City Industrial and Cultural Facilities Trust for these arrangements. The efforts made by John Michael Williams, counsel for the Oklahoma City Industrial and Cultural Facilities Trust, also are appreciated for working with the Memorial Foundation in the structuring of the transactions.

In addition to acquisition of the several properties mentioned above, Fifth Street needed to be permanently closed, the Murrah Federal Building site needed to be acquired from the U.S. General Services Administration (GSA), and a perpetual easement from GSA covering the Murrah Federal Building Plaza located south of the former Murrah Federal Building had to be received. Those efforts proved to be difficult.

Closing of Fifth Street

Dialogue was initiated regarding the closing of Fifth Street with the City Manager of Oklahoma City in February 1996, knowing that the final decision regarding such matter would rest with the City Council of Oklahoma City.

We were aware that not only were there elevated raw emotions among the victims' families and survivors, but there also was anger among the many business and property owners that had been adversely impacted by the bombing, including those that relied on Fifth Street for their access and for access by their customers and clients. After the Mission Statement was adopted, a Fifth Street Sub-Committee composed of volunteers and the surrounding property and business owners, including people on both sides of the street closure issue, was formed. The Sub-Committee was co-chaired by Rowland Denman, Kenny Walker, who had a business in the immediate area, and Bud Welch, whose daughter had died in the bombing. In addition to the meetings of the Sub-Committee, in which a viable solution for everyone was sought, a door-to-door campaign was launched to visit everyone on Fourth, Fifth and Sixth streets who might view the closing of Fifth Street as averse to them. It was important for everyone to understand that the closing of that one block of Fifth Street was essential to the fulfillment of the consensus views reflected by the Mission Statement, including the desired serenity of the Memorial.

The first step in the process with the City of Oklahoma City was a study and recommendation by the Oklahoma City Traffic Commission. In its report on July 15, 1996, the Traffic Commission staff report stated that the vitality of the area was dependent upon adequate vehicle and pedestrian circulation and that the need to move motorists toward the interstate highway and provide adequate circulation throughout the central business district was critical to the future economic success of Oklahoma City and the downtown area. The Traffic Commission staff recommended opening Fifth Street and reducing it to two lanes rather than permanently closing it. At the meeting of the Traffic Commission on August 1, 1996, the vote was evenly split for and against closure.

Following the Traffic Commission vote, the Oklahoma City Planning Commission considered the request on September 12, 1996, and voted five to three in favor of permanently closing Fifth Street.

In preparation for the City Council meeting, at which the final decision on Fifth Street would be made, individual meetings were had with each of the members of the City Council. However, given the split vote of the Traffic Commission, the slim majority vote of the Oklahoma City Planning Commission, and the non-committal responses we had received from some City Council members, the outcome was unknown.

On October 22, 1996, in fulfillment of the obligations contained in the Intergovernmental Letter of Understanding, the City Council of Oklahoma City unanimously approved permanently closing Fifth Street as requested. Those visiting the Memorial can readily understand why the City Council's vote on that day was a pivotal moment in the history of the Memorial. After the Council meeting, Bud Welch said, "I'm in tears of joy that we had a nine-nothing vote. It's really important that this community be completely unified." I believe this comment illustrates that the chaos in the early meetings of the victims' families and survivors had been transformed into a focus on unity.

Murrah Building Footprint and Plaza

The memorial site was to include both the footprint of the former Murrah Federal Building and also the plaza located above the parking garage and south of the footprint. The Intergovernmental Letter of Understanding provided that all parties signatory, including GSA, agreed to: (a) Recognize and abide by the Task Force Mission Statement adopted by the Advisory Committee of the Task Force on March 26, 1996, and (b) Recognize the importance of working together to accommodate the Memorial design selected pursuant the International Design Competition. For instance, should the selected design call for using a portion of the Murrah Building site, its plaza and/or acquiring a parcel of land near the site of the former Murrah Building, all participants agree to cooperate in making such efforts possible.

In addition to the covenants made by all parties to the Intergovernmental Letter of Understanding, GSA agreed that "upon receiving from the Foundation notification that (1) the Foundation has selected the final Memorial design and (2) the Foundation is prepared to commence construction of the Memorial, GSA shall deliver to whomever is ultimately going to maintain the property the deed to the land on which the footprint of the Murrah Federal Building is located" and GSA will "enter into a separate agreement with the Foundation providing for the use of the Murrah Federal Building Block Plaza as a part of the Memorial complex." In addition, the Oklahoma City National Memorial Act of 1997 enacted by Congress provided for the transfer of the Murrah Federal Building footprint land for inclusion in the Memorial.

Based on GSA's covenants in the Intergovernmental Letter of Understanding and the Congressional Act, one would think that the process of obtaining a deed to the parcel of land on which the Murrah Federal Building was located and obtaining a perpetual easement for Memorial visitors across the elevated Murrah Federal Building Plaza south of the planned Memorial would have been relatively easy, but it was not.

When GSA was contacted to set the wheels in motion to obtain the deed and easement, the Memorial Foundation was referred to a gentleman outside of Oklahoma who, in a word, was difficult. His position was that if a deed to the Murrah Federal Building footprint were granted by GSA it would include a stipulation that if GSA subsequently determined the land was needed for some other federal purpose, the property would be conveyed back to GSA. After several attempts at reasoning with the gentleman and reiterating the GSA covenants contained in the Intergovernmental Letter of Understanding and the provisions of the Congressional legislation, relief from his superiors was the only alternative. After several months of frustration, the deed covering the Murrah Federal Building footprint and the perpetual access easement covering the adjoining plaza were received. Other than the deed and easement challenge, GSA was helpful throughout the memorial journey.

CHAPTER 11

International Design Competition

In November of 1996, after assembling the memorial site, an open international design competition was launched to discover a design for the Memorial that would fulfill the requirements of the Mission Statement. Such process was carried out under the careful guidance of Jackie Jones and Beth Tolbert, co-chairs of the Design Solicitation Committee.

The Washington Post stated that the initial design competition advisor, Paul Spreiregen, saw the inclusion of victims' families and survivors in the selection process as a "recipe for disaster." He was quoted as saying, "The entries have to be evaluated by a group of designers who are eminently respected or you are not going to draw from the field you want. It would be a mess and not result in quality. I couldn't in good conscience accept the way they wanted it done."

Although the Task Force continued to have respect for Spreiregen, his philosophy regarding the composition of the selection committee and structure of the selection process did not support the commitment to involve victims' family members and survivors in every aspect of the memorial process. One of the hallmarks of the memorialization process was that the Task Force honored its word every step of the way.

The Task Force engaged a trio of capable design competition consultants—Paul Morris and Don Stastny from Portland, Oregon and Helene Fried from San Francisco, California. Such engagement was made only after making certain they agreed that victims' families and survivors would be involved in the selection of the Memorial design. Their contacts with design professionals around the world and their assistance in refining our design competition were invaluable.

To the knowledge of the Task Force leadership, this was the most widely participated open international design competition held to

The 624 designs for the Oklahoma City National Memorial were displayed in a building in downtown Oklahoma City for public viewing. People stood in long lines awaiting an opportunity to catch a glimpse of "remembrance" and "hope" that the designs portrayed.

date. There were 624 high quality design entries received from all 50 states, in addition to the Commonwealth of Puerto Rico and 23 foreign countries, including Australia, Bahamas, Belgium, Bolivia, Brazil, Canada, Costa Rica, Denmark,

England, France, Germany, Guam, Guatemala, India, Israel, Italy, Japan, the Netherlands, Norway, Mexico, Singapore, Slovenia, and Switzerland. The Design Selection Committee was impressed by the meaningful thought that had been integrated into each of the designs.

Some of the participants said they entered the competition as a means of dealing with their feelings about what happened in Oklahoma City. One participant stated:

"For me, an entry in the design competition was an effort to cope with the tragedy. Through it all, one thing was clear. The people of Oklahoma City were doing everything they could to heal, to move on. Not forgetting the losses they suffered, but also not willing to allow those losses to control their lives. Their scars were fresh, but that was not what you saw, not what you heard when you talked to them. Rather, there was hope and determination, and a kind of grace. The people of Oklahoma City taught me much and gave me a kind of hope that all of us need."

A nine-member Evaluation Panel had the responsibility of selecting five finalist designs. The panel consisted of six internationally eminent design professionals, and three representatives of the victims' families and survivors. Serving on the panel were Jaune Quick-To-See Smith, an artist from New Mexico who had lectured internationally at more than 100 universities and been a tireless advocate of a sense of community; Adèle Naudé Santos, an architect and urban designer from Philadelphia, Pennsylvania who was raised in South Africa and educated in London, winner of six international design competitions and published work in journals worldwide, and an academic career that included professorships within the graduate programs of Harvard, Rice, and the University of Pennsylvania; Bill Moggridge, a Senior Fellow of the Royal College of Arts, a Trustee of the Design Museum in London, and a lecturer at Stanford University; and Richard Haag, a practicing and teaching landscape architect from Seattle, Washington who was educated at Harvard and the only person to twice receive the American Society of Landscape Architects President's Award for Design Excellence.

Other members included Michaele Pride-Wells, an architect from Kentucky who had received awards for design, planning, and community advocacy from the Los Angeles Cultural Affairs Commission, the National Organization of Minority Architects, the American Planning Association, and the American Institute of Architects; Robert Campbell, a writer and architect from Cambridge, Massachusetts, architecture critic of *The Boston Globe*, where he received the 1996 Pulitzer Prize for Distinguished Criticism, a Fellow of the American

Members of the Evaluation Panel and staff, from left, seated, Don Stastny and Helene Fried, middle row, Adèle Santos, Polly Nichols, Michaele Pride-Wells, and Yvonne Maloan, and, standing, Richard Williams, Toby Thompson, Bill Moggridge, Robert Campbell, Jaune Quick-to-See Smith, and Richard Haag.

Academy in Rome, the American Institute of Architects, and the American Academy of Arts and Sciences, and an advisor to the National Endowment for the Arts Mayors Institute for City Design; Polly Nichols, executive director of the Oklahoma Foundation for Excellence and a survivor of the bombing who suffered life threatening injuries in the Journal Record Building and whose cousin, Doris "Adele" Higginbottom, died in the bombing; Richard Williams, a survivor of the bombing and assistant building manager for the Murrah Federal Building; and Toby Thompson, whose brother, Michael Thompson, was killed in the bombing, a local consultant for the arts and non-profit communities in Oklahoma City, and co-chair of the Victims' Families and Survivors Liaison Committee.

The five finalist designs were announced on April 19, 1997, the second anniversary of the bombing.

Members of the Evaluation Panel and staff reviewing designs for the Oklahoma City National Memorial.

Members of the Evaluation Panel and staff reviewing the five designs selected as finalists. From left, Toby Thompson, JoAnn Pearce, Jaune Quick-to-See Smith, Robert Campbell, Kari Watkins, Richard Williams, Michaele Pride-Wells, and Bill Moggridge. Holding the designs for review are, from left, Sydney Dobson, Yvonne Maloan, Beth Tolbert, and Helene Fried.

Members of the Evaluation Panel and staff reviewing designs for the Oklahoma City National Memorial from left, standing, Sydney Dobson, Cheryl Vaught, Kari Watkins, Bob Johnson (seated), Beth Tolbert, and JoAnn Pearce. Seated, Polly Nichols, Richard Williams, Robert Campbell, Richard Haag, Bill Moggridge, Jaune Quick-to-See Smith, Toby Thompson, Michaele Pride-Wells, and Yvonne Maloan, and Helene Fried, standing right.

Models of the five finalist designs unanimously selected by the Evaluation Panel from the 624 submitted for the Oklahoma City National Memorial.

"OKLAHOMA CITY MEMORIAL"
 Hans Ekkchard-Butzer,
 Torrey Butzer, and Sven Berg
 Locus Bold Desaign
 Berlin, Germany

"OKLAHOMA CITY MEMORIAL"
 Hanno Weber and Kathleen Hess
 Hanno Weber & Associates
 Chicago, Illinois

**"THE LEANING WALL
 OF REMEMBRANCE
 AND REBIRTH"**
 Richard Scherr and
 James Rossant
 New York City, New York

"FOOTFALLS ECHO THE MEMORY"
Susan Herrington and Mark Stankard
Ames, Iowa

"CELEBRATION OF LIFE"
J. Kyle Casper and Brian Branstetter
Dallas, Texas

Members of the design Selection Committee and staff on the grounds for the Oklahoma City National Memorial. From left, kneeling, Bud Welch, Helene Fried, Dave Lopez, Laurie Beckelman, Don Stastny, and Crystal Radcliff. Second row, Ignacio Bunster-Ossa, Jeannine Gist, Cheryl Scroggins, Kimberly Ritchie, John Cole, Douglas Hollis, Tom Hall, Mayor Ron Norick, and Karen Luke, and, back row, Luke Corbett, Dr. Paul Heath, Calvin Moser, Phillip Thompson, Kari Watkins, Richard Williams, Lars Lerup, and Bob Johnson.

Members of the design Selection Committee and staff, from left, front row, Dr. Paul Heath, Don Stastny, Kimberly Ritchie, Helene Fried, Mayor Ron Norick, Laurie Beckelman, Cheryl Scroggins, Cheryl Vaught, and Crystal Radcliff, and, back row, Jeannine Gist, Dave Lopez, Bob Johnson, Jackie Jones, Karen Luke, Tom Hall, Kari Watkins, Ignacio Bunster-Ossa, John Cole, Bud Welch, Luke Corbett, Calvin Moser, Douglas Hollis, Phillip Thompson, Lars Lerup, Sydney Dobson, and Beth Tolbert.

After three-dimensional models of the five finalist designs were completed, a fifteen-member Selection Committee, consisting of a blend of victims' family members, survivors, design professionals, and community leaders, convened for the final selection.

The members of the Selection Committee were John Cole, whose godchildren, Aaron and Elijah Coverdale, died in the bombing; survivors Tom Hall, Dr. Paul Heath, Calvin Moser, and Kimberly Ritchie; Jeannine Gist, whose youngest daughter, Karen Gist Carr, died in the bombing; Cheryl Scroggins, whose husband, Lanny Scroggins, died in the bombing; Phillip Thompson, whose mother, Virginia Thompson, died in the bombing; Bud Welch, whose daughter, Julie Marie Welch, died in the bombing; Mayor Ron Norick; Luke Corbett, chairman and CEO of Kerr-McGee Corporation; Dave Lopez, president of Oklahoma Southwestern Bell; Laurie Beckelman, an internationally recognized advocate of significant monuments and historic landmarks; Ignacio Bunster-Ossa, an internationally respected urban designer and landscape architect; Lars Lerup, dean of the Rice School of Architecture; and Douglas Hollis, an internationally respected artist of public works.

The Selection Committee reviewed comment cards of victims' families and survivors that were completed during a two-day viewing period of the three-dimensional finalist designs. Also reviewed was the report on the finalist designs prepared by the Evaluation Panel.

The first vote of the Selection Committee was conducted by secret ballot, solely for the purpose of gauging the prospects of a consensus selection. The ballots revealed one design received the vote of every committee member—unanimous selection. My feeling after that vote was indescribable.

The recommendation of the Selection Committee was next presented to a joint meeting of the Memorial Foundation's Board of Directors and

Chairman Bob Johnson announces the winning design of the International Design Competition for the Oklahoma City National Memorial on July 1, 1997.

the Victims' Families and Survivors Committee. Members of both unanimously approved the design.

On July 1, 1997, three young architects, Hans Butzer, Torrey Butzer, and Sven Berg, who were practicing in Berlin, Germany, were introduced as the designers of the Oklahoma City National Memorial. The design has been featured in hundreds of publications around the world and received widespread international architectural acclaim. Hans Butzer became dean of the University of Oklahoma College of Architecture, and Hans and Torrey practice design and architecture in Oklahoma City.

Oklahoma Governor Frank Keating, Oklahoma First Lady Cathy Keating, Oklahoma City Mayor Ron Norick, and representatives of the Memorial Foundation were invited to the White House for a presentation of the Memorial design to President Clinton and other dignitaries on August 13, 1997. Preceding the design presentation ceremony, Governor Keating, Mayor Norick, and I had an

opportunity to spend time in the Oval Office with President Clinton. In his remarks at the April 23, 1995, Memorial Prayer Service in Oklahoma City, President Clinton stated, "America would stand with us for as many tomorrows as it takes." We thanked the President for having made that commitment, and he reaffirmed that such heartfelt promise remained important to him. I believe political considerations were set aside during the aftermath of the bombing and the memorialization process.

During the presentation ceremony in the White House, President Clinton said:

"I have been terrifically impressed by the design of this memorial. It is elegant. It is symbolic. It manages to focus on this act of unconscionable violence and still honor the valor of the people of the community and the lives of the victims in a setting of reflection and peace that should leave people, when they go through

The Memorial Design is presented to President Bill Clinton in a ceremony in the White House in August 1997. *Courtesy the White House.*

Attending the Oklahoma City National Memorial design presentation ceremony at the White House were from left to right: Cheryl Vaught, Kathleen Treanor, Kari Watkins, Torrey Butzer, Hans Butzer, Michael Treanor, Judy Kelley, Bob Johnson, Gennie Johnson, Toby Thompson, Bud Welch, George Hozendorf, Richard Williams, Polly Nichols, Phillip Thompson, and Brenda McDaniel. Not pictured are Frank and Cathy Keating, Ron Norick, Luke Corbett and Tom McDaniel.
Courtesy the White House.

it, feeling stronger rather than weaker. I have no doubt that the totally open and democratic nature of this process, the reaching out to the family members and the survivors every step of the way, was absolutely indispensable to the healing of the people who were affected by what happened. I also have no doubt that it gave you a better memorial—a more powerful, more profound, more lasting memory."

Reflective of the richness and international praise of the Oklahoma City National Memorial design is an article that appeared in the August 1, 2000, edition of *The Irish Times* a few months after the completion and dedication of the Memorial. The author, Fintan O'Toole, stated:

"Recently, I happened to be passing through Oklahoma City. What I saw was one of the most moving, dignified and beautiful responses to violence I have ever seen. It made me wonder why America can produce such a powerful and restrained memorial to those killed by a terrorist bomb when Ireland, which prides itself on its rich artistic and spiritual history, has managed nothing of the kind."

REFLECTIONS
HANS AND TORREY BUTZER

REFLECTIONS ON MEMORIAL DESIGN SELECTION

Hans and Torrey Butzer
CO-DESIGNERS OF
THE OKLAHOMA CITY NATIONAL MEMORIAL

The Oklahoma City National Memorial stands out from the architects' perspective because of a community's commitment to the values of inclusion, process, and empathy. The Memorial Foundation insisted family members and survivors, along with other non-professionals, should work side-by-side with design professionals to select the shortlist of designs and eventually the selected design. The original competition advisor hired by the Memorial Foundation conversely believed only design professionals and advocates should help select the design. Ultimately, the competition jury members, comprised of design professionals and those most closely affected by the bombing, taught one another about their respective experiences and insights and, together, made good decisions for posterity. This new format for sharing important design decisions has become a template for subsequent memorial competitions in the United States, among them the September 11 Memorial at Shanksville, Pennsylvania, the Texas A&M Bonfire Memorial, and most recently the National Pulse Memorial & Museum.

The Mission Statement developed by family members, survivors, and community leaders became a visionary framework for the memorial and its creation. It offered a reference point that could be shared by all. The Mission Statement secured a transition plan that started with victims' family members and survivors but finished with architects and builders.

"Gates of Reflection", a watercolor sketch by Torrey Butzer.

For the architects who were wading through public meetings and others' perspectives, the Mission Statement became a litmus test of sorts that protected the unanimously selected design from being blurred by important yet at times conflicting suggestions for refinement. It gave the architects space in which to work, and to refine the original concept so that its integrity and depth could be experienced in built form and by future generations.

Most significant is the manner in which the Mission Statement fostered design experiences in which empathy for the visitor is placed on near equal footing with the history embodied in the memorial itself. It formalized a way of thinking about places of remembrance that made the Vietnam Veterans

Memorial so endearing in retrospect. In Oklahoma City, competition design concepts were born from the disciplines of art, lighting design, architecture, landscape architecture, and urban design in ways that foster a sense of invitation for visitors. All five finalists submitted proposals layered in spatial sequences, landscape materials, and formal anchor points, each balancing actualities with abstraction. The document called for a memorial space that is connected to its urban context in both a literal and figurative sense. The richness of the Mission Statement's language invited a contemporary approach to how different visitors might experience the same tragedy physically and intellectually. It could help the memorial become a place of equity.

The Oklahoma City National Memorial is the result of a process that welcomed diverse perspectives and types of expertise. The Mission Statement protected the inclusivity of the memorial's selection process as well as the integrity of the architects' developing work. The built design is an acknowledgement that we experience loss and hope in different ways, and that the participation of visitors is welcome even in the most solemn places of reflection.

CHAPTER 12

Symbolism of the Memorial Components and Continued Relevance of The Fence

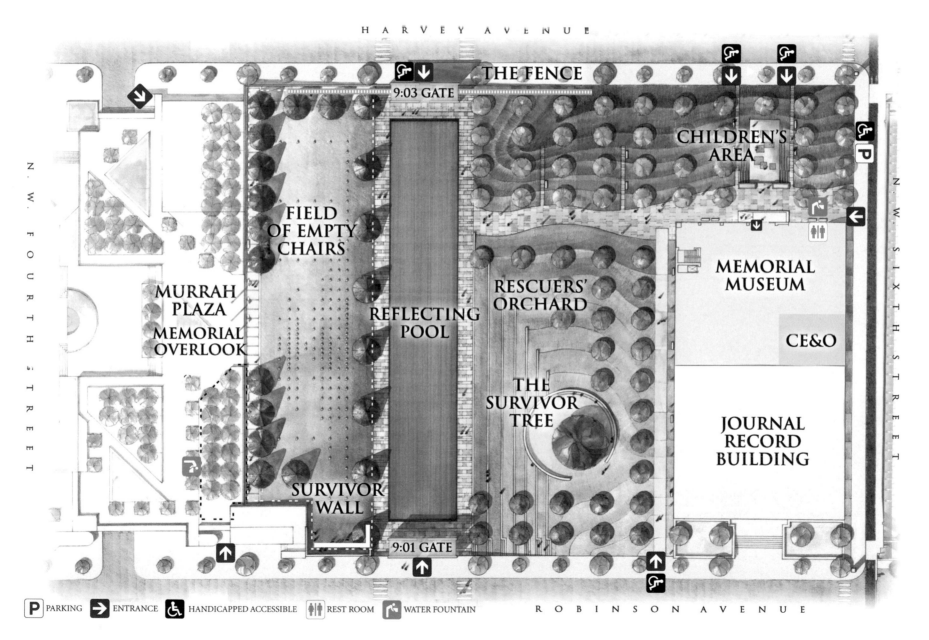

HARVEY AVENUE

THE FENCE

9:03 GATE

CHILDREN'S AREA

FIELD OF EMPTY CHAIRS

MURRAH PLAZA

MEMORIAL OVERLOOK

REFLECTING POOL

RESCUERS' ORCHARD

MEMORIAL MUSEUM

CE&O

THE SURVIVOR TREE

SURVIVOR WALL

JOURNAL RECORD BUILDING

9:01 GATE

N. W. FOURTH STREET

N. W. SIXTH STREET

P PARKING ➤ ENTRANCE ♿ HANDICAPPED ACCESSIBLE 🚻 REST ROOM ⛲ WATER FOUNTAIN

ROBINSON AVENUE

The Gates of Time

The Oklahoma City National Memorial contains a number of components with deep symbolic significance.

THE GATES OF TIME

The east gate of the "Gates of Time" represents 9:01 a.m. on April 19, 1995—the innocence of the city before the attack. The west gate represents the moment that hope sprang from horror and healing began at 9:03 a.m.

THE REFLECTING POOL

A block long shallow depth of gently flowing water is located where Fifth Street once existed and the truck containing the bomb was parked. What once was the location of the most horrific tragedy in Oklahoma City's history has been replaced with the "Reflecting Pool"—the most serene place in our city.

The designers envisioned that a person who peers into such pool would see a reflection of a person changed forever by April 19, 1995, and the days that followed.

The Reflecting Pool

THE FIELD OF EMPTY CHAIRS

Each of the 168 chairs symbolizes one of those killed, with the smaller chairs representing the 19 children. The "Field of Empty Chairs" are arranged in nine rows, one for each of the nine floors of the building. The chairs are placed according to the floor on which the 168 were working or visiting at the time of the bombing. By day, the chairs seem to float above the translucent bases. By night, the glass bases illuminate as beacons of hope.

The
Field of
Empty
Chairs

THE SURVIVOR TREE
The American Elm bent, but did not fall on the day of the bombing. The iconic Survivor Tree symbolizes strength, endurance, and the ability of the human spirit to overcome great adversity.

The Survivor Tree

The Survivor Wall

THE SURVIVOR WALL

On the east end of the Memorial stands the only remaining walls of the Murrah Federal Building. The "Survivor Wall" reminds us of those who survived the attack. Attached to the walls are more than 600 names of survivors inscribed on salvaged pieces of granite from the Murrah Federal Building lobby.

THE CHILDREN'S AREA

In the aftermath of the bombing, countless expressions of encouragement were received from children. Janet Langsam, director of the Westchester County (New York) Arts Council contacted Jackie Jones, Executive Director of Arts Council Oklahoma City, and inquired as to how the children of New York could reach out to the children of Oklahoma City. Her medium became ceramic tiles hand painted by "children sending messages of hope and caring to other children." Langsam contacted arts councils in the nation's fifty largest cities and encouraged them to join in the effort. She also formed a partnership with the World Organization of China Painters to bake the tiles to make the messages of hope permanent.

The project spread beyond the original cities encouraged to participate, and more than 5,000 tiles were produced in the United States and Canada. Many of the tiles came from schools in

The Children's Area

Oklahoma City. The project became much more than messages of compassion; it became a means for the children to express their emotions.

The Mission Statement provides: "The Memorial Complex should have a special place for children. The Memorial Complex should have a component designed to reach kids on 'their level,' both physically and cognitively. The component should help children learn and feel something they can carry with them as they grow and should offer them assurance that the world holds far more good than bad." The "Children's Area," located west of the Museum entrance, includes a wall of the hand-painted tiles and a series of chalkboards for children to continue to share their feelings.

Tiles were sent to Oklahoma City from children around the world as tokens of support. *Courtesy Jackie Jones.*

131

The Rescuers' Orchard

THE RESCUERS' ORCHARD

In honor of the first responders who rushed in to help, the "Rescuers' Orchard" surrounds and protects the Survivor Tree. An inscription encircling the Survivor Tree reads: "To the courageous and caring who responded from near and far we offer our eternal gratitude."

CONTINUED RELEVANCE OF THE FENCE

In his comments on the day of the Ground-breaking Ceremony, Vice President Al Gore said, "Open your eyes and your hearts and you will see that on the chain link fence all around us—filled with flowers and prayers and teddy bears—is written the real story of our democracy."

During the media viewing of the 624 designs, ABC's *Good Morning America* host Charles Gibson said, "Perhaps your greatest challenge will be selecting a memorial design that will adequately replace The Fence."

After the design for the Oklahoma City National Memorial was selected, several victims' family members and survivors asked that the design be modified to incorporate "The Fence." The discussions that followed offered differing opinions. Some believed The Fence would not be needed upon completion of the Memorial, while others believed it would always be relevant as a component through which visitors could express themselves. Both opinions were strongly held.

After several emotional meetings and discussion with the Memorial designers, a plan was developed to place a section of The Fence along the west exterior of the Memorial. It was concluded that only time would tell whether The Fence would remain an important component for visitors. The Fence continues to be a vital element for those visiting the Oklahoma City National Memorial & Museum. We are very thankful for the cooperative manner in which Hans and Torrey Butzer, Tom Kight, whose daughter, Frankie Merrell, died in the bombing, numerous other victims' family members and survivors, and dedicated volunteers were instrumental in amicably resolving this issue.

CHAPTER 13

National Memorial Designation by Congress and the Challenges Faced

In 1997, as required by the Mission Statement, a designation as a National Memorial and a $5 million appropriation to defray a portion of the capital costs of the Oklahoma City National Memorial were sought from Congress.

In support of our efforts, President Clinton said, "We all know that the Oklahoma City bombing was an attack, not just on the people, a city, a state, but the nation, ...on what we stand for, how we govern ourselves and the values we live by. The tragedy was a national one, and the memorial should be recognized and embraced and supported by the nation."

In April 1997, a meeting occurred with the leadership of the Senate Subcommittee on National Parks, Historic Preservation and Recreation to discuss the desired Congressional legislation that would designate the Oklahoma City National Memorial as a National Memorial and turn it over to the National Park Service

(NPS) to operate at the time of completion. We were told that because the NPS had a deferred maintenance deficit of approximately $8 billion, which Congress did not plan to fund, Congress would not be willing to add another facility to the already overburdened NPS budget. We also were advised it would not be in the best interest of the Memorial to turn it over to the NPS to operate due to a shortage of funds necessary to assure quality care. We were asked to consider taking a different approach—accept the National Memorial designation without adding the Memorial to the list of annually funded NPS sites.

After further study, Senator Don Nickles' staff and the Congressional Subcommittee leadership proposed that the legislation be structured similarly to the Congressional Act covering The Presidio, a former military installation in San Francisco, California that was converted to a facility operated by the Presidio Trust—a

Oklahoma City bombing survivor Polly Nichols addressed the U.S. Senate Subcommittee on National Parks, Historic Preservation and Recreation regarding the designation of the Oklahoma City National Memorial as a National Memorial.

wholly owned government corporation created by Congress—and partially staffed by NPS.

It was determined that the only realistic chance of obtaining the Congressional recognition of the Memorial as a National Memorial and the requested Congressional appropriation would be to create a unit of the NPS to be operated by a wholly owned government trust created by Congress without impact on the NPS budget. We were advised that we could likely obtain a one-time $5 million appropriation as part of such legislation.

With this determination, two primary concerns arose. First, there was apprehension about the economic feasibility of operating the Memorial without annual government appropriations. Second, we were told that if a trust was established by Congress the Trust Board would be limited to nine trustees. As a result, not all members of the Foundation Board of Directors could serve as Trustees of the Trust Board.

We returned home to Oklahoma and began studying the feasibility of private, self-supporting operations of the Memorial. The budgets and visitation experience of several other memorials and museums, including The Sixth Floor Museum in Dallas which operates without government subsidy, were studied. We then made conservative adjustments to the likely visitation differences between our Memorial and the others we studied and developed a business plan for operations based on the projected earnings on our endowment, revenue from the Museum, and annual contributions. The operating expense forecast included staffing and budget information provided by the NPS, which included a supervising interpreter, two full-time interpreters, two seasonal interpreters, and one curator.

After much discussion of the Congressional Subcommittee's recommendation, the proposed Congressional legislation structure was approved by the Memorial Foundation's Government Liaison Committee and the Foundation's Board of Directors before proceeding further in pursuit of such legislation.

On October 9, 1997, Congress passed the Oklahoma City National Memorial Act of 1997. This legislation was not perfect as it created a second Memorial entity—the Oklahoma City National Memorial Trust. Although we made every effort to have all members of the Foundation Board of Directors appointed as trustees of the Oklahoma City National Memorial Trust, the White House staff indeed opposed having more than nine members of the Trust Board. In determining whether the Foundation Board could serve as an advisory board to the Trust, we were told by the Department of Interior staff that such structure would create a conflict of interest and that all members of the Trust Board would have to resign as members of the Foundation Board.

The U.S. Senate Subcommittee on National Parks, Historic
Preservation and Recreation.

The decision to create the Oklahoma City
National Memorial Trust was a difficult one,
as having a small number of trustees was
inconsistent with the inclusive nature of the
memorial process. While painful to agree to have
only nine trustees appointed by the President,
there was no viable alternative to obtain
the National Memorial designation required
by the Mission Statement and the $5 million
congressional appropriation.

The selection of trustees also was difficult.
Ultimately, through the constituency suggestions
of members of the Oklahoma congressional
delegation, the nine trustees included Luke
Corbett, chairman of Kerr-McGee Corporation,
who represented a leader in the Oklahoma City
business community; Larry Brummett, chairman
of ONEOK, who represented a leader in the
Tulsa business community; Hannah Atkins, a
statewide community leader; John Cook, director

of the Intermountain Region of the National Park Service (NPS); Don Ferrell, father of victim Susan Ferrell; Richard Williams, survivor and assistant building manager for General Services Administration at the Murrah Federal Building; Oklahoma City Fire Chief Gary Marrs who represented the first responders; Linda Lambert, treasurer of the Oklahoma City National Memorial Foundation; and myself, chairman of the Oklahoma City National Memorial Foundation.

Although challenging, the complexity of having two separate entities did not deter us from continuing the memorial process in a relatively seamless manner.

When the business plan for operation of the Memorial and Museum was developed in 1997, we were unaware that the NPS staff and the resulting operational costs would be significantly increased by NPS after the Memorial was completed.

On January 23, 2004, President George W. Bush signed a law that dissolved the Oklahoma City National Memorial Trust, transferred ownership and operating responsibility of the Memorial and Museum to the Oklahoma City National Memorial Foundation, limited the NPS staff to interpreters on the outdoor Memorial site, and removed all National Park Service expenses from the Foundation's budget. The Memorial continues to be recognized as a National Memorial, an affiliated site of the National Park System.

Oklahoma City Memorial Foundation Chairman Bob Johnson, Ann Simank, and Tom McDaniel addressed the U.S. Senate Subcommittee on National Parks, Historic Preservation and Recreation in April 1997.

CHAPTER 14

Funding of the Memorial and Museum

Believing a major fundraising campaign should not be commenced until after the Memorial design was selected, a line of credit was secured from BancFirst in Oklahoma City to cover the design competition and related expenses. We are grateful for H.E. "Gene" Rainbolt of BancFirst having confidence in our subsequent fundraising efforts. In preparing for public fundraising the Memorial Task Force was transformed into the Oklahoma City Memorial Foundation. It is known today as the Oklahoma City National Memorial Foundation, a non-profit foundation.

After the design of the Memorial was selected, a capital fundraising effort was launched to cover the $24.1 million budget for the Memorial, the Museum, the initial endowment, and design selection and related expenses. Polly Nichols was chosen to lead the campaign because she brought three important perspectives to the task—she was a survivor, a victim's family member, and was widely respected as a community volunteer. Mayor Ron Norick and former Vice President Dick Cheney, then chairman of Halliburton, also led the capital campaign alongside Polly Nichols. Governor Keating made numerous calls to donors within and beyond the borders of Oklahoma.

The lead gift that created momentum for our fundraising efforts was made by Kerr-McGee Corporation. The contribution included a letter in part stating:

"Our proximity to the explosion, the heroic and unselfish response by our employees in the aftermath, and the unbearable loss of loved ones by our people and many others, all weighed heavily in the decision to make a gift that will underscore our deep feelings, support, and continuing commitment to all those affected.

"Kerr-McGee also has a tradition of leadership in helping with worthwhile projects that are important today and that will have a significant impact on succeeding generations. The memorial is such a project for our community, our state, our nation, and the entire world.

"Therefore, on behalf of Kerr-McGee Corporation and our employees around the globe, we hereby pledge the sum of $1,000,000 to help build a fitting memorial as an enduring reminder of the indomitable human spirit that rose above the tragedy."

The announcement of the lead gift from Kerr-McGee Corporation at a public ceremony on July 1, 1997, was emotional. Without that lead gift we might have encountered incredible difficulty meeting our fundraising goal.

The second gift came from Sonic Corp., in the amount of $250,000, which was the largest donation made by Sonic to that date. Their gift was further

evidence of the community's selfless response.

During the nine months between the announcement of Kerr-McGee Corporation's lead gift and the third anniversary of the bombing, nearly half of the $24.1 million goal was raised.

In addition to the private fundraising efforts, the State of Oklahoma and Congress played major roles in funding the Memorial and Museum. The initial appropriation by the State of Oklahoma was $5 million. As the 5th Anniversary and the dedication of the Memorial neared, Governor Keating led the effort for a second appropriation from the State of Oklahoma to cover the remaining $2.3 million. On the day before the dedication, Governor Keating and Oklahoma legislative leaders personally delivered the message that the $2.3 million supplemental appropriation had been approved.

Of the $24.1 million campaign, approximately $11.8 million was raised from private donations.

Those gifts ranged from pennies from children and small and large personal gifts to large corporate and foundation gifts Congress appropriated $5 million and $7.3 million was appropriated by the State of Oklahoma.

The unprecedented cooperative public-private partnership during the aftermath of the bombing continued uninterrupted during the totality of the memorialization process.

From left, Tom McDaniel, Vice-Chairman of Kerr-McGee, Luke Corbett, Chairman of Kerr-McGee, Bob Johnson, Vince Gill, and Linda Cavanaugh at the ceremonial presentation of the $1 million contribution made by Kerr-McGee Corporation—the lead gift to support the Oklahoma City National Memorial.

REFLECTIONS
POLLY NICHOLS

REFLECTIONS ON THE MEMORIAL CAPITAL CAMPAIGN

Polly Nichols, Survivor
CO-CHAIR OF THE MEMORIAL FUNDRAISING
COMMITTEE AND 2002-2003 CHAIRMAN OF THE
OKLAHOMA CITY NATIONAL MEMORIAL FOUNDATION

After I was asked to co-chair the fundraising effort, we began our campaign by leaning on the very able and knowledgeable Lee Allan Smith for planning and fundraising advice. A dedicated group of volunteers sat around his conference room table for hours, with an agenda of funding a memorial and museum free of debt to fulfill the objectives set forth in the Memorial Mission Statement. It was clear that we would need a compelling grass roots effort that placed emphasis on Oklahomans, but also involved all Americans. I believed the selected memorial design would positively influence gift giving, because, in my opinion, it was clear, non-controversial, and interactive.

The announcement of the lead gift by Kerr-McGee in 1997 of $1 million made Chairman Bob Johnson's voice crack as he announced it during a ceremony on the memorial grounds. It was the catalyst for the larger corporate and individual gifts that would ensure the building and maintaining of our Memorial and Museum.

From the beginning, I believed children would be the most-affected of those touched by the bombing (in losing a parent, they had lost their world). I also believed children could be involved in fundraising in a manner that would have a positive impact on them.

Immediately after the bombing, children from around the world responded by sending drawings and cards. They also gave pennies. Of all of the donations received, the donations that touched our hearts the most were those that came from children. A "168 Pennies Campaign" was a concept based on a similar effort by Nancy Krodel, at Coronado Heights Elementary School in Oklahoma City, who raised more than $51,000 for the Memorial during the weeks after the bombing by asking each student to contribute 19 pennies, one for each of the children who died in the bombing. "Pennies for My Mom Campaign" was a program we started when 10-year old Clint Seidl, who lost his mother in the bombing, volunteered to help. He wanted to make sure people who visited the Memorial could sit on his Mom's chair and get to know her. In schools we visited, he would stand in front of us and drop one penny in a jar for his mom, Kathy, and then 167 pennies for each of the others who were killed. The children would then line up to add their pennies for the Memorial. Clint was joined by fellow Oklahoman and Miss America Shawntel Smith and Teleflora, a locally headquartered floral wire company.

Together, the 168 Pennies Campaign and the Pennies for My Mom Campaign drew participation from 892 schools from 38 states, and over 46 million pennies—$460,373.78—were received to help build the Memorial and Museum. These campaigns not only helped us reach our capital campaign goal, but equally as important they provided participating elementary teachers a platform for teaching their children the many lessons that emanated from the tragedy, including the senselessness of violence and the goodness of humanity.

Governor Keating, Mayor Norick, victims' family members, first responders, and survivors were asked to speak of their experiences across the country, and they sent their speaking honorariums to the Memorial Foundation. Also, famous Oklahomans came home to headline events to raise money.

So many were so generous. Large gifts, small gifts, we needed both. Foundations, large businesses, small businesses, individuals. People gave what they could. I'm very pleased the names of all of the donors are still listed in the Museum lobby. We all came together to build this special place.

CHAPTER 15

Definition of Survivor

One of the most difficult tasks in the memorial process was to define "survivor" in order to determine whose names would be included on the granite wall on the former Murrah Federal Building site and whose names and stories would be included in the Museum. The complexity of such definitional task is brought into focus by acknowledging that arguably all are survivors, because there were concentric rings of impact radiating out from the bombing.

The definition was developed through a consensus process which took approximately eighteen months. The process was co-chaired by two survivors—Richard Williams and Earnestine Clark. Beth Shortt, the facilitator for the Memorial Mission Statement Drafting Committee, also served admirably in that capacity for the Survivor Definition Committee. She said, "Occasionally, some committee members felt we could never solve it and that we should just include all of downtown. I reminded them that such decision would trivialize the horrific experiences of so many grievously wounded people who came out of the Murrah and other buildings."

The adopted "survivor" definition for the purpose of whose names would be included on the wall on the Murrah Federal Building site included those most at risk at the time of the bombing. This included those who were located in the Murrah block, the Journal Record Building block, on the half blocks to the east and west, and on streets within the area.

Also included were those who were admitted to a hospital as a result of the bombing and were not released on the same day, regardless of their location at the time of the bombing. An expanded definition of "survivor" was adopted for the purpose of stories told in the Museum for those who worked or resided within the area, but were not present at the time of the bombing.

The map used to determine those defined as a "survivor" in planning for the Oklahoma City National Memorial & Museum.

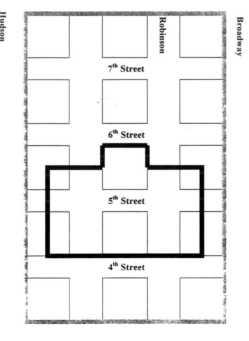

PERIMETER BOUNDARIES
FOR PURPOSES OF RECOGNIZING SURVIVORS
IN THE OKLAHOMA CITY MEMORIAL

BLACK Perimeter: All those physically within the **BLACK** Perimeter at 9:02 a.m. on April 19, 1995, and who do not object to being included, are to be identified on the site of the Murrah Building and in the Memorial Center. In addition, all those who suffered an injury which caused them to be held for care at a hospital (not "treated and released"), regardless of their physical location at 9:02 a.m., and who do not object to being included, are to be identified on the site of the Murrah Building and in the Memorial Center.

The buildings within the BLACK Perimeter are:
Alfred P. Murrah Building
Oklahoma Water Resources Building
Journal Record Building
Center City Station Post Office Building
First Methodist Church
YMCA Building
St. Joseph's Catholic Church and Rectory

REFLECTIONS
RICHARD WILLIAMS

REFLECTIONS ON THE DEFINITION OF SURVIVOR

Richard Williams, Survivor
CO-CHAIR OF SURVIVOR DEFINITION COMMITTEE

My involvement in the memorial process was two-fold. The first part of that was being a buildings manager for the General Services Administration (GSA). The site of the bombing was on a Federal complex overseen by the GSA office housed in the Murrah Building.

Second, as a survivor whose office was on the first floor of the building, I had been personally affected physically and emotionally. My need for the victims to be remembered also included the building itself, which had been my place of employment since just prior to its opening in 1977. My friends, co-workers, the agencies, and other entities there had been like a second family to me. When Bob Johnson became the leader for the memorial process, he recognized those who needed to be consulted and included in that work. Community leaders ensured all of those affected were given a voice—victims' families, survivors, and first responders.

As I served on the Oklahoma City National Memorial Trust, and numerous committees, it was clear that those most affected would contribute to the end result. When I was asked to serve as co-chair of the Survivor Definition Committee, I had no idea the difficulty of defining survivors as set forth in the Mission Statement. As a survivor, I was given the opportunity to share my experience. As someone who had been responsible for the Federal complex and its occupants, I had knowledge that allowed me to contribute in unique ways in the memorialization process.

CHAPTER 16

Groundbreaking and Fence Moving Ceremonies

The official groundbreaking for the Oklahoma City National Memorial was held on October 25, 1998. Dignitaries in attendance included Vice President Al Gore, U.S. Attorney General Janet Reno, director of the National Park Service Robert Stanton, U.S. Senator Don Nickles, Governor Frank Keating, Oklahoma First Lady Cathy Keating, Mayor Ron Norick, and sitting Mayor Kirk Humphreys.

During the groundbreaking, Vice President Gore said, "Today, in the dark shadow of memory, we gather to seek the light, to find in this soil, nourished with a million tears, the harvest of God's healing grace. To those who are ever tempted to denigrate the labor of our self-government, come here and be silent and remember."

Oklahoma City Mayor Kirk Humphreys remarked, "We dedicate this ground to the memory of the past, and to a vision of the future . . . a future vastly different than that envisioned

Oklahoma City National Memorial Foundation Chairman Bob Johnson and Vice Chair Karen Luke visit with U.S. Attorney General Janet Reno prior to the groundbreaking ceremony.

by the bombers . . . a future of compassion instead of cruelty. . . brotherhood instead of bitterness . . . reconciliation instead of revenge . . . harmony instead of hostility . . . faith instead of fear . . . renaissance instead of ruin. Today, as we dedicate

Clint Seidl, who lost his mother Kathy in the bombing, and Vice President Al Gore break ground on the Murrah Federal Building footprint.

this ground, let us dedicate ourselves anew to one another . . . a bedrock faith, a ready smile, a can-do attitude and a helping hand."

Vice President Gore and other dignitaries led thousands of participants as they took shovels to help turn the sacred soil on which the Murrah Federal Building stood. As shovels turned the earth, from atop the Murrah Plaza the 100-member Ambassadors' Concert Choir sang the very meaningful and soulful hymn, "Holy Ground".

The evening after the Groundbreaking Ceremony hundreds came to the site for The Fence Moving Ceremony. All participants stood hand in hand for a candlelight prayer service on the sacred soil on which the Field of Empty Chairs and the remembrance of the survivors would be constructed. The Fence Moving Ceremony was capped off with the victims' family members, survivors, first responders, and volunteers physically moving The Fence to its present location on the west edge of the Memorial site to make way for construction. The emotions evidenced that evening reaffirmed beyond any doubt the decision to retain The Fence as a vital component of the Memorial.

Victims' families, survivors, first responders, and volunteers move The Fence from Fifth Street to its permanent location on Harvey Avenue. *Courtesy Oklahoma Publishing Company.*

Oklahoma City National Memorial Foundation Chairman Bob Johnson participates in The Fence Moving Ceremony. *Courtesy David Allen.*

CHAPTER 17

Memorial Construction and Dedication

To lead the construction of the Memorial, we were blessed to have two people, Rowland Denman and Hardy Watkins, with great people and organizational skills, a deep devotion for the Memorial effort, a thorough understanding of construction, and the keen ability to keep costs within the budget.

To set the tone of how the construction process would proceed, Denman and Watkins conducted a Partnering Meeting and Scheduling Review with the parties who would be involved in the construction. Participants were reminded that the Mission Statement provided, in part, that "the Memorial Complex, and especially where the Murrah Federal Building stood, is 'sacred ground'— a hallowed place deserving of great respect and solemnity associated with great loss." In addition, each participant signed a Commitment Statement which established a tone of devotion, sensitivity to protecting the integrity of the site, mutual respect, open communication, teamwork, quality workmanship, timely and efficient performance, and the importance of the Memorial to help all visitors understand the tragedy, its impact, and the ability of people to triumph over evil. With such commitment, everyone on site was honored to participate and approached the construction of the Memorial as a labor of love and respect.

Great care was taken in all aspects of the construction of the Memorial. For example, Mark Bays, an urban forester, personally guided volunteers and construction workers as they hand-dug the 100 concrete promontory pier placements around the Survivor Tree to assure the tree's roots were not damaged. He also arranged structural design alterations to protect major roots.

Just as people around the world responded to assist Oklahoma City in the aftermath of the bombing, we searched near and far for the finest materials with which to build the Memorial.

From the east and west, the Memorial's most striking features are the Gates of Time. Clad with 26 tons of bronze panels milled in Japan due to the large, single-panel sizes required, the panels were finished in New Jersey. The black granite within both Gates of Time and on the one-block long Reflecting Pool surface was quarried in Quebec, Canada. The flagstones in the pathway around the Reflecting Pool were quarried in Arkansas, while the large sandstone benches on the Memorial grounds are from eastern Oklahoma. The reinforced lawn product used for the Memorial's immaculate zoysia grounds was manufactured in London, England.

The Loblolly Pines that represent sentinels around the Field of Empty Chairs were selected from a tree plantation in McLoud, Oklahoma. The glass bases of the chairs were fabricated in Oakland, California and the bronze chair backs were cast in Oklahoma City. The mechanical and

Before the Dedication of the Memorial on April 19, 2000, President Bill Clinton was given a tour of the Memorial grounds by Executive Director Kari Watkins, family members Doris Jones and Jeannine Gist, survivor Florence Rogers and Oklahoma City Fire Chief Gary Marrs. They stopped at the Reflecting Pool for a moment of silence. *Courtesy the White House.*

structural elements of the chairs were designed in New Hampshire. The granite panels on which the survivors' names are etched and the granite stones that make up the pathway around the Field of Empty Chairs were salvaged from the Murrah Building.

The Oklahoma Redbud, Amur Maple, Chinese Pistache, and Bosque Elm trees were grown in Oklahoma, Texas and Georgia. The oversized in-ground chalkboards in the Children's Area were quarried in Vermont and the hand-painted tiles incorporated into the Children's Area were received from children throughout the United States and Canada.

Although the construction timeline was tight, the commitment to the public was to dedicate the Memorial on April 19, 2000—the 5th Anniversary of the bombing. The final element was installed three days prior to the dedication. In addition, the Memorial was built within the original budget despite being unlike any project the contractor, its

subcontractors, and vendors had experienced.

As promised, the Oklahoma City National Memorial was dedicated on the 5th Anniversary of the bombing. Media credentials were issued to 770 media representatives from throughout the world.

To honor and reflect respect for the victims' families, survivors, and first responders, a private dedication ceremony was held on the morning of April 19, 2000. It was acknowledged that during the preceding five years the journey had been a difficult one for all involved, and the choice of the victims' families and survivors to be the guiding force in shaping the planning of the Memorial had been monumental. The victims' families and survivors chose to take a stand against terrorism and raise a lasting tribute to the innocent who perished, the survivors, the first responders who came from near and far, and all whose lives were impacted by the tragedy.

Above and Facing: Victims' families visit the Field of Empty Chairs during the private ceremony preceding the Dedication of the Oklahoma City National Memorial on April 19, 2000.

Doris Jones, who lost her daughter, Carrie Lenz, and unborn grandson, Michael Lenz III, helped shape the Memorial through her grace, dedication, and thoughtfulness, including serving as Co-Chair of the Dedication of the Memorial. After she recited the Preamble of the Mission Statement, several other respectful presentations were made, including "Where do we go from here?" followed by the singing of "Holy Ground." As church bells rang, 168 seconds of silence were observed to remember each of those killed.

It is the custom on each anniversary to remember the 168 who were killed by reading their names aloud. As those names were read during the Dedication, each of the victims' families were escorted by first responders onto the Memorial grounds to their loved one's chair for a few moments of private personal reflection before the survivors joined them. The remaining first responders followed, many of whom were returning to the site for the first time since the days following the bombing. They were able to see the transformation of the site, including the orchard of trees dedicated to remembering the valor of their efforts.

As bagpipes played "Amazing Grace," the private respectful ceremony was concluded with the raising of three flags over the Memorial to represent the unity of our city, state and nation in helping us endure during our greatest hours of need. Phillip Thompson, one of the victim's family members, said, "When we walked in that first day to see the Memorial, it was an emotionally stunning moment."

Kathleen Treanor, whose in-laws and daughter were killed in the blast, waited until the dedication ceremony to see the finished Memorial. She said, "When I first stepped through the gate, it was like a demarcation, a line between grief and being able to live again. I really believe it's holy ground."

In her article "Love Among the Ruins," Mamie Healey said, "Maybe the purpose of commemorating a loss with a physical monument is . . . that by its very presence, it testifies, it reminds, it shocks, it teaches. And most important, for those whose pain weighs heaviest, it assumes some of the burden of remembering."

A public Dedication was held later that afternoon. It was led by President Bill Clinton and a long list of dignitaries, including U.S. Attorney General Janet Reno, National Park Service Director Robert Stanton, U.S. Senator Don Nickles, Governor Frank Keating, First Lady Cathy Keating, and Mayor Kirk Humphreys. Following the presentation of colors, 1996 Miss America from Oklahoma, Shawntel Smith, performed "The National Anthem."

The preamble of the Mission Statement was recited by John Cole, the godfather of Aaron and Elijah Coverdale who died in the bombing, Priscilla Salyers, a Murrah Federal Building survivor, and Oklahoma City Police Chief M. T. Berry, representing the first responders. The reading was followed by the Oklahoma City Philharmonic Brass performance of "Fanfare for The Common Man" and the Memorial Community Choir and everyone in attendance singing "O God, Our Help In Ages Past".

Those most deeply touched by the tragedy were the victims' families, the survivors, and the first responders. They were an essential part of the memorialization process from the very beginning. They gave their time, courageously shared their personal experiences and feelings, and came together in unity to guide the creation of the Memorial.

Jeannine Gist, whose youngest daughter Karen died in the bombing, was instrumental in shaping the memorial journey. Jeannine responded time and again with quiet strength and grace. She offered a message from the hearts of the victims' families as part of the ceremony surrounding the Dedication. Jeannine Gist shared:

"After the Memorial Task Force was appointed by then Mayor Ron Norick, the many meetings that followed brought together victims' family members, survivors, rescue workers and members of the community to discuss how best to remember and honor all those involved.

"At first it was a very difficult process. Emotions were raw, we were hurt, angry and still in shock. At times it seemed like we would never get anything done, but we did. Thanks to a consensus building process and the dedication of all those involved, we were able to come together. We developed the Mission Statement and helped choose the design of this beautiful Memorial. We hope all of you are as proud of it as we are."

The survivors also courageously contributed to the arrival of Dedication Day. Florence Rogers was one of hundreds who suffered the horror of the tragedy and miraculously survived. On the morning of the bombing, Florence, President of the Federal Employees Credit Union, had just convened a weekly meeting with her staff when the bomb ripped half of the building away. The floor beneath her desk and chair held, but the eight fellow employees who were sitting across the desk from her disappeared and died. Florence Rogers said:

"To our city, state and nation, thank you for understanding that this Memorial had to be created, that that this place had to be sacred, and that the memory had to exist so that all will remember and learn from what happened here.

"Today, we give this place to the world so you will know we are united to prove that acts of terrorism will not dampen the American spirit, not here, not anywhere."

On April 19, 1995, our nation was inspired by the unselfish example of the first responders. The man who quickly organized and led the rescue and recovery effort in such a remarkable manner was Oklahoma City Fire Chief Gary Marrs. The first responders will tell you that on that fateful day they were not trying to inspire us, they were simply doing their job. On that day, their "job" became unthinkable, but our police, fire, rescue, and medical personnel, alongside fellow citizens, demonstrated extraordinary valor. Chief Marrs delivered the following message:

"To the courageous and caring who responded from near and far we offer our eternal gratitude. That quote will forever be in stone set in the wall surrounding the Survivor Tree and overlooking the Rescue Workers' Orchard. It is fitting that an orchard was selected as a symbol of the hundreds of rescue workers who came to this site and gave their all for the rescue and recovery of our people, because they gave of themselves then and they continue to give of themselves year in and year out.

"When we speak of rescue workers on that day the term transcends the usual meaning of first responders. It includes all who represented the resources of this entire city and ultimately the entire nation. It includes all of those who made available their services so that the workers on the front line could give their best.

"The scene encountered on April 19, 1995, by the hundreds of rescue workers was heartbreaking . . . the effort they made was monumental. All of them left a piece of themselves here. We hope that this Memorial will be a place of peace and comfort for them . . . not just in remembrance of April 19th, but for all of the problems these first responders will face in their professional lives. Perhaps here they can gain a peace that will walk beside them as they face each day."

During the five years following the bombing, the City of Oklahoma City, first under the leadership of Mayor Ron Norick and then Mayor Kirk Humphreys, was a valued partner in the community's work to rebuild not only our neighborhood, but our lives; not to replace, but to remember; not to erase, but to educate. The City helped us secure the land on which a portion of the Memorial is built. The City helped transform Fifth Street from a site of great violence to the serene Reflecting Pool there today. On behalf of the City of Oklahoma City, Mayor Kirk Humphreys said:

"We come here today to dedicate this Memorial so that all Americans, indeed, all mankind, can come here to remember, reflect and find renewal. The Reflecting Pool in the center of the Memorial helps us reflect on what happened here and its meaning. How fitting that the reflecting pool of serenity is the very place where the bomb exploded. And, that's the message of this place. . .in this place love conquered hatred and sacrifice overcame selfishness."

On the 5th Anniversary of the bombing, the character and resilience of Oklahomans remained as symbols of courage and hope for the nation. Frank Keating became the Governor of Oklahoma just three months before the bombing, yet in a calming and steady manner he led our state through recovery and securing funding from the State of Oklahoma to defray a significant portion of the cost of the Memorial. Governor Keating stated:

"On April 19th, another spring Wednesday like today, the flag of our nation was flying over the Murrah Building. It is flying over the Memorial today and I know it flies proudly in all of your hearts. For those who perpetrated the act we have one message . . . if you think you can bring that flag down, there is your answer. May God continue to bless our beloved land."

Throughout the democratized memorial planning process, much was accomplished. However, it could not have happened without congressional support. Leading the effort to secure a $5 million appropriation and to designate the Memorial as a National Memorial by passing the Oklahoma City National Memorial Act was our entire Congressional Delegation. Representing them at the Dedication was U. S. Senator Don Nickles, who stated:

"Today, we pay tribute to the spirit of recovery and faith that has been an example and encouragement to everyone across our country. This Memorial will stand as a testament of hope, generosity, and courage shown after the tragedy by Oklahomans and our fellow Americans."

In recognition of the Memorial's designation as a National Memorial, National Park Service Director Robert Stanton offered the following:

"This place represents a principal element of the heritage of America. It gives us hope and courage to become better citizens. This is a very special place to honor, to learn and to remember. Here, America has chosen to take a stand for the values that past generations have taught us.

"Because of what happened here, we shall dedicate our efforts to find better ways of meeting and resolving the discontent of conflict, fear and uncertainty. This National Memorial shall always stand as a beacon on the watchtower of human endeavor, reminding us of our individual and collective responsibilities to achieve that which is set forth in the Preamble of the U.S. Constitution, namely to form a more perfect union, establish justice, insure domestic tranquility, provide for the common defense, promote the general welfare, and secure the blessings of liberty. In the memory of those we honor on this very special place, we shall not, as a community, as a nation, as a people, do less. We cannot afford to do less."

Echoing that which was written on the wall of the Journal Record Building by first responder and law enforcement teams, "The discovery of truth and the pursuit of justice" were important to all who were touched by the bombing. The nation's top law enforcement official, U.S. Attorney General Janet Reno, extended her heart to Oklahoma, acted as our advocate, and led the pursuit of truth and justice on our behalf. On behalf of the United States Department of Justice, Attorney General Reno said:

"To all of the people of Oklahoma, thank you for showing America how to stand up to evil. You have helped us renew our spirit and our love of this country. We come to reaffirm our faith that binds us together is stronger than the evil that would tear us apart. You have proven that again.

"This Memorial, like this community, will always stand for justice. Justice is that deep and abiding peace that comes when wrong is righted and when hurt begins to heal.

"In the face of an evil ... an evil that staggers the soul, you demonstrated the triumph of the human spirit. This Memorial and the peace it will bring stands for your triumph.

"Five years ago we were bound together by sheer tragedy. Now we are bound together not merely by the memories of what was lost, but also their spirit and by the knowledge that men and women of good will can come in tragedy and in crisis to stand against evil and hate . . . to stand for justice and love . . . to stand for this nation and all that we hold dear. Thank you for leading the way."

On April 23, 1995, President Bill Clinton attended the Memorial Prayer Service in Oklahoma City and told Oklahomans that he and the nation would be by our side until our work is done. With President Clinton's assistance, Oklahoma City reminded the world that ours is a great nation capable of repelling terrorism and its insidious effects, a nation capable of great compassion. On behalf of all people across our great nation, President Clinton proclaimed:

"This is a day both for remembrance and renewal. I know the last five years have not been easy. I hope you can take some comfort knowing that America is still with you, and with this Memorial, America will never forget.

"There are places in our national landscape so scarred by sacrifice that they shape forever the soul of America. This place is such sacred ground.

"Five years ago the cowards made a choice to attack this federal building and the people in it, because they wanted to strike a blow at America's Heartland, at the very core of our nation's being. This was an attack on America and every American. Five years later, we are here because you made a choice. A choice to choose hope and love over despair and hatred. It is easy for us to say today, but I know that this wise choice was also a very hard one, especially for the families of the victims.

"I know there are still days when the old anger wells up inside you . . . still days when tears fill your eyes . . . when you think your heart will surely break. On those days in the future I hope you can come here and find solace.

"You taught us how much stronger we are when we all stand together in our common

President Bill Clinton addressed the thousands of people attending the Oklahoma City National Memorial Dedication to honor those who were killed, those who survived, and those changed forever. *Courtesy the White House.*

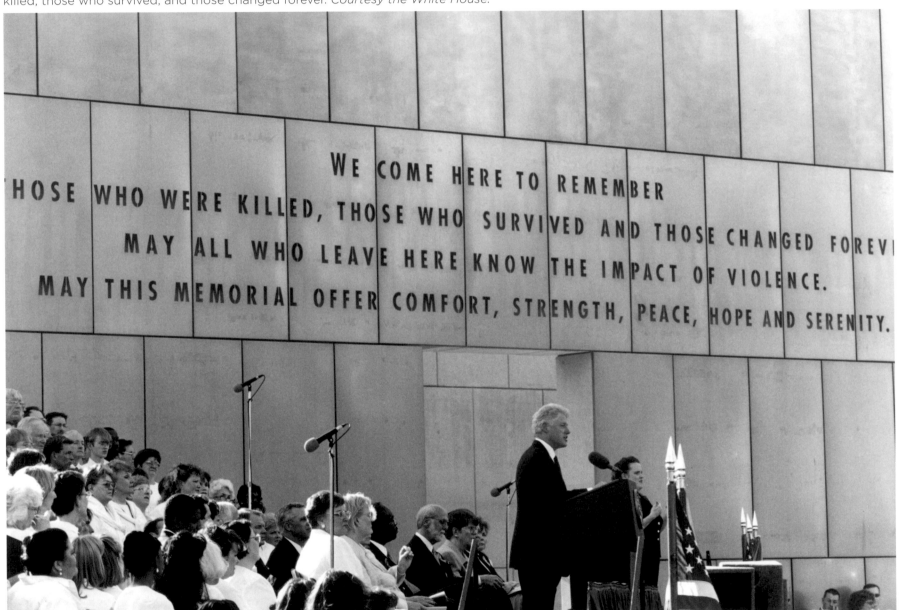

humanity. One truth is clear. What was meant to break has made you stronger.

"All of your fellow Americans and, indeed, decent good people all over the world are grateful to you and grateful to God for the grace that led you on.

"In Romans it is said, 'The night is far spent. The day is in hand. Let us cast off the works of darkness and let us put on the armor of light.' May you keep on your armor of light. May you keep your light shining on this place of hope where memories of the lost and the meaning of America will live forever.'"

Following President Clinton's remarks, Karen Luke and I recited the following to dedicate the Memorial:

"Today, in keeping with the occasion that brings us together, we come here first to remember. We remember the tragedy that has taken from us our loved ones, our civil servants and our fellow citizens. We come here to honor those who have gone before us as well as those who have overcome this tragedy. We honor each family and individual who was victimized by the bombing. We honor those who came to their rescue and who have continued to support and comfort those individuals affected. We commit ourselves to making our nation safer. In creating this Memorial, we are living witness of our dedication to this task. This Memorial represents the commitment of the people of Oklahoma and the Nation to the preservation of peace and sanctity of life. We humbly dedicate this Memorial."

Keeping with the tradition for all Memorial ceremonies, 168 seconds of silence were observed in remembrance of the 168 victims of the attack.

The Oklahoma City National Memorial in the heart of downtown Oklahoma City.

Following the Memorial Community Choir's performance of "To Remember," an original anthem composed for the Memorial Dedication, President Clinton, Memorial designers Hans Butzer, Torrey Butzer, and Sven Berg; John Cole, representing the victims' families; Priscilla Salyers, representing the survivors; Oklahoma Police Chief M.T. Berry, representing the first responders; and Memorial leaders participated in a ribbon-cutting ceremony to officially open to the world the Oklahoma City National Memorial.

The value of the Oklahoma City National Memorial was underscored in an article which appeared in the May 29, 2000, issue of *TIME* Magazine. The article reported an interview of Jeannine Gist. In the early stages of the memorial planning process Jeannine was justifiably angry. She was quoted in the article as saying, "After Karen died, I couldn't function. I couldn't handle big things. I lost my concentration. In a way, I dreaded seeing the memorial. Yet when it opened, it took me by surprise. I never thought I could be happy again. Then I walked in, and suddenly I felt good."

In 2018, PBS designated the Oklahoma City National Memorial as one of the Top Ten Monuments in the United States.

SHE TOOK MY HAND . . .

On the evening of the Dedication day, my wife, Gennie, and I were standing by the Reflecting Pool visiting with National Park Service visitors when I felt someone take my hand. When I looked, I saw a young girl who I would guess was about seven years old. I leaned down to listen to her, and she said: "Mr. Johnson, thank you for helping. I lost my mother here." I was unable to ask her name, because my heart was in my throat. If there were no other reasons, that very poignant, moving moment, standing alone, made my commitment to the Memorial effort so very rewarding and, more importantly, it validated the importance of the Memorial and the cathartic process by which it was created.

Bob Johnson

REFLECTIONS
ROWLAND DENMAN

REFLECTIONS ON CONSTRUCTION OF THE MEMORIAL

Rowland Denman
CO-CHAIRMAN OF THE MEMORIAL CONSTRUCTION COMMITTEE
AND CHAIRMAN OF THE OKLAHOMA CITY NATIONAL MEMORIAL
FOUNDATION, 2001-2002.

Having experienced many construction projects during my career, the construction of the Memorial stands out as a project that was much more than just a job to all who participated as vendors, contractors, or construction workers. From the referenced Partnering Meeting and Scheduling Review to the completion of construction, all parties involved in the construction conducted themselves in a manner that yielded the very best results of which they were capable. Each construction meeting commenced with a moment of silence to remember those who lost their lives, the survivors, and those changed forever to remind everyone that this was a very special project located on "Sacred Ground." When an occasional memorial service was conducted prior to completion of construction, all construction workers would stop their work and stand at attention during the service. Also, it was noticeable that everyone focused not only on their work but also on the work of others to minimize mistakes, avoid delays, and ensure the highest quality. Upon completion of the Memorial, the sense of pride of all involved was readily apparent. It was a high honor to be involved in such a remarkable construction process and project.

CHAPTER 18

Creation of the Museum

One of the resolutions adopted by the Advisory Committee of the Memorial Task Force and appended to the Mission Statement required that one of the components of the Memorial must be an information center. In part, the center would include a living memorial segment consisting of photographic representations and biographies of the victims written by the families and stories of the survivors and their photographic representations.

Most museums are created by the organizing group's engagement of museum and exhibit consultants and architects to develop a plan for consideration by the organizing group. The approach taken to create the Museum was very different from the norm. Over a period of multiple months, a grassroots consensus-building approach in developing the storyline for the Museum was deployed before engaging any museum design professionals.

The storyline was comprised of the following:

Chapter 1—Description of the morning of April 19, 1995, as a typical beautiful spring day in Oklahoma City.

Chapter 2—History: Alfred P. Murrah Federal Building and the surrounding area.

Chapter 3A—Replica of the Water Resources Board Hearing Room: playing of the audio of a hearing that began at 9:00 a.m. and ended with the sound of the bomb exploding and the ensuing moments of panic.

Chapter 3B—Confusion: exiting the Hearing Room, visitors see the CBS affiliate (KWTV) news helicopter video of the Murrah Federal Building just moments after the explosion.

Chapter 4A—Chaos: the first frantic moments after the bombing reflected.

Chapter 4B—Survivor Experiences:

ordinary citizens, co-workers became rescuers, survivors.

Chapter 5A—Media reporting around the globe.

Chapter 5B—Rescue and Recovery: stories of trapped survivors, first responders, medical personnel, construction volunteers and others, and discovery of the axle of the truck that contained the explosives.

Chapter 6—Watching and Waiting: rescue and recovery continues, the FEMA Teams, the Family Assistance Center, national outpouring of care and concern, the Oklahoma Standard, Memorial Prayer Service, and the ceremony marking the closing of rescue and recovery.

Chapter 7—Gallery of Honor: honoring the lives of the 168 who were killed.

Chapter 8—Impact and Healing: Oral Histories of victims' families, survivors and first responders, changes in our community and nation after the bombing, passage of congressional legislation regarding justice and victims' rights, the community rallied to remember and memorialize the tragedy, and the public response.

Chapter 9—Investigation, Evidence and Justice: trail of evidence and justice.

Chapter 10—Responsibility and Hope.

As described in the following Reflections on the Creation of the Museum by Hardy Watkins, the collaborative process by which the Museum was created was filled with challenges; however, as was the case with the Memorial, the challenges were successfully embraced to create an exceptional Museum on time and within budget.

One of the hallmarks of the Museum is the Gallery of Honor, honoring the lives of the 168 who perished in the bombing.

REFLECTIONS
HARDY WATKINS

REFLECTIONS ON THE CREATION OF THE MUSEUM

Hardy Watkins
CO-CHAIRMAN OF THE MEMORIAL AND MUSEUM CONSTRUCTION
COMMITTEE AND OWNER'S REPRESENTATIVE

Like the Outdoor Symbolic Memorial; planning, design, and construction of the Oklahoma City National Memorial Museum was a complex and collaborative process bringing together the very best talents of construction professionals, world-class designers, and video story tellers, as well as strong, dedicated leadership from the Memorial's Board and staff.

An early and fortunate decision was Lippert Bros., Inc. General Contractors selection through competitive bidding for the construction and rehabilitation phases of the bomb-damaged Journal Record Building. Because early construction of the Museum overlapped completion of the symbolic memorial by several months, it was important that construction activity taking place inside the building not hamper in the final critical months of work to complete the outdoor site. Guernsey & Company assisted with engineering and building design.

Douglas|Gallagher (DG), an internationally respected museum design firm, was selected through a competition to tell the story of the bombing in the Museum. DG was supported in its design by highly regarded Hillmann & Carr for the video elements that would be used throughout. DG was selected by a review panel that included family members, survivors and first responders; in addition to local community museum professionals, Memorial board and staff members. The five finalists were invited to create story boards and those boards were placed on display in the 2nd floor atrium of Leadership Square in downtown Oklahoma City for public comment.

After final analysis, the DG exhibit design team was selected because its proposed storyline stayed closest to the outline proposed by the Memorial's Content Committee and helped guide the visitor from beginning to end in an easy-to-understand chronological and compelling manner, and the proposal was within budget. The DG team also retained an important artifact; the audio recording of the Water Resources Board Meeting, as part of its storyline.

A final team member that was instrumental in the success of the Memorial Museum was Exhibit Concepts as builders of the infrastructure and exhibits that would become what visitors would see and touch as they walked through the completed museum.

Looking back, there were three significant challenges that could have derailed the ultimate success of the museum's opening. However, because of the Memorial's steady leadership and the professional team selected, the project was delivered to great acclaim.

The first challenge arose as construction crews were able to get into the Journal Record Building and fully discover the amount of damage the building had sustained. It would require more reinforcement than originally planned. The primary ramification of this was the timeline. Because the Memorial & Museum were to be self-sustaining and would not receive federal funds to operate—even though it had

been designated part of the National Park System, the original pro forma included a museum opening date of August 2000, just four months after the outdoor Memorial's opening. The building's condition required a six-month delay which was agreed to by all parties involved. This new schedule was still aggressive. However, the families, survivors, first responders, and general public were told of the new timeline and the reasons for the delay. Looking back, it was helpful this decision and announcement were made after the opening of the outdoor symbolic site. Because the symbolic memorial had opened to such strong reviews and offered such quality; families, survivors, first responders, city leaders, news media and the general public had come to trust the Memorial's board and staff. As in all things, we were transparent and shared reasons for the delay. Nonetheless, the pressure remained, and everyone understood there would not be an additional delay. Plans were on for a February 2001 (Presidents' Day) Museum opening.

A second challenge completely outside Memorial leadership and staff control arose shortly thereafter. DG, the design team chosen, split and the senior partner who worked with the Oklahoma City project and his design team left that organization. They had initially hoped the Oklahoma City National Memorial Foundation would sign on as a client. However, given the short construction schedule, the prior completion of the design phase of the project, and legal issues, Memorial leadership continued the project with DG working with a new senior designer and team. Hillmann & Carr's agreement as a subcontractor was also with DG which meant we were able to continue working with that group to complete oral histories and video elements showcased in the Museum.

The final major challenge was a dissatisfaction with the general tone and storytelling of the different chapters within the Museum. First drafts were coming back very academic and detached from the emotion. The proposed words on the panels lacked connection to the families, survivors, and first responders—in general the people of Oklahoma and Oklahoma City. Memorial Leaders decided the Museum panels and photo captions should all be written by someone local. As Owner's Representative, I was assigned the responsibility of following the design plan and writing the information presented on panels and captions throughout the Museum.

That process, in reality, became much more collaborative. I wrote a first draft of every Museum panel and photo caption within the suggested word count to fit the space allocated. Members of the Content Committee agreed to meet to review and make suggested edits and content corrections based on their experiences. Initially, the group was asked to meet for a couple of hours on two successive Wednesday evenings. Those meetings proved invaluable, and in the end, the Content Committee actually ended up

meeting over ten successive Wednesday evenings for several hours.

Every photo, every word, every claim was read aloud and reviewed for accuracy. Team Members included: Bob Johnson, Chairman; Karen Luke, Vice Chair; Jeannine Gist, family member; Richard Williams, survivor; Fire Chief Gary Marrs and Police Major Ed Hill, first responders; Cheryl Vaught, Co-Chair of Victims' Families and Survivors Liaison Committee; Sue Hale, editor of *The Daily Oklahoman*; and Memorial team members including Kari Watkins, Jane Thomas, Pam Neville, Joanne Riley, and myself. Each week, edits would be made, fact-checking assigned as needed and photos approved or replacements suggested. At each meeting, the entire team would revisit the changes

from the week prior then move on to the first drafts of the upcoming chapter. Reviews occurred in order to help ensure the timeline and photos appeared in the correct chronological order and information would not be presented too soon or too late. It was important to everyone that future visitors would have the opportunity to easily follow along as they moved through the Museum. In the end, it was hoped there would be a universal understanding of the senselessness of violence as well as the significant loss, pursuit of justice and eventual recovery and healing of Oklahoma City by future visitors to the Museum. As each section was completed and approved, text and photos were shipped overnight to Exhibit Concepts in Ohio for fabrication.

Everyone involved in the project proved to be incredibly talented and dedicated. In the months between opening of the Outdoor Symbolic Memorial in April 2000 and the Museum opening in February 2001, Christmas Day was the only day when no one worked. Even on New Year's Day, 2001, and with snow on the ground in Oklahoma City that year, elements of the Museum were being installed. In the end, all exhibits and components of the Museum came together as planned— and beautifully—in those final days and weeks. In February, family members, survivors and first responders were given the opportunity to preview the Museum. Despite the difficulty of the story and the very personal connections to the artifacts, oral histories and mementos included as part of the Gallery of Honor, the Museum was well received by those most important.

Team members worked collaboratively at each stage of the project to ensure plans, design, construction, fabrication and visitor experience would be recognized as world-class. There have been subsequent updates to the story and Museum as needed over time, and technology upgrades have also occurred. To Memorial leadership's credit, many original team members have been invited back to help lead and accomplish planned updates in an effort to ensure consistency of voice, understanding of the story and its timeline as well as connection to the families, survivors, first responders and community leaders who were there to help Oklahoma City and the country heal and always remember the high cost paid at a place that remains the site of the largest domestic terrorist attack in United States history.

CHAPTER 19

Dedication and Importance of The Museum

On Presidents' Day, February 19, 2001, President George W. Bush, First Lady Laura Bush, and Secretary of State Condoleezza Rice led the list of dignitaries attending the Dedication of the Oklahoma City National Memorial Museum.

In his remarks at the Dedication of the Museum, Oklahoma City Mayor Kirk Humphreys said:

"Today, we dedicate this museum where all Americans, indeed all mankind can see, hear and feel the effects of terrorism, especially as it visited us and invaded our lives at this place. May we all learn anew the lessons taught here. . . that terrorism should never be the answer for conflict and that friends and family in every day of life are precious gifts from God."

From the very beginning of the memorialization process Governor Frank Keating was a consistent and supportive partner in the efforts to develop the Memorial and Museum. In his Museum Dedication remarks, Governor Keating stated:

"On April 19, 1995, this was a place of unspeakable horror and tragedy. We experienced every conceivable emotion that day, including anger, hope, hopelessness, frustration, fear and futility . . . but we are a believing people. We know that out of evil good comes . . . and good came. That day and the following days were characterized by goodness and heroism.

"Rebecca Anderson gave her life so others could live. Goodness and heroism.

"The rescue workers, firefighters, police, highway patrol, national guard, medical personnel, crane operators and construction workers came here and risked everything to rescue survivors and recover the bodies of those who died so they could be returned to their loved ones. Goodness and heroism.

"The message of this place should be that

President George W. Bush and First Lady Laura Bush toured the Museum prior to its dedication on Presidents' Day, 2001.

we as human beings should care for each other and not permit evil or selfishness to depreciate or deprave us."

During the introduction of the Nichols Hills Elementary Varsity Choir, I noted that the last of the ten chapters in the Museum speaks of hope, and that the message of this group of young people is for each of us to take responsibility to reduce violence of any kind. . . that our hope for peace on earth is dependent on each of us. Their extraordinary performance of "Peace on Earth" brought the first standing ovation of the day.

Before the Museum dedication ceremony began, President George W. Bush and First Lady Laura Bush were given a tour of the Museum by Jeannine Gist, representing the victims' families; Richard Williams, representing the survivors; and

Oklahoma City Police Major Ed Hill, representing the first responders. President Bush provided the following remarks:

"I appreciate so very much the tour of the Museum Laura and I just took. It is a really well done place. It is powerful. A lot of Americans are going come and be better people for having walked through this Museum.

"Americans found a lot to admire in Oklahomans in those days in 1995. You suffered so much and you responded with courage. Your losses were great and your pain was deep, but far greater and deeper was your care for one another. That is what brings us back to this place today.

"A mother who lost her daughter here will be working in the Museum. She said when she comes down here, she always has a good feeling. A time for mourning may pass, but a time for remembering never does.

"Here we remember one act of malice. The Gates of Time record the very moment of it. Yet, we also remember many acts of human kindness, heroism and love. By 9:03 on that morning a new and hopeful story was being written.

"The truth of Oklahoma City is the courage and comfort you found in one another. It began with the rescue effort. It continues with this Memorial. It is recorded in this Museum.

"Oklahoma City will always be one of those places in our national memory where the worst and the best both came to pass.

"You in Oklahoma City are victims of tragedy and witnesses of hope. You have suffered with courage, and you have fulfilled Apostle Paul's admonition to the Romans: 'Do not be overcome by evil, but overcome evil with good.' For that your nation is grateful."

At the conclusion of President Bush's remarks,

President George W. Bush spoke to those in attendance, and to the nationally televised audience, during the dedication of the Oklahoma City National Memorial Museum.

I commented that he had emphasized the importance of education, that no child should be left behind. Included in the educational outreach emanating from within the walls of the Museum is teaching children the life lessons relating to the tragedy and its aftermath. The Museum opened that day is timeless in that the lessons learned within it will likely be just as important in 100 years as they were that day.

As part of the Dedication Ceremony, the importance of the Museum was validated by a senior statesman, teacher, and student. The first message was from Don Ferrell, former Oklahoma State Senator and Adjutant General of Oklahoma. Ferrell, who lost his daughter Susan in the bombing, said:

"In the weeks following the bombing, I feared the nation and the world would soon forget the senseless sacrifice of 168 lives, including our daughter, Susan. The dedication of this Museum ensures that the world will not forget.

"Like others, I come here to remember and celebrate a life that was snuffed out needlessly on that promising spring morning almost six years ago.

"This Museum brings hope that all will learn from the horrors of violence and hope that such tragedy will not be repeated."

Sharing an educator's perspective was Talita DeNegri, Oklahoma's 2001 Teacher of the Year. She said:

"I am a teacher, but like all of us who come here and will continue to come here to this hallowed ground, we do not come here to teach. We come here to study the lessons learned and to ponder the lessons to be learned.

"As we walk the hallways of this Museum, we must remember that each display, each narrative and each photograph begs us to learn just a little bit more and challenges us to live a better life.

"As a classroom teacher, I ask all my fellow teachers, not only in Oklahoma but across this great nation, as well as all parents and grandparents who are our students' best and most important teachers, to never let your students, our children, forget what happened here."

It is beyond debate that our nation's greatest natural resource is our children. The third message was delivered by Carmen Ponder-Moore, a sixth grade student. With great confidence and enthusiasm, she delivered the following message:

"This Museum assures that everyone will remember the bombing and the devastation and hurt that it caused. We must remember what hate, violence and terrorism can do.

"I was 6 years old when this terrible tragedy happened. I remember watching on television how all the people were helping each other no matter what color they were, because they had a mission. I learned from the tragedy that people should continue to come together and help each other.

"Today, we still have a mission. I think children should be encouraged to do the right thing and make a difference in the world. Violence is not a solution or the way to make your voice heard. We must remember that love overcomes hate and love and respect should be taught in our homes and schools.

"We must always pray and have faith and trust in God. We must live everyday with an attitude of gratitude.

"People must have hope for the future, and I believe if people have goals, ambitions and dreams, they will have hope for the future. I have a dream today about people coming together and being able to live peacefully and grow in a safe tomorrow.

"We must make choices, not excuses.

"I challenge everyone today to let there be peace on earth and let it begin with us."

Carmen Ponder-Moore received a standing ovation.

As the 168-voice Memorial Choir performed the Memorial's Anthem, "To Remember," President Bush joined in a ribbon cutting ceremony to officially open to the world the Oklahoma City National Memorial Museum.

The Museum opened that day to large crowds. To date it has been visited by nearly five-million people. The reactions written in the visitor book, as well as ratings and comments on social media, remain overwhelmingly positive.

In 2006, the Museum was awarded accreditation by the American Association of Museums (AAM) and reaccredited in 2016.

The Museum is among the elite museums in the United States as only 3% of the approximate 35,000 museums have received such accreditation. The AAM Accreditation Committee Report stated:

"A response to a tragic moment in our nation's history, the Oklahoma City National Memorial Museum stands as a model for building consensus among stakeholders and for skillfully linking museum interpretation and memorialization. At a moment when there is much discussion and debate about the politics of memory and memorialization, we know what they have achieved was not a given."

TripAdvisor has designated the Museum as one of the Top 10 Museums in the United States.

The Museum houses the story of the bombing and the hope that sprang from people stepping forward selflessly to make a difference.

Chief Gary Marrs said the Museum "does a very good job of wrapping you up at the end with a feeling that despite what you've seen [earlier in the Museum], there's always hope. There's a community spirit that came through and bound us together. I think that people who go through there walk out being emotionally drained from the first part of it, but being energized from the hope in the last part of it."

Frances Leonard, a teacher and sister of one of the bombing victims, Secret Service Agent Don Leonard, visited the Museum just after its dedication. She followed up in a letter that read:

"As a family member of one of the victims of the bombing, I was apprehensive about revisiting the events of that day—the longest and worst day of my life! But, as I listened to the video coverage and read accounts from other families involved, rescue workers, and survivors, I was able to fill in the missing pieces of that day. We were frantic that day to find Don and were unaware of all that was happening.

"My favorite chapter of the Museum was the last chapter—the hope of the future. As a teacher, how well I know that our hope for the future lies in our children. It is so important for me and others to teach tolerance and conflict resolution as well as academics. I found this chapter to be a renewal of my spirit in hopes that I can make this a better world in which we live."

If each visitor to the Museum takes to heart the messages within it, he or she will be changed by those lessons. Further, if those lessons are taught by each, by word or example, the hope generated by the Museum will continue to multiply. This is how the Museum is changing the world.

An important message offered by the Museum is that each of us can make a positive difference for others and thereby create hope. Tom McDaniel accurately described a message of the Museum as being, "Man's resilience to deal with whatever life brings ... and a remarkable resilience to rise above the fray and bring hope to the future."

In addition to stories within the walls of the Museum, it is through Called2Change and other educational outreach programs the promise of hope is being fulfilled by teaching our young people the lessons of responsible citizenship, the importance of community involvement, solid core values, the senselessness of violence as a means of achieving government or societal change, and creating hope by making a difference for others. In short, the Museum is seeking to replace meanness with meaning, hate with love, and ugliness with grace.

The Museum is instilling in young people courage to make good decisions. They are being taught that there are times when each of us alone must test our principles, make moral choices, and stand by an idea or an article of faith even when under pressure to do the easy, expedient, and, sometimes, wrong thing. I believe this is what Andrew Jackson was referencing when he said:

> "Sometimes one person with courage makes a majority."

To date, educational curriculum guides and materials have reached students and educators in thousands of schools located in all 50 states and Afghanistan, Brazil, Egypt, India, Ireland, Japan, Kenya, Puerto Rico, Spain, and the United Kingdom. Since its inception, the annual student essay contest has received more than 11,000 entries from all 50 states.

In 2010, a middle school teacher from a poverty stricken area in eastern Oklahoma obtained a grant to bring her middle school class to visit the Memorial and Museum. In her grant application, she stated:

MAKING A DIFFERENCE CREATES HOPE

Creating hope by making a difference for others is well illustrated by a story that arose out of the earthquake in Haiti in January 2010. A Haitian violinist named Romel Joseph has been blind since childhood, but the nuns in the school he attended in Haiti recognized his remarkable musical talent. Ultimately, the culmination of his education occurred at The Juilliard School in New York. Although he had many opportunities after graduating from Juilliard, he chose to return to Haiti and build a school of music for Haitian children. On January 12, 2000, his New Victorian School was destroyed by fire. On January 12, 2010, precisely ten years later, the school was destroyed by earthquake.

An eight-year-old violin prodigy in Florida, Brianna Kahane, read of the destruction of the school and how Joseph was trapped in the rubble for 18 hours, not knowing that his wife and unborn child had perished. She was saddened by the story and decided to do something to help rebuild the school. She held fundraising performances and also donated her first violin. She sent letters to several famous violinists, resulting in benefit concerts across America.

The efforts of this young girl raised approximately $5 million to assure the New Victorian School in Haiti would be rebuilt. On September 6, 2011, the New Victorian School opened its doors to 257 Haitian students and resumed classes. In an interview Brianna Kahane said her dream is to make the world a better place one song at a time. The story of the difference made by this 8-year-old girl confirms that each of us has the capacity to make a difference in the world and thereby create hope.

"I am planning on implementing the Memorial's Called2Change Program into our reading and writing curriculum. Hope is going to be the character trait instilled into my students. Our school system lies in a poverty stricken community. Drugs and alcohol are something my students face every day, many times in their own homes. I truly believe visiting and feeling the impact of the Memorial will change their lives."

As this teacher was departing the Memorial and Museum, she said that she was so grateful for her students' experience that day, because it confirmed for them that notwithstanding their limited resources each of them has the capacity to make a difference in the world.

Without the Museum, future generations would have been short-changed. Without it, the future could not learn of the horror of the tragedy and the innocence we lost. Without it, the future could not go there to learn and resolve to do what they can in their own lives to help prevent violence. Without it, the future could not learn of the pain and suffering brought about by hate. Without it, the future could not learn of how much good can be done when we work together. The Museum is a very special, prestigious, preeminent place of learning that remembers Oklahoma's losses and inspires hope and excellence.

As a community we could have responded to the forces of hate with more hate; we did not. Rather, the Museum captures the public response consisting of thousands of acts of virtue. Very simply, on April 19, 1995, evil did not triumph in Oklahoma City.

CHAPTER 20

Worldwide Pilgrimage to the Memorial and Museum

The Oklahoma City National Memorial & Museum continues to be the most visited site in Oklahoma by out-of-state travelers. On average, each year the Memorial and Museum welcomes visitors from almost all 50 states and 81 countries.

Typical of comments by visitors from outside of Oklahoma are the following:

"I had never been to Oklahoma City before the bombing and, truthfully, had never paid much attention to your city. The events of April 19, 1995, changed all of that. Not only did Oklahoma City garner international attention from the tragedy itself but also from the way it responded to it. Now you have set another precedent. This memorial moved me beyond words even as I struggled to comprehend what had occurred on that spot. The world will never understand why, but you have shown us how to heal. Be very proud of what you have accomplished and what you will accomplish.

I'd be very proud to call Oklahoma City my home. I will be back soon."

The Oklahoma City National Memorial & Museum was created in and from the heart of America. A worldwide pilgrimage to the Memorial and Museum continues because they have become universal symbols of a strong worldwide resolve to reject the forces of terrorism and serve as the greatest example of how profound loss was met with profound love. What once was the site of the most horrific violence in Oklahoma City's history is now the most serene.

Professor Jonathan Turley, a nationally-recognized legal scholar from Washington, D.C., visited Oklahoma City and in his Blog stated:

"The success of Oklahoma City is evident in its memorial. The city came together after the bombing, and in true Oklahoma style, created a massive effort to collectively consider and

The Oklahoma City National Memorial after a winter storm. *Courtesy Steve Johnson, KFOR-TV.*

approve a design for the memorial. The result is in my view the single greatest modern memorial in the United States ... a moving and simple space at the site of the former Oklahoma City federal building. This was done without rancor and without debt. It was done as a unified community to express profound sorrow and continued unity."

The Memorial, in all of its power and beautiful grandeur, is not about the monumental or the spectacular. Rather, it is about people, and the celebration of the triumph of the human spirit. Through the Museum, visitors from around the world are exposed to the soul of Oklahoma. Out of the chaos grew unprecedented resilience, courage, strength, generosity, and unity. The Memorial and Museum will continue to teach that terrorism cannot be tolerated. They will forever remember the losses and the erosion of our senses of innocence and security. And, for the

generations, they will represent the commitment of the people of Oklahoma and the nation to the preservation of peace and the sanctity of life.

It is my hope that the Memorial and Museum will touch the lives of visitors in a way that will cause each to ask: "What would I do in the circumstances of April 19, 1995? Would I step forward to make a difference and provide hope to someone in need? What can I do to help make the world a better, more peaceful and less violent place?"

People from around the world also have been drawn to the Memorial and Museum as a result of the creation of the Oklahoma City Memorial Marathon. In the spring of 2000, a call from Art Swanson and Chet Collier was received to discuss the possibility of creating an annual marathon that would be held in April of each year. After discussing the proposed event with the Board and victims' families and survivors, it was decided that the marathon and related activities

A runner begins the inaugural OKC Memorial Marathon in April 2001.

could be conducted in a respectful manner that would enhance the remembrance and education missions of the Memorial and Museum.

The mission of the Oklahoma City Memorial Marathon is to celebrate life, reach for the future, honor the memories of those who were killed, and unite the world in hope. Through the guidance provided by Collier, David Hill, and Thomas Hill, and the dedication and efforts of the Memorial staff and hundreds of volunteers, the inaugural event was held in 2001 with just shy of 5,000 participants. The 2019 event hosted 23,789 runners and walkers from all 50 states and 13 foreign countries. As a result of the incredible selfless efforts of all involved, the "Run To Remember" has become a significant financial contributor to the operation and maintenance of the Memorial and Museum. More important, it has continued to broaden the exposure of the Memorial and Museum to people around the world.

The 2019 Run to Remember boasted more than 23,000 participants.

3

REFLECTIONS
KAREN LUKE

REFLECTIONS ON THE MEMORIALIZATION PROCESS

Karen Luke
CHAIRMAN OF THE OKLAHOMA CITY NATIONAL MEMORIAL
FOUNDATION, 1998-2001

Much has changed in our city since the bombing, but the Oklahoma City National Memorial continues to Remember, to Listen and to Include, these words, as ever, the very foundation of our process and beginning.

The intrepid Bob Johnson stepped up first. He volunteered to help build a memorial before the city knew what that was. The Murrah Federal Building had not even yet been imploded. Bob worked tirelessly for years and his strong leadership carries on today.

The incredible Kari Watkins was the miracle first hire and continues 25 years later as Executive Director. She not only guides our work but has helped hundreds of others facing disasters and terrorism in our country since 1995.

Polly Nichols, a dear friend and survivor, agreed to co-chair the fundraising committee with Vice President Dick Cheney, then Chairman of Halliburton. We began that effort before we had a design, a staff or an office. But Polly said "yes." She too has continued to serve the Memorial in so many gentle, gracious and generous ways.

Countless others came forward... on the streets, in lines to donate blood, and to meet with us for hours to craft and shape the Memorial we built and love today.

This was a journey of faith made easier by the words of our Mission Statement. Inclusion was the keynote after the bombing. Family members deep in grief were encouraged to participate in spite of experts and consultants who said it should be otherwise.

In the horrific aftermath of the bombing we discovered that we are stronger than we thought, we reaffirmed that Americans respond to almost unanimity when freedom is challenged and that we all share a core belief that all people should be free from fear and violence. That commitment drove us through the process.

The Mission Statement which has guided us since the beginning was another miracle of listening, collaboration and leadership, this time led by Beth Shortt and the writing of Yvonne Maloan.

A grieving mother said we could not include the word HOPE in the Mission

Statement as then, in her world, there was no hope. Later, she said that her participation in the Memorial process was her greatest gift and created hope. The words prevailed in the statement to guide the design but also to appear in bronze on the Gates of Time.

Tireless and countless volunteers listened, captured ideas and presented to our city the hundreds of designs submitted to the final design competition. And, miraculously, a consensus was achieved.

From the beginning we wanted to be a beacon of hope and proactive against violence as a means of societal change. This effort, thanks to so many, continues.

Creating and building was a challenge, but some would say maintaining has been an even greater challenge. So to the current and future board members AND STAFF, thank you for continuing to serve and to lead the Memorial and Museum for the next 25 years.

CHAPTER 21

Leadership Invested

Thinking Forward

BY KARI WATKINS

" It is important that such a tribute in no way dismiss the tragedy, but rather that it offer an inspiring contrast between the brutality of evil and the tenderness of the response..." some key words from the Mission Statement that are etched in our core beliefs as we look back and think forward about the content, the education, and the programs taught at the Oklahoma City National Memorial & Museum. With every major decision made we go back to our founding documents to reread to make sure we are staying on mission as we move forward.

Being a part of this process from the early days has taught me so much about the people this story is about and the lessons we must continue to teach. There is not one part of the Memorial design or one word or one picture, artifact, or video told in the Museum that wasn't vetted through stakeholder groups most closely impacted by the Oklahoma City bombing.

This has made the story both emotional and compelling. The story told on this site and within the walls of the Museum is not easy and was never meant to be. Visitors who come through the Museum won't see this story anywhere else in the country. Sure, there are other monumental stories at historical sites told about hard days in history, but the story told here is one about the people... the people impacted, the families torn apart by terrorism, survivors who had to rebuild their lives, and first responders who had to act strong on the outside while inside they were hurting, and a community who decided we would not be defined by the bombing, but our response to it.

The Memorial and Museum exist today because of countless hours of volunteer work and the leadership of some great men and women whom I have had the honor to work with and learn from. Bob Johnson, Karen Luke, Rowland Denman, Linda Lambert, Polly Nichols, Luke Corbett, Frank

CHAIRMEN OF THE OKLAHOMA CITY NATIONAL MEMORIAL & MUSEUM

Bob Johnson
Foundation Chair
1995-1998
Trust Chair
1998-2001

Karen Luke
Foundation Chair
1998-2001

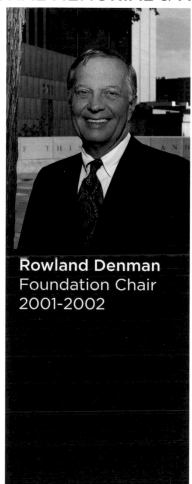

Rowland Denman
Foundation Chair
2001-2002

Linda Lambert
Trust Chair
2001-2002

CHAIRMEN OF THE OKLAHOMA CITY NATIONAL MEMORIAL & MUSEUM

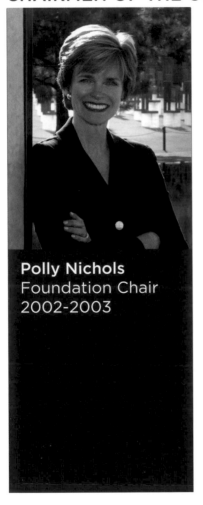

Polly Nichols
Foundation Chair
2002-2003

Luke Corbett
Trust Chair
2003

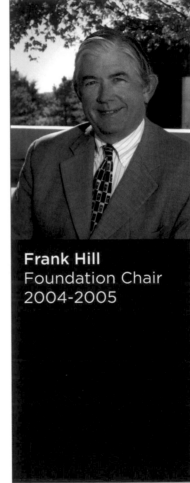

Frank Hill
Foundation Chair
2004-2005

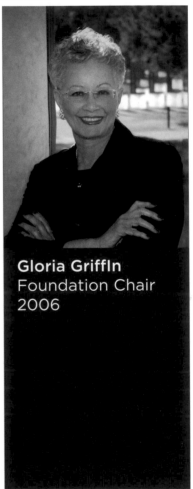

Gloria Griffin
Foundation Chair
2006

CHAIRMEN OF THE OKLAHOMA CITY NATIONAL MEMORIAL & MUSEUM

Burns Hargis
Foundation Chair
2007

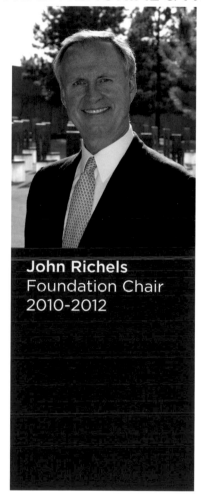

Bill Scheihing
Foundation Chair
2007-2009

John Richels
Foundation Chair
2010-2012

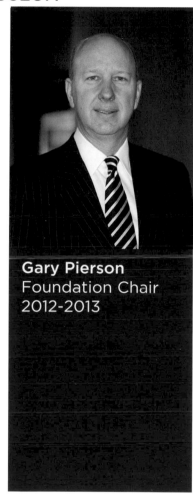

Gary Pierson
Foundation Chair
2012-2013

229

CHAIRMEN OF THE OKLAHOMA CITY NATIONAL MEMORIAL & MUSEUM

Susan Winchester
Foundation Chair
2014-2015

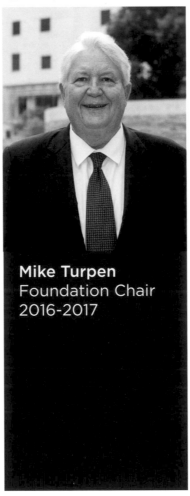

Mike Turpen
Foundation Chair
2016-2017

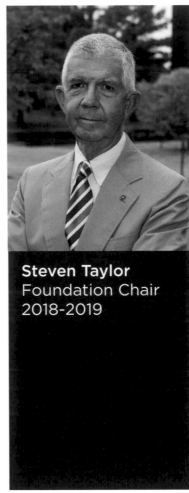

Steven Taylor
Foundation Chair
2018-2019

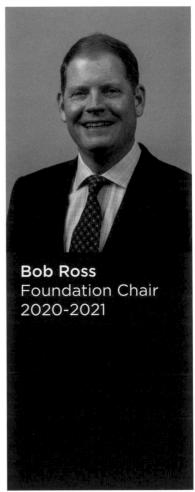

Bob Ross
Foundation Chair
2020-2021

Hill, Gloria Griffin, Burns Hargis, Bill Scheihing, John Richels, Gary Pierson, Susan Winchester, Mike Turpen, Justice Steven Taylor, and Bob Ross have all proven to be critical leaders at just the perfect time. Each, serving as chairman, have brought their own expertise to the table and with everything in this process, the right people have come to the table at the right time.

These men and women have helped lead the Memorial and Museum and have guided the staff in a way that was both selfless and visionary. All while holding full-time and demanding jobs, these leaders stepped in to work through tough decisions, look at changing trends, and help raise money to make telling this story possible. Most important, they would talk through emotional situations day or night to get to the right decision. They each knew we could never stop looking back, but also each had the vision to help us think forward.

CHAPTER 22

A Classroom

The future of this story is critical to teaching the senseless of violence to a generation that did not live through this historical event. Learning this story is a different experience for them. When we were first building the Memorial and Museum we would talk about how someday we would teach a generation of kids that did not live through the bombing. That day seemed to come very quickly.

Today we are teaching thousands of students each month that this event is truly history. They did not live through it and for some of their parents it is a faint memory. Today more than 50% of the people in Oklahoma City either were not alive or did not live here in 1995. Our mission is as important today as it was the day we opened. We must continue to be on the cutting edge of teaching even if sometimes it is not a typical Museum education program. We are a different institution and not necessarily a traditional museum. We have been challenged by some traditionalists in the Museum business, but we believe we are impacting the world in a different way through our educational opportunities and using technology to enhance their experience. Teaching the lessons of STEM (Science, Technology, Engineering and Math) and how each was used in the rescue and recovery and in building the Memorial and Museum are innovative in a history museum. The key lessons learned here make this story relevant in the mind of young visitors. We knew we could not be so arrogant to think that everyone knew of this story or would want to know, we had to meet our visitors where they were willing to learn.

Sometimes people are surprised when I say this Memorial was not built to be a cemetery but rather to be a living breathing Memorial— a classroom.

When we built the Memorial and Museum, today's smart phones and tablets were not even publicly being talked about, much less being sold. Today on their way to a class field trip, students and visitors can pull up information on the Memorial and Museum or other facts about the Oklahoma City bombing.

Why is the Museum visit important? Why would someone want to pay to learn this story? Why should they care? How do we use "new" technology to enhance the telling of this story? These questions motivate us as we develop programs and exhibits for this special place. We have learned quickly that we have to meet our visitors where they are and not assume everyone will interpret this story the traditional way of most museums through text panels and artifacts. We knew that when we designed the Museum the first time, and believe it even more today after watching millions interact with both the Memorial and the Museum.

Having a National Park Service Ranger share the symbolism of the Outdoor Symbolic Memorial has proven to be one of the visitor's favorite experiences. While the Memorial doesn't receive annual government funding and we are not a traditional national memorial, we believe there are lessons to be learned by private citizens and the government working together. If ever a partnership should work, it should be on the site of where an American thought he could bring down his government. We have worked very hard to make this partnership work and I'm grateful it does. We are proud of the lessons it teaches.

I have been fortunate to have been raising two kids through this process. So between Ford and Caroline and their friends, they have served as our primary focus group. They have given us a front row seat to how different learning styles are today versus what they were when we originally designed the Memorial and Museum. So much so,

I sometimes think if I hadn't seen it, I'm not sure I would believe it. The staff through the years has been focused and dedicated. We have been blessed by a visionary board and Museum design groups that have seen our concerns and helped us stay on mission yet change technology and never ever depart from the original story line, just different ways to teach it.

CHAPTER 23

The Second Decade

As we took a fresh look at the Museum ahead of the 20th anniversary, we went back to our original museum designer Patrick Gallagher. I knew he was following the changing trends in Museum design and understood our concern in meeting our visitors where they were willing to learn. So with the Museum design teams of Gallagher & Associates and Hillmann & Carr, we brought back the "Wednesday night groups" to look at our plans and envision a repurposed Museum and added the knowledge of veteran Oklahoman reporter Nolan Clay who had covered this story since day one and knew nearly every detail. We brought together new groups that weren't ready the first time or couldn't because of the federal and state trials to meet and share their experiences. We also added Cortina Productions, a new video and interactive group, to help us think through and design new technology. We stayed with our original exhibit fabricators Exhibit Concepts and our long time contractor Lippert Bros. to help bring all the dreams to reality. These teams, combined with our staff that does great work on preserving history, figuring out how to teach the story in new and creative ways, creating videos and understanding and helping design the interactive components, has been an incredible experience few people get to do much less have an impact on actually producing and executing museum exhibits. Even for the designers, they are not used to working with such active participatory staffs and governing boards. I am grateful we have chosen partners who allow us use of our skills, know our stakeholders, and use their expertise to create what I think is a one-of-a-kind museum in our country.

The Museum enhancements took an advertising campaign to explain. It also took a Visitor Services staff and facilities and security teams to execute daily as we would work night and day to rebuild all while remaining open during the process. There were two times in the 18-month process to ensure visitor safety

As part of the Museum enhancements, an Investigators Round Table of city, state, and federal law enforcement who worked the Oklahoma City bombing were brought together. This was one of several groups that came to the table to give their stories and experiences during the Museum remodel.

that we had to close for a day or two at a time, but between the designers and contractors and our staff, those days were kept to a minimum and the work was completed. We reopened different galleries in stages with the main grand reopening in January 2015. We studied The Ronald Reagan Presidential Library plan as our design teams had worked on that project a few years earlier. Visiting with their staff and understanding how they designed their plan, helped us understand how visitors liked being a part of a rebuilding process as long as there was transparency in the project.

Temporary glass walls so construction could be seen, educating staff with daily up-to-date information each morning about the timeline and the process, and a token given to each visitor to come back for free to see the finished project were just a few of the things we did to bring visitors along in this enhancement project.

The process of rebuilding the Museum and staying true to its original storyline was not easy, yet critical. Educating new staff and trustees on why the storyline was written as it was proved critical during this process. Artifacts and stories

were now available to us that were not when the Museum was designed and built. We had to include these stories.

We continually look at what and how we are telling the story and making sure it is kept up to date. Museums sometimes feel outdated, but then you take a look at how visitors are interacting with it and begin to make plans on what if anything needs to be changed. Changes have only been made to the Museum to enhance or enrich the story. Adding technology is critical to teaching this story. We talk a lot about teaching this story to people from eight to eighty. Each of those generations learn differently so to have a traditional museum panel or an artifact in a case proves critical as the basis of the story. Then add a video of those who were killed, a story of those who survived, or a story of someone changed forever, and all of a sudden the story becomes real. With experience and insight, decisions were made to add the layer of an interactive and instead of showing one artifact you can literally show every single piece of evidence shared in the trials at the touch of your fingertips. These each play

239

Trustees Ann-Clore Duncan, Susan Winchester, and Founding Chairman Bob Johnson took a hard hat tour with Oklahoma City National Memorial & Museum Executive Director Kari Watkins during the 2014-2015 Museum enhancements.

Middle and high school students tested the Uncover Discover Stem Lab for the Memorial as the finishing touches were put on a new area of the Museum designed to teach the lessons learned in the rescue and recovery of the Oklahoma City bombing with relevant lessons taught today.

an important role and as the institution, it cannot and should not dictate how people learn—you just want to provide the tools for learning.

Selecting artifacts and stories that are sensitive and hard to tell, and even more difficult to process, was very important as we enhanced the Museum. We are teaching this story to a new generation and the vision of the Board and the Conscience Committee was critical as we looked to the future. I am grateful for the candid discussions and wisdom of the designers who see museums around the world, the board, the staff and, most important, the Conscience Committee who saw the importance of including items that we could have never even thought about when we originally built the Museum.

Adding interactive touch screens and stories in the Museum has allowed multi-generations to learn the story together in ways never seen before. It is not uncommon to see kids with their parents and grandparents sitting down together learning this story and hearing their experiences.

REFLECTIONS
SAM PRESTI

REFLECTIONS ON THE OKLAHOMA STANDARD

Sam Presti
EXECUTIVE VICE PRESIDENT & GENERAL MANAGER OF
THE OKLAHOMA CITY THUNDER

The water surrounded my ankle forming a perfect circle around my skin. A thin, clear line separated the water drenching my ankle and the air-filled atmosphere above the line. It was April 19, 1995.

As an eighteen-year-old boy sitting in front of the television in Concord, Massachusetts, soaking my twisted ankle from a basketball game earlier that day with hopes that my body would find the resiliency to take the court tomorrow. I watched image after image of despair flash before me from what seemed to be a far off land: Oklahoma.

Fast forward to the year 2020, my ankles are still sore, albeit for different reasons. I have gone from the boy in front of a television, to a man watching image after image of progress and hope flash before me from what has become my home: Oklahoma.

Each moment I spend thinking about the transformation of Oklahoma City and how it is rooted in response, resilience, and optimism is more informative than the next.

Some things are always present, they are just waiting to be named.

From what I can tell, this was the case with what we now term the Oklahoma Standard. In a land, that in 1995, seemed far off for so many, exhibiting Service, Honor, and Kindness was as natural as the land itself.

In the year 1995, our world was not as fast, it was not as technologically advanced. Solitude was possible without extraordinary effort and discipline. We still looked to certain trusted voices to make sense of our current events in a way that could steady our fears, yet build hope in what may be in the waiting. Tom Brokaw served in this role of communicator/translator, and that April, gathered himself and spoke to those of us who were not all that familiar with this place called Oklahoma.

He introduced the world to Oklahoma in its newest form, it was a somber recognition. A new member to the areas of the world where domestic terrorism was now a possibility. Brokaw brokered the relationship with a quote that still serves its purpose: "Oklahoma has earned its place in American folklore as cowboy tough and proudly self-reliant. Oklahomans may feel more vulnerable now and little disoriented by what's happened to them, but in their response to this madness they have elevated us all with

their essential sense of goodness, community, and compassion."

In 2008, the first time I saw this quote on the walls of the Oklahoma City National Memorial & Museum, it penetrated me. It not only served as an introduction to the place I would now call home, but it was also a catalyst for learning about the people that I would be calling my neighbors going forward. It set a standard in and of itself for community citizenship, an unspoken seemingly unattainable bar to meet for any new arrival.

Today, our world presses on all of our communities to advance rapidly, expand themselves, and raise the tempo and bustle of everyday life. All local communities bare two essential burdens as they push to keep

pace with an ever-changing world around them. First, is preservation of the values that built the foundation and identity from which we have the opportunity to build and advance in the modern age. Second is allowing those historic values to remain adaptable enough for future leaders to take with them into the future and the history they will be writing.

Oklahoma City is no longer a far-off land to many in this world, far from it. It was thrust into the global spotlight on April 19th, 1995. It too has been asked to expand and grow at rapid rates as a result of its meteoric rise into one of the United States greatest success stories for thriving mid-sized cities.

We must revisit Brokaw now, and again. As he introduced the world to Oklahoma City, he used the term "essential

For the 2019-2020 season of the Oklahoma City Thunder, a new City Edition uniform was designed in partnership with the Oklahoma City National Memorial & Museum in honor of those impacted by the April 19, 1995, bombing of the Alfred P. Murrah Federal Building in downtown Oklahoma City.

sense of goodness." At the time, he was speaking about the great people here. Today, I believe those words are speaking to our great people here.

As we seek to recruit the best and brightest of all industries to help our forward progress, it is imperative that we scale our growth with an equal amount of education about the history of the Oklahoma Standard. Without an intentional focus that helps to introduce our new neighbors to associate with and carry-on the actions and thinking that draw them here in the first place, Oklahoma City will run the real risk of diluting its greatest natural resource: the essential sense of goodness.

Oklahoma City must preserve its identity intentionally by raising awareness of all that has come before, yet in the ultimate sign

of courage, must cede control of what the Oklahoma Standard will come to be in the future by allowing future generations to express it authentically to their generation and changing times. This is how true growth and sustainability can be born, and the Oklahoma Standard can live yet another life.

The thin clear line of ice and water that encapsulated my ankle in 1995, and created one world under water and another above, is as thin as the line that separates the past from the future of the Oklahoma Standard. The essential sense of goodness in all of us should recognize the necessity and opportunity before us.

There is someone, somewhere, in what may seem a far-off land to all of us here in Oklahoma, that knows very little of our history yet could find themselves one day immersed in it.

CHAPTER 24

Challenges and Responsibilities

In a day where people can pull up any information in a matter of seconds on their smart devices and kids can "kill" more people on their video games each day after school in a war game than died on this site makes our mission difficult. Teaching that each of these people whom they didn't know and were killed or sustained lifelong injuries were living purposeful lives and giving back to their communities is worth learning. But so is the story of the perpetrators and how they got crossways with the country they served and thought by their actions they could divide their country yet failed. Telling the story of these individuals teach and demonstrate meaningful life lessons; all worth capturing and sharing in whatever way the future holds. I have always said in guiding this institution, we cannot remember without teaching and we certainly will not teach without remembering.

There is a video in the Museum where a widow tells of rebuilding her family and she says "teaching my teenage boys we were still a family even though their dad was gone was very hard but I had to do it." This sound bite reminds me that anyone can relate to this Museum. You didn't have to lose a family member in the bombing to be impacted. Many have lost dads and moms in other tragedies or sickness. These words by the key stakeholders speak important meaning into everyday lives.

The story of this Memorial and Museum will never be completely written. The way we look back and think forward will be the next chapter and the next and the next.

Remaining relevant and teaching this story to future generations will be critical to making sure this story is not forgotten and the lessons learned are taught forever. Continuing to work with families, survivors, and first responders and their families are what make this job unique and meaningful. Capturing their stories to tell in the Museum and through our social media channels are captivating to our visitors. They help us make people understand the "why" and the importance of each individual impacted and are likely the most life-changing.

One other major area of making an impact has been the Memorial and Museum helping other cities torn apart by major acts of terrorism or violence. The fact that people call here as one of their first calls gives us a great sense of pride, yet it also awes us with the great sense of responsibility. What worked for us in Oklahoma City may certainly not be the prescription other cities need, but the fact they are willing to let us share our successes and challenges is the first step. We have walked through the darkest days with the people of 9/11 in all three cities impacted; we have helped the people in Oslo, Norway, after a shooting at a summer camp; Orlando, Florida, with the Pulse Night Club Shooting; Boston, Massachusetts, after the Boston Marathon bombing; Las Vegas, Nevada, after the mass shooting; and Newtown, Connecticut, after the school shooting; and NASA turned to us following the last space shuttle explosion. Each of these cities received a Survivor sapling. Numerous other cities have asked us for help or to send people impacted here to help them. We are proud to share our lessons learned and help them through their rebuilding, sharing with them the strength and resilience of the people of Oklahoma. This is an outreach we will always do as long as people need our help and can learn from us.

May we always work together as we have the first 25 years to teach these stories and teach the true meaning of comfort, strength, peace, hope, and serenity...the core tenets of the Oklahoma City National Memorial & Museum.

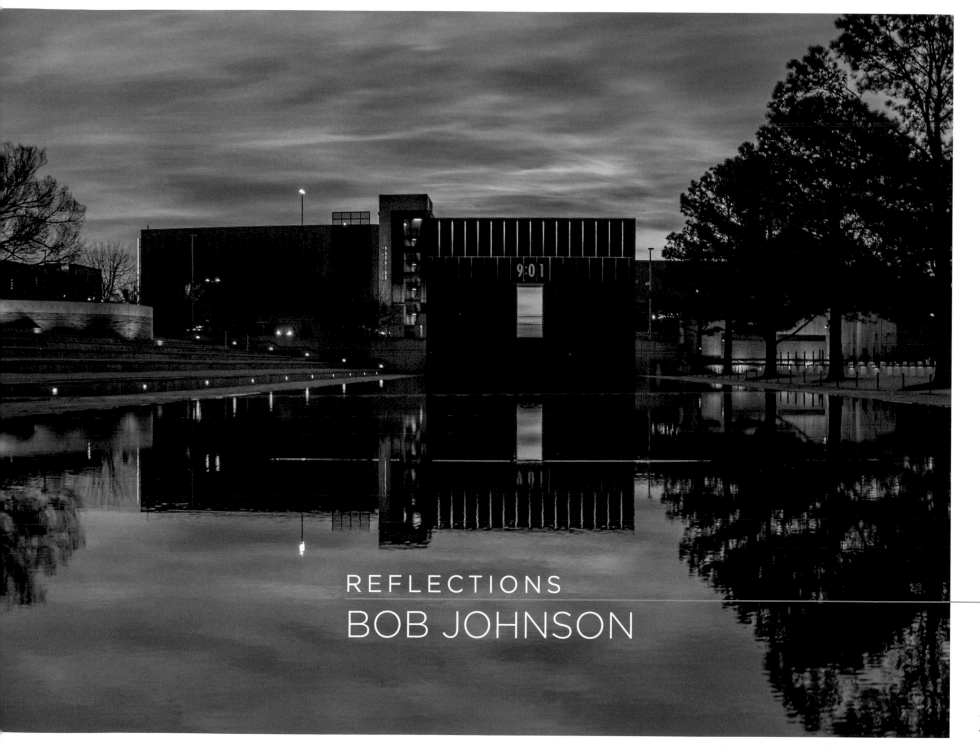

REFLECTIONS
BOB JOHNSON

REFLECTIONS

Bob Johnson
FOUNDING CHAIRMAN,
OKLAHOMA CITY NATIONAL MEMORIAL AND MUSEUM

April 19, 1995, was a day overshadowed by tragedy, but out of chaos arose a coming together of people of all walks of life to memorialize both the tragedy and the altruistic aftermath in a manner that is truly unique in the history of America's memorials. Just as its embedded roots gave the Survivor Tree the strength to endure the explosion, the character of Oklahomans, rooted in resilience, integrity, sensitivity, and compassion, provided the resolve to create a Memorial and Museum that signaled to the world that those who sought terror to divide us were neither victorious in our society nor in our hearts.

The Memorial and Museum are testaments to our faith, to the fragile nature of our freedom from fear and violence, and to the reaffirmation that Americans always respond in unity when their freedom is challenged. The Memorial journey was a pilgrimage of faith, and without our faith to sustain us it would have been a most difficult journey to complete.

The memorialization process presented several daunting challenges. First, there was no precedent for memorializing a tragedy so soon after its occurrence. Second, each raw emotion, integral to the healing and grieving processes, was encountered. Third, because of the elevated emotions there were a multitude of ideas regarding what should be memorialized, how it should be done, and who should do it. Fourth, the process involved a blend of those both familiar and unfamiliar with community processes. Finally, as has been the case with other memorials, there was a great risk that the memorialization process might be plagued by politically generated controversy.

The early meetings of victims' family members and survivors were marked with a venting of raw emotions and a feeling of distrust of the volunteers. In addition, some of the victims' family members did not think the survivors should participate in those meetings, because they had survived. In short,

"Nothing is wrong with America that cannot be cured through faith, love of freedom and energy of her citizens."
PRESIDENT DWIGHT D. EISENHOWER

"Courage is what it takes to stand up and speak. Courage is also what it takes to sit down and listen."

WINSTON CHURCHILL

anger was very prevalent in the meetings, but the volunteers listened, learned and maintained a focus on fostering healing.

Although these meetings were chaired by victims' family members, in many cases I was asked to respond to the group regarding questions or concerns, and sometimes I became a lightning rod for the anger that prevailed. As I reflect on those experiences, I am reminded of Josh Groban's song "You Raise Me Up", which includes the following lyrics: "I am strong when I am on your shoulders. You raise me up to more than I can be." During the difficult times in the Memorial journey, my faith provided strength and patience to be more than I could otherwise be.

A few years ago I read Max Lucado's

book *Outlive Your Life*. One of the more profound statements in the book is: "God does not always call the qualified, but he always qualifies the called." Such statement clearly resonates with me regarding my experience of chairing the memorialization process.

An uncharted path was forged to create the Memorial and Museum, because The Memorial Task Force leadership firmly believed that the memorialization process, as envisioned, could promote healing, hope, and unity.

I believe our memorialization process represented the first time in history such a process was democratized. Hopefully, a legacy of our memorial process will be that a consensus on difficult issues can be established if the participants are representative of the community

"No man can get from one end of life to the other by following another's path."

MARK TWAIN

as a whole and if time is taken and patience is deployed to work through the challenges. There are no limits to the value of the decisions resulting from a successful consensus building process.

In his book *The Unfinished Bombing: Oklahoma City in American Memory,* Edward T. Linenthal said of the memorial journey:

"The memorial process served as an ingeniously designed model of community consensus building. It brought together a wide cross-section of the community. Some spoke in public for the first time, most learned the art of compromise, most learned how grief became manifest in so many different ways, most learned to listen and to be patient. That people seared by immediate loss could practice

the arts of democracy in the work of memorial making is a significant achievement."

It would have been easy to fail, but through the assistance of so many caring people, the challenges were successfully embraced and a Memorial and Museum were created that have touched the world.

The noted philosopher, physician and humanitarian Albert Schweitzer said: "As the sun makes ice melt, kindness causes misunderstanding, mistrust and hostility to evaporate." I believe kindness constitutes a universal language that transcends adversity, crosses any frontier and knits humanity together in a very positive way. If asked to describe with one word the predominate characteristic of the volunteers and staff who made such extraordinary efforts to create the Memorial and Museum, that word would be kindness.

A couple of years ago a group of Wisdom Community leaders chose Oklahoma City for its annual meeting. Following their time spent at the Memorial and Museum, Steve Hannon, a member of the group, included the following in his "Mind the Gap" Blog:

"The lessons learned from my time in Oklahoma City are far too numerous for this blog entry. However, focusing on the challenges of company or project team leadership that you and I face on a regular basis, I have three takeaways:

1. Take the time to clearly define your team's mission. The time will be well spent. Down the road, the vision and principles articulated will govern decisions and keep you on track.

2. Walk the talk when it comes to inclusiveness. Paying lip service to diversity of thought and opinion will not cut it. Identify your stakeholders and err on the side of too many rather than too few. Be open and listen and thereby foster trust. This may take time. It certainly did not happen overnight . . . (in Oklahoma City). In the end the outcome will be superior.

3. Tap into your pillars of support to persevere. These pillars may be a mentor or two or it could include an outside advisory committee. It is a difficult downward spiral when you as a leader believe, and act as though, you are isolated and alone.

Bob Johnson will be the first person to

tell you that he did not lead alone and that his pillars got him through some very dark days.

These three takeaways cannot be cherry picked. It's all or nothing. For example, if you adhere to #2 without tackling #1, you'll be mired in dysfunction and discord. And even if you adhere to #1 and #2, you'll not have the stomach to survive the program or project if you ignore #3."

Two months after 9/11, a team from the Memorial and Museum had the opportunity to tell our story to the memorial organizing groups in New York City, New York, Shanksville, Pennsylvania, and the Pentagon in Washington, D.C. Without the extraordinary efforts of the multitude of devoted victims' family members, survivors, first responders, and volunteers who contributed in so many valuable ways, we would not have this story to share.

I believe the creation of the Oklahoma City National Memorial & Museum elevated the bar of excellence for all memorials and museums, but more importantly, our memorialization process fostered healing and evidenced the essential goodness of humanity. It is worth repeating what one of the victim's family members said: "Through the memorial process, chaos was transformed into hope and unity."

My experience in chairing the creation of the Oklahoma City National Memorial & Museum confirmed for me that volunteer service to others outside my comfort zone is the pathway to the greatest sense of fulfillment. As Winston Churchill said: "You make a living from what you receive, but you make a life from what you give."

Poet Robert Browning Hamilton wrote the following about the legacy of loss and sorrow:

"I walked a mile with pleasure;
She chatted all the way;
But left me none the wiser
For all she had to say.
I walked a mile with Sorrow;
And ne'er a word said she;
But, oh! The things I learned from her,
When Sorrow walked with me."

In 1995, as our community walked with sorrow, many, both far and near, learned that Tim Russert, NBC's *Meet the Press* host, was right when he said: "The best

exercise of the human heart is reaching down and picking someone else up."

The people of Oklahoma City responded with Service, Honor and Kindness as sorrow walked with us, and we were strengthened by the adversity we confronted. By preserving the memory of the incredible selfless and compassionate public response that became known as the Oklahoma Standard, collectively the Memorial and Museum will continue to serve as a catalyst for people dealing with one

another with respect and responsibility in times of misfortune and in everyday life, and serve as a reminder that no act of kindness is ever wasted.

Hopefully, as people from around the world continue to visit the Memorial and Museum, they will return home empowered with a desire to make a positive difference in the lives of others and will thereafter teach by word or example the lessons of goodwill toward humankind that we are striving to impart. It is my hope that someday the Oklahoma Standard will become a universal standard of human relationships far beyond the borders of our state and nation.

"In the world we live in today, we seem trapped in a never-ending storm of rancor, divisiveness, and distraction. How much could we accomplish though, if we were able to see the world everyday the way we see it after a disaster? Neighbors in need. People with resources. All of us in this together."

PRESIDENT JIMMY CARTER, 1977-1981

262

EPILOGUE

Jon Meacham

The New York Times Bestseller and Pulitzer Prize–Winning Author
From the Keynote Speech at Oklahoma City National Memorial & Museum
Day One Luncheon, November 4, 2019

Let's begin with a story that is ever ancient, ever new. The great prophet of Israel, Moses, has come to the end of his life. He has led God's people out of bondage in Egypt and into the wilderness, heading step by painful step, year by anguishing year, toward the Promised Land. Now Moses is dying, and he realizes he will not live to dwell in the land of the Lord. In his great, final song, Moses tells the ages: "Remember the days of old, consider the years of many generations; ask thy fathers and they will tell thee, their elders and they will show thee."

Remember the days of old: You and I are gathered here now, so many millennia from the Song of Moses, yet we hear its notes still. Remember the days of old: it is commandment that, like Jesus's injunction at the Last Supper, on the night he was handed over to suffering and death, to break bread and drink wine "in remembrance of me."

We are, then, taking part in a primeval tradition as we contemplate what has come before and, crucially, what may come next. For remembrance is not static; it is not academic; it is not isolated from the hurly burly of the present and from the unknown mysteries of what lies ahead. Remembrance is, rather, the means by which the work of the future begins. As Abraham Lincoln reminded us, we cannot escape history nor should we want to try to. Americans are charged with a sacred duty: to fulfill the injunction that to whom much is given, much is expected.

And as Americans we have been given much—gifts of liberty and of opportunity, of self-government and of what Lincoln called an "open field and a fair chance." And of Oklahoma City far, far too much has been expected, and so, so much has been nobly given. You gave the blood of your blood, the flesh of your flesh. You did not do so willingly; fate and tragedy brought this upon you, and you rose to the grimmest of hours with courage and grace and love and endurance.

I stand in awe of your strength in the face of the worst kind of adversity. Your country honors you. Your country reveres you. And your country needs you—for in remembering the cataclysm and the courage of Wednesday, April 19, 1995, we are able to learn about faith, about bravery, and about resilience. This is your story. And it matters enormously to your country. I know everyone here would have given everything to have this cup pass from you. But it did not. So now we are left to make the best of the worst day any of us can imagine—a day you don't have to imagine, for you experienced it.

To know what has come before is to be armed against despair. Consider: if the men and women of previous generations, with all their flaws and limitations and ambitions and appetites, could press on through ignorance and superstition, racism and sexism, selfishness and greed, to create a freer nation, then perhaps we can, too.

History teaches us that we've always grown stronger the more widely we've opened our arms and the more generously we've interpreted the most important sentence ever originally rendered in English: Thomas Jefferson's assertion that all men are created equal.

This isn't a Republican point or a Democratic point. It's not a red point or a blue point. It's just a true point. Think about it: We don't tend to erect monuments to people who build walls; we erect monuments to people who open doors. We honor liberators, not captors. Here, in this place, we honor the people of Oklahoma City, not the terrorists who brought death and devastation to an

American city and to its people.

From Seneca Falls to Fort Sumter; from Omaha Beach to the Edmund Pettus Bridge; from Soviet-occupied Berlin to Stonewall; from Oklahoma City to New York City, Washington, and Shanksville, Pennsylvania, where passengers brought down United Flight 93 before it could reach the Capitol or the White House, Americans have sought to perfect our Union and to nudge the world toward an ethos of liberty rather than tyranny. The future belongs to the men and the women, in power and far from it, who choose to heed Lincoln's "better angels"—people like you. How do I know the future belongs to such people? Because the best of the past belongs to those who did precisely that.

Think about the act of remembrance in our nation's capital. There is a monument to Washington, who gave up power and preserved the sacred fire of liberty. There is a monument to Lincoln, who saved the Union. There is a monument to the veterans of World War II, who projected force around the globe in defense of human rights. And is there anything more American than the fact that Martin Luther King, Jr., and Thomas Jefferson now stare at each other in perpetuity across the Tidal Basin?

What do all these monuments have in common? They're there to commemorate the fulfillment of the spirit of the Declaration of Independence and of the Constitution—the devotion to the

American Founding that was unfolding in your federal building so many Aprils ago and which is commemorated in the Memorial we are honoring today. Such monuments and memorials don't celebrate fear; they celebrate hope. And your Memorial here in this city, telling your story, is a vital element in the mechanics of American memory. For without memory we are lost, disoriented, and more vulnerable to despair.

I know this may seem counter-intuitive. To remember what is painful, you might say, is disorienting and desperate. So why not just move on? Because to fail to commemorate the experience of April 1995 risks obscuring the lives and lessons of that day and of all the days since: The lives that were devoted to the service of the nation. The lives that were simply going about their business. The lives of the first responders, and of the kith and kin left behind.

And what of the lessons? A lesson of Oklahoma City is that evil is real and so is goodness. A lesson of Oklahoma City is that the world is a fallen and tragic place and we are called, like Moses, to keep faith even in years of pain and in the face of a Promised Land that seems perennially just out of reach. A lesson of Oklahoma City is that the mystery of suffering, the mystery of untimely death, the mystery of how a providential universe can be in the grip of forces that bring sorrow and agony cannot be resolved until that day beyond time when all things shall be made new.

In the meantime—and that's where so much of our lives is lived, in the meantime—in our search—in our hunger—for a way forward, the beginning of wisdom lies in an appreciation of the past—which, as William Faulkner taught us, isn't dead; it isn't even past. And what can we learn from history? That the perfect should not be the enemy of the good. That compromise is the oxygen of democracy. That hate and fear might prevail for a day or even a season, but not for long, and never forever.

The risk we always face—the risk that became all too real here in 1995—often grows out of the anger of loners and of crowds (literal and, in our own time, also virtual) of the alienated. The better presidents, the better citizens, do not cater to such forces; they conquer them with a breadth of vision that speaks to the best parts of our soul.

Socrates believed the soul was nothing less than the animating force of reality. In Genesis, the soul was life itself: "And the Lord God formed man of the dust of the ground, and breathed into his nostrils the breath of life; and man became a living soul." In the New Testament, when Jesus says, "Greater love hath no man than this, that a man lay down his life for his friends," the word for "life" could also be translated as "soul."

Martin Luther King, Jr., dwells in the American soul; so, alas, does the Ku Klux Klan. History hangs in the balance between good and evil. And the contest between light and dark within that national soul is, as Wellington said of Waterloo, the closest-run thing you ever saw in your life. For that contest is ferocious not only for "We the People," but for you and me.

To get things right 51 percent of the time as a nation is a pretty good thing— for, if we're being honest with ourselves, isn't a 51 percent success rate on getting things right in our own lives a pretty good—and perhaps all too rare—day? I'd think so, for I know it's true in my own life—in my own struggles of the soul. And given that a republic is the most human form of government—it is the broad manifestation of the individual dispositions of all of our hearts and minds—why wouldn't our story be one in which our personal decisions have a collective impact on the way we live now?

Telling that story is remembrance. It is history. And history, therefore, isn't stifling or limiting but thrilling, hopeful, and ennobling, for it reminds us that the most American thing we can do is to try and when we fail, which we will, we must try again and again, and again, and again. For only in trial is progress possible.

The past wasn't easier and simpler. You know that, for your past surely wasn't. If we believe that our forebears faced less complicated times, we foreclose the possibility of learning from what came before—if they had it so easy, what can they teach us?—and we fail to do proper honor to those who lived and fought and toiled and died to give us a nation that, as President Reagan put it, would be a rest and a refuge for "all the lost pilgrims from all the lost places who are hurtling through the darkness, toward home."

Let's end where we began, with Moses in the desert. "Rejoice, O Nations, with His people: for he will avenge the blood of his servants ... and will atone for His land and his people." And the truth of that time is the truth of all time: that we have been promised that the gates of Hell shall not finally prevail.

In our own time, our nation is at her best when our better angels take flight against all odds and against all enemies. If anyone wants to see those better angels, they should come here to Oklahoma City. If anyone wants to know what it is to endure the death of innocents yet to press on, in faith and hope and love, they should come here to Oklahoma City. If anyone wants to see the best of us, they should come here to Oklahoma City.

And once here, let them pause and remember: remember what makes us good and what makes us strong and what makes us us. For that is your story, and in your story lies our hope.

EPILOGUE

Larry Nichols

Chairman Emeritus, Devon Energy Corporation
and Husband of Survivor Polly Nichols

When we reflect on the bombing 25 years ago, we generally focus on the deceased, the survivors and the first responders. Their stories are both tragic and heroic at the same time. It is also important for us to recognize the unsung heroes of our event. Those heroes are the good people of Oklahoma City, and their instinct to do the right thing, at the right time, for the right reasons. We call that the Oklahoma Standard.

My favorite example is when the Oklahoma City Mayor, Ron Norick, was told that the first responders were running out of work gloves. He went to the media and asked the citizens of our City to bring any surplus work gloves they might have down to City

Hall. Our citizens did not do just that. They also went to every store in town, purchased all the work gloves they could find and brought those downtown. The shelves were bare. They did not seek any recognition or awards. A very simple story. They were just doing the right thing. They learned of the need and rushed to help.

My other favorite story is a personal one that you will not read or hear about anywhere. When I was running to the hospital's emergency room, I saw a line of seven or eight ambulances—their red lights blinking, their sirens going. In the middle of that line was a pickup truck driven by a young man with a cowboy hat. The back of his pickup truck was loaded with injured, bloody people. He had been driving down the road, minding his own business, and saw people who had not yet been picked up by an ambulance. He did not think, "They need to do something about that. They need more ambulances." He wheeled around, loaded them up in his pickup truck, and got them to the emergency room. He did not do it for fame or glory. We do not know his name and never will. That does not matter. That is not why he did it. I picture him as a teenager who went home that afternoon and his mom said, "What'd you do today?" His likely response was, "Oh, nothing."

Our citizens knew how to respond.... at least, they did 25 years ago. However, today's younger generation was not alive at the time of the bombing. Half of the people in this city were not here on that fateful day. How would they respond? How would they respond if this event took place tomorrow? We of course hope that such a tragedy will never happen. But how would our City respond now?

It is incumbent upon each of us to teach the surviving generations, the younger generations, what doing the right thing means. This is where our Memorial plays a huge role in our community and indeed in our nation.

As you see busload after busload of grade school kids and high school kids coming to our Memorial; as you see people from outside our community being brought there, like the Thunder does; as we bring our own children and our friends and neighbors to that Memorial, they see the riveting story of the explosion, the capture of Timothy McVeigh, the nationwide response of first responders, the worldwide response of sympathy and help. And all of those are highly engaging stories. But then they delve into the part of our Memorial that really has take-home value, the part that reminds us what basic human values should be, the part that shows how regular, ordinary people of Oklahoma City responded. Not just our Mayor, Governor and first responders. Not just those with special positions and special training— they were all great. But all the selfless acts of compassion and caring by the regular people of Oklahoma City. That's when our Memorial is at its greatest. When it is educating people about what doing the right thing looks like. What doing the right thing feels like. What those fancy words the Oklahoma Standard really mean. I sense when visitors go to the Memorial, they look at that behavior of ordinary people, and are impressed by what they did. They think, "Yes, I would like to do that. I would like the pride of holding myself to that standard."

That is when our Memorial is at its best. That is why we should do everything we can to support it.

APPENDIX I

THOSE WHO WERE KILLED

LUCIO ALEMAN JR.   TERESA ANTIONETTE ALEXANDER   RICHARD A. ALLEN   TED L. ALLEN   MISS BAYLEE ALMON   DIANE E. (HOLLINGSWORTH) ALTHOUSE   REBECCA NEEDHAM ANDERSON

PAMELA CLEVELAND ARGO   SAUNDRA G. (SANDY) AVERY   PETER R. AVILLANOZA   CALVIN BATTLE   PEOLA BATTLE   DANIELLE NICOLE BELL   OLETA C. BIDDY

SHELLY D. BLAND   ANDREA YVETTE BLANTON   OLEN BURL BLOOMER   SERGEANT FIRST CLASS LOLA BOLDEN U.S. ARMY   JAMES E. BOLES   MARK ALLEN BOLTE   CASANDRA KAY BOOKER

CAROL LOUISE BOWERS

PEACHLYN BRADLEY

WOODROW CLIFFORD "WOODY" BRADY

CYNTHIA L. BROWN

PAUL GREGORY BEATTY BROXTERMAN

GABREON D. L. BRUCE

KIMBERLY RUTH BURGESS

DAVID NEIL BURKETT

DONALD EARL BURNS SR.

KAREN GIST CARR

MICHAEL CARRILLO

ZACKARY TAYLOR CHAVEZ

ROBERT N. CHIPMAN

KIMBERLY KAY CLARK

DR. MARGARET L. "PEGGY" CLARK

ANTHONY CHRISTOPHER COOPER II

ANTONIO ANSARA COOPER JR.

DANA LEANNE COOPER

HARLEY RICHARD COTTINGHAM

KIM R. COUSINS

AARON M. COVERDALE

ELIJAH S. COVERDALE

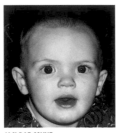

JACI RAE COYNE

KATHERINE LOUISE CREGAN

RICHARD (DICK) CUMMINS

STEVEN DOUGLAS CURRY

BRENDA FAYE DANIELS

SERGEANT BENJAMIN LARANZO
DAVIS USMC

DIANA LYNNE DAY

PETER L. DEMASTER

CASTINE BROOKS HEARN DEVEROUX

TYLOR SANTOI EAVES

ASHLEY MEGAN ECKLES

SUSAN JANE FERRELL

CARROL JUNE "CHIP" FIELDS

KATHY A. FINLEY

JUDY J. (FROH) FISHER

LINDA LOUISE FLORENCE

DON FRITZLER

MARY ANNE FRITZLER

TEVIN D'AUNDRAE GARRETT

LAURA JANE GARRISON

278

JAMIE (FIALKOWSKI) GENZER

SHEILA R. GIGGER-DRIVER AND
BABY GREGORY N. DRIVER II

MARGARET BETTERTON GOODSON

KEVIN "LEE" GOTTSHALL II

ETHEL L. GRIFFIN

J. COLLEEN GUILES

CAPTAIN RANDOLPH A. GUZMAN
USMC

CHERYL E. HAMMON

RONALD VERNON HARDING SR.

THOMAS LYNN HAWTHORNE SR.

DORIS "ADELE" HIGGINBOTTOM

ANITA CHRISTINE HIGHTOWER

THOMPSON EUGENE "GENE"
HODGES JR.

PEGGY LOUISE HOLLAND

LINDA COLEEN HOUSLEY

DR. GEORGE MICHAEL HOWARD
DVM

WANDA LEE HOWELL

ROBBIN ANN HUFF AND
BABY AMBER DENISE HUFF

DR. CHARLES E. HURLBURT

JEAN NUTTING HURLBURT

PAUL D. ICE

CHRISTI YOLANDA JENKINS

NORMA "JEAN" JOHNSON

RAYMOND "LEE" JOHNSON

LARRY JAMES JONES

ALVIN J. JUSTES

BLAKE RYAN KENNEDY

CAROLE SUE KHALIL

VALERIE JO KOELSCH

ANN KREYMBORG

RONA LINN KUEHNER-CHAFEY

TERESA LEA TAYLOR LAUDERDALE

MARY LEASURE-RENTIE

KATHY CAGLE LEINEN

CARRIE ANN LENZ AND
BABY MICHAEL JAMES LENZ III

DONALD RAY LEONARD

LAKESHA RICHARDSON LEVY

DOMINIQUE RAVAE (JOHNSON) –
LONDON

RHETA BENDER LONG

MICHAEL L. LOUDENSLAGER

AURELIA DONNA LUSTER

ROBERT LEE LUSTER JR.

MICKEY B. MARONEY

JAMES K. MARTIN

REVEREND GILBERT X. MARTINEZ

JAMES A. MCCARTHY II

KENNETH GLENN MCCULLOUGH

BETSY J. (BEEBE) MCGONNELL

LINDA G. MCKINNEY

CARTNEY J. MCRAVEN

CLAUDE ARTHUR MEDEARIS S.S.A.

CLAUDETTE (DUKE) MEEK

FRANKIE ANN MERRELL

DERWIN W. MILLER

EULA LEIGH MITCHELL

JOHN C. MOSS III

RONOTA ANN NEWBERRY-
WOODBRIDGE

PATRICIA ANN NIX

JERRY LEE PARKER

JILL DIANE RANDOLPH

MICHELLE A. REEDER

TERRY SMITH REES

ANTONIO "TONY" C. REYES

  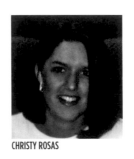   

KATHRYN ELIZABETH RIDLEY   TRUDY JEAN RIGNEY   CLAUDINE RITTER   CHRISTY ROSAS   SONJA LYNN SANDERS   LANNY LEE DAVID SCROGGINS   KATHY LYNN SEIDL

LEORA LEE SELLS   KARAN HOWELL SHEPHERD   CHASE DALTON SMITH   COLTON WADE SMITH   VICTORIA (VICKEY) L. SOHN   JOHN THOMAS STEWART   DOLORES (DEE) STRATTON

EMILIO TAPIA   VICTORIA JEANETTE TEXTER   CHARLOTTE ANDREA LEWIS THOMAS   MICHAEL GEORGE THOMPSON   VIRGINIA M. THOMPSON   KAYLA MARIE TITSWORTH   RICK L. TOMLIN

LARUE A. TREANOR

LUTHER H. TREANOR

LARRY L. TURNER

JULES A. VALDEZ

JOHN KARL VAN ESS III

JOHNNY ALLEN WADE

DAVID JACK WALKER

ROBERT N. WALKER JR.

WANDA LEE WATKINS

MICHAEL D. WEAVER

JULIE MARIE WELCH

ROBERT G. WESTBERRY

ALAN G. WHICHER

JO ANN WHITTENBERG

FRANCES "FRAN" ANN WILLIAMS

SCOTT D. WILLIAMS

W. STEPHEN WILLIAMS

CLARENCE EUGENE WILSON SR.

SHARON LOUISE WOOD-CHESNUT

TRESIA JO "MATHES" WORTON

JOHN A. YOUNGBLOOD

APPENDIX II

MEMBERSHIP OF MEMORIAL TASK FORCE
APPOINTED BY OKLAHOMA CITY MAYOR RON NORICK
350 TOTAL: 322 APPOINTED ON 6/28/1995, 28 APPOINTED LATER

NAME	ORGANIZATION/CAPACITY	COMMITTEE/S	NAME	ORGANIZATION/CAPACITY	COMMITTEE/S
Div. Chief Steve Abraira	City of Miami, Fl Fire and Rescue	ADV	Ms. Marcela Banks	General Services Administration	ADV
Ray Ackerman	Ackerman McQueen	PR	Mr. John E. Barry	Conner & Winters, Tulsa, OK	IDS
Father Ray K. Ackerman	Our Lady's Cathedral	PR	Mr. Williams M. Bell	Liberty Bank & Trust Company	ADV / FIN
Dr. Ann Ackerman	Oklahoma City Community College	IDS	Ms. Deniece Bell	Survivor	FSL
Ms. Jonie Alderton	YMCA	ADV	Mr. Ed Beltram	AT&T	ADV
Rev. Don H. Alexander	First Christian Church	ADV / FSL	Mr. Clayton I. Bennett	Oklahoma Publishing Company	ADV
Ms. Ann Allen	Principal, Emerson Alternative School	IDS	Honorable Loyd Benson	Oklahoma State Representative	GVT
Ms. Ann Alspaugh	Community Volunteer	ADV / COR / PFR Co-Chair	Ms. Sally Bentley	Community Volunteer	ADV / IDS
Mr. Fred Anderson	Victim's Family Member	ADV / VFS	Mr. Leonard Benton	Urban League	ADV
Ms. Nancy Anthony	Oklahoma City Community Foundation	ADV / PPG	Ms. Pat Bishop	Community Volunteer	IDS
Ms. Joelda Aragon	Thrifty Office Supply	ADV	Mr. Ray E. Bitsche, Jr.	OK County Juvenile Center	FSL
Ms. Anita Arnold	BLAC,Inc.	ADV / COR / ARC Co-Chair	Honorable Debbie Blackburn	Oklahoma State Representative	ADV
Mr. Michael J. Ash	Canine Rescue Volunteer	IDS	Mr. Bob Blackburn	Oklahoma Historical Society	ARC
Mr. Hannah Atkins	Statewide Leader	ADV / GVT	Ms. Shirley Blaschke	Community Volunteer	ARC
Mr. Keith Bailey	The Williams Companies, Tulsa, OK	ADV	Ms. Maureen Bloomer	Community Volunteer, Moore, OK	IDS
Mr. Clark Bailey	Southwestern Bell Telephone Company	PR / IDS	Mr. Bruce Bockus	Bockus, Payne & Associates	ADV
Mr. Paul Bailey	Marion County, IN USAR Team	ADV	Mr. Ron Bogle	Oklahoma City University	ARC
Mr. Currie Ballard	Coyle, OK	ARC	Honorable Richard L. Bohanon	Federal District Judge	FIN

284

APPENDIX II: MEMBERSHIP OF MEMORIAL TASK FORCE

NAME	ORGANIZATION/CAPACITY	COMMITTEE/S
Ms. Ann Bohanon	Community Volunteer	ADV
Ms. Natalie Bonney	Bonney, Percival & Sheets	ADV
Asst. Chief Frank Borden	City of Los Angeles, CA Fire Department	ADV
Ms. Ruth Boss	Re/Max Associates, Edmond, OK	ADV
Dr. John R. Bozalis	President, Oklahoma County Medical Society	ADV
Mr. Lee B. Brawner	Metropolitan Library System	ADV
Mr. Philip Bread	Community Volunteer	FIN
Ms. Anita Bridges	Litigation Alternatives, Inc.	ADV
Mr. William J. Bross	Oklahoma City Community Foundation	PFR
Senator Ben Brown	Oklahoma State Senator	ADV
Ms. Cheryl Browne	Community Volunteer	PFR
Mr. Charles Bryant	West Tennessee E.M.A	ADV
Mr. Joe Van Bullard	Assistant City Manager, City of Oklahoma City	GVT
Honorable Bernest H. Cain, Jr.	Oklahoma State Senator	ADV
Mr. Tommy Carr	Montgomery County, MD Fire Department	ADV
Division Chief Charles Castillo	Metro-Dade County Florida Fire & Rescue	ADV
Mr. Sherman Catalon	Survivor	FSL / ARC
Ms. Jean Cate	Community Volunteer	ADV
Mr. Sam Cerny	Oil & Gas Investments	ADV
Mr. Terry Childers	Childers Construction	ADV / COR / GVT Co-Chair
Mr. Robert L. Chumard	Midwest City, OK	FSL

NAME	ORGANIZATION/CAPACITY	COMMITTEE/S
Ms. Earnestine Clark	Oklahoma City Downtown Library	ARC
Mr. James C. Clark	B. C. Clark Jewelers	IDS
Mr. Milford Clayton	Community Volunteer	GVT
Mr. William B. Cleary	Cleary Exploration, L.L.C.	ADV / DSN Co-Chair
Mr. Dennis Clowers	Clowers Engineering	ADV
Mr. Sam Cole	Cole & Reed	FIN
Mr. John Cole	Victims' Family Member	ADV / FSL
Ms. Ann Cong Tang	Rio Algon Mining Corporation	IDS
Dr. Thomas Coniglione	St. Anthony Hospital	FSL
Ms. Kaye L. Cook	Community Volunteer	ADV / PFR
Rev. Lee Cooper	Prospect Baptist Church	IDS
Ms. Cynthia Cope	Southwestern Bell Telephone Company	PPG
Mr. Luke R. Corbett	Kerr McGee Corporation	ADV
Ms. Lisa Crowell	Community Volunteer	ADM
Mr. Douglas R. Cummings	Cummings Oil Company	PFR
Ms. Elcena Cummings	Survivor	FSL
Ms. Deborah Dalton	University of Oklahoma College of Architecture	ARTC
Mr. Khalil Dana	Spiritual Assembly of the Baha'i of OKC	ADV
Mr. Jim Daniel	South Oklahoma City Chamber of Commerce	ADV
Ms. Nancy Deaver	Commission for Community Service	ADM
Mr. Rowland Denman	The Denman Companies	ADV / COR / ADM Co-Chair

APPENDIX II: MEMBERSHIP OF MEMORIAL TASK FORCE

NAME	ORGANIZATION/CAPACITY	COMMITTEE/S
Mr. James Denny	Survivors' Family Member	ADV / FLS
Ms. Marion Devore	Community Volunteer	DSN
Ms. Chris Dillon	Oklahoma State Arts Council	DSN / PR
Mr. Paul Dillon	Denver, CO	ADV
Ms. Sydney Dobson	Oklahoma City Beautiful	ADV / COR / IDS Co-Chair
Ms. Tiana Douglas	Second Century, Inc.	ADV / GVT
Mr. Ray Downey	New York City Police, Fire & Rescue	ADV
Mr. Tom Dulaney	Community Volunteer	PFR
Honorable Stuart Earnest, Sr.	Oklahoma County Commissioner	ADV
Mr. Gary Easton	San Diego, CA USAR Team	ADV
Mr. K. M. Eaton	Phillips Petroleum Company	ADV
Mr. Ed Eckenstein	Oklahoma Water Resources Board	ADV / GVT
Mr. W. A. Drew Edmondson	Oklahoma Attorney General	ADV / GVT
Mr. Carl E. Edwards	Price Edwards & Company	FIN
Dr. Ronald C. Elkins	University of Oklahoma Health Sciences Center	ADV / FSL
Lt. Governor Mary Fallin	Lt. Governor of Oklahoma	GVT
Ms. Patricia B. Fennell	Latino Community Development	FSL
Ms. Suzie Fentriss	Community Volunteer	IDS
Mr. Don Ferrell	Victim's Family Member	ADV / FSL
Ms. Deb Ferrell-Lynn	Victim's Family Member	ADV / COR / ARC Co-Chair
Ms. Pam Fleischaker	Oklahoma Gazette	ADV

NAME	ORGANIZATION/CAPACITY	COMMITTEE/S
Ms. Marca Floyd	Community Volunteer	ADM
Chief Don Forsyth	Orange County, CA USAR Team	ADV
Mr. Chip Fudge	Community Volunteer	PFR
Ms. Jeanette Gamba	Jordan Associates	ADV / COR / PR Co-Chair
Dr. Gene Garrison	First Baptist Church	ADV
Mr. Steve J. Gentling	VA Medical Center	ADV
Mr. Marshall Gesner	Salvation Army	ADV
Mr. Gilbert Gibson	Citizens Bank, Lawton, OK	GVT
Ms. Joan Gilmore	Journal Record	PR
Ms. Jeannine Gist	Victim's Family Member	FSL / IDS
Mr. Charles Givens	Givens Interests, Inc.	DSN
Mr. Jack Gobin	U.S. Department of Agriculture	FSL
Dr. Kay Goebel	Psychologist and Community Volunteer	ADV / FSL Co-Chair
Ms. Kathi Goebel	Community Volunteer	ARC
Mr. Sam Gonzales	Oklahoma City Police Chief	ADV
Dr. Debby Goodman	Community Volunteer	ADV / COR / FSL
Mr. Jimmy Goodman	Crowe & Dunlevy	ADV / COR / IDS Co-Chair
Ms. Cheryl Gottshall	Victim's Family Member	FSL / PFR
Mr. Kevin Gottshall	Victim's Family Member	ADV / COR / FSL / GVT
Mr. Alan Greenberg	Bear Stearns & Co, New York, NY	ADV
Dr. Loren Gresham	President, Southern Nazarene University	IDS

APPENDIX II: MEMBERSHIP OF MEMORIAL TASK FORCE

NAME	ORGANIZATION/CAPACITY	COMMITTEE/S
Ms. Jean Gumerson	Presbyterian Health Foundation	ADV / COR / PPG Co-Chair
Ms. Marcia L. Hale	White House, Dir. of Intergovernmental Affairs	ADV / GVT
Ms. Sue Hale	Oklahoman	ADM
Mr. Fred J. Hall	Fred Jones Companies, Inc.	ADV
Ms. Patty Hampton	Oklahoma City 89ers	ADV
Ms. Debbie Hampton	American Red Cross	ADM
Mr. Jon Hansen	Assistant Fire Chief, City of Oklahoma City	FSL
Ms. Mariana Hanska	Bentley's	PFR
Mr. Steve Hanson	Clark County, NV Fire Department	ADV
Mr. James G. Harlow, Jr.	Oklahoma Gas and Electric Co.	ADV
Ms. Penny Harper	Community Volunteer	FSL
Reverend Nick Harris	First United Methodist Church	ADV
Captain Daniel Hartman	Bureau of Operations, Harrisburg, PA	ADV
Mr. Jeff Hayden	Community Volunteer	ADV
Mr. Dick Hefton	Oklahoma County Newspapers, Inc.	PR
Ms. Joyce Henderson	Principal, Classen School of Advanced Studies	IDS
Mr. Lawrence Herbster	KOCO TV	ADV
Mr. Ray Hibbard	Edmond Life and Leisure	ADV
Mr. Frank Hill	McAfee & Taft	ADV / COR
Ms. Carolyn Hill	Oklahoma City Art Museum	ARC
Mr. Randy Hogan	Survivor, Hogan Property Co.	ADV

NAME	ORGANIZATION/CAPACITY	COMMITTEE/S
Ms. Elizabeth Holmes	Mental Health Association of Oklahoma City	FSL
Ms. Ann Holzberlein	Community Volunteer	FSL
Ms. Ann Hoover	Community Volunteer	PFR
Mr. Charles Hooper	Oklahoma Natural Gas Company	ADV
Ms. LeAnn Horton	Community Volunteer	IDS
Ms. Hilda Pattie Howell	Community Volunteer	ARC
Ms. Effie Hudson	Victim's Family Member	FSL
Mr. Cliff Hudson	Sonic Corp	ADV / GVT
Deputy Chief John Huff	Lincoln, NE Fire Department	ADV
Mr. Dick Hunter	Community Volunteer	GVT
Mr. Steven Hunter	St. Anthony Hospital	ADV
Mr. Stanley Hupfeld	Integris Hospital	ADV
Ms. Sue Ann Hyde	Community Volunteer	ADV / ARC
Ms. Judy Jack	Community Volunteer	PR
Ms. Jane Jayroe	Oklahoma Health Center	ADV
Mr. Larry Jeffries	AT&T	IDS
Ms. LeAnn Jenkins	Federal Executive Board	ADV / COR / GVT / PFR
Mr. Marty Jennings	Community Volunteer	ARC
Mr. Kirk Jewell	The Oklahoman	PFR
Mr. Carlos Johnson	KPMG	GVT
Ms. Gennie Johnson	Community Volunteer	DSN

APPENDIX II: MEMBERSHIP OF MEMORIAL TASK FORCE

NAME	ORGANIZATION/CAPACITY	COMMITTEE/S
Mr. Glen Johnson	Speaker of Oklahoma House of Representatives	ADV / GVT
Mr. Herb Johnson	Office of U.S. Senator James Inhofe	ADV / GVT
Mr. Robert Johnson	Crowe & Dunlevy	ADV / COR Chair
Mr. William Johnstone	City Bank & Trust	ADV / COR / IDS
Ms. Doris Jones	Victim's Family Member	ADV / COR / FSL
Ms. Jackie Jones	Arts Council of Oklahoma City	ADV / COR / DSN Co-Chair
Ms. Lynne Jones	Community Volunteer	PR
Mr. Will Jones	Enterprise Square, USA	IDS / DSN
Ms. Kim Jones-Shelton	Survivor	ADV / COR / IDS Co-Chair
Ms. Diane Joy-Sizemore	City Bank & Trust	ADM
Ms. Carol Kaspereit	Community Volunteer	DSN
Mr. Ben Kates	Midwest Wrecking Co.	ADV
Mr. Bill Katsafanas	KFOR TV	ADV
Ms. Wanene Keener	Community Volunteer	IDS
Mr. Ed Keller	Bank IV, Tulsa, OK	PFR
Mr. John Kennedy	Irish Realty Corporation	ADV / IDS
Mr. Joe Kernke, Jr.	Smith & Kernke	IDS
Ms. Lou Kerr	Community Volunteer	ADV
Ms. Barbara Kerrick	Community Volunteer	ADV / COR / PFR Co-Chair
Ms. Robbie Kienzie	American Institute of Architects	DSN
Ms. Marsha Kight	Victim's Family Member	FSL / IDS

NAME	ORGANIZATION/CAPACITY	COMMITTEE/S
Mr. Tom Kight	Victim's Family Member	ADV / FSL
Mr. John Kilpatrick	Kilpatrick Investment Company	ADV
Mr. Klaholt Kimker	Liberty Bank & Trust Company	DSN
Ms. Jill King	Community Volunteer	PFR
Ms. Mary Krodel	Principal, Coronado Heights Elementary School	PFR
Ms. Lee Ann Kuhlman	Community Volunteer	FIN
Ms. Linda Lambert	Lasso Corporation	ADV / COR / FIN Co-Chair
Mr. Dale Lanzone	General Services Administration	GVT
Mr. V. Z. Lawton	Survivor	FSL
Mr. Randy Ledger	Survivor	ADV
Mr. Paul LeFebvre	Counsel, City of Oklahoma City	IDS
Senator Keith Leftwich	Oklahoma State Senator	GVT / FSL
Mr. Barney Lehmbeck	Liberty Bancorp	PR
Mr. Harrison Levy	Harrison Levy Company	PPG
Ms. Judy Liebmann	Community Volunteer	IDS
Ms. Kay Lindsey	Community Volunteer	IDS
Mr. Bill Lissau	Bank of America	ADV
Mr. Ed Livermore	Edmond Evening Sun	PR
Mr. James Loftis	James Loftis Architects	ADV
Mr. J. Duke Logan	Oklahoma Bar Association	IDS
Mr. Bill Lokey	Dept. of Emergency Management, Tacoma, WA	ADV

APPENDIX II: MEMBERSHIP OF MEMORIAL TASK FORCE

NAME	ORGANIZATION/CAPACITY	COMMITTEE/S
Dr. Robert Long	St. Luke's United Methodist Church	ADV
Mr. David Lopez	Southwestern Bell Telephone Company	ADV
Mr. Sam Armstrong Lopez	Integris Hospital	ADV / COR / PR Co-Chair
Mr. Robert Lorenz	Arthur Andersen & Company	ADV / FIN
Mr. Bob Lorton	Tulsa World	ADV
Mr. Tom Love	Love's Country Stores, Inc.	ADV
Ms. Karen Luke	Community Volunteer	ADV / COR Vice-Chair
Mr. Dan Mahoney	Office of Oklahoma Governor	ADV / GVT
Mr. Abe Marrero	University of Oklahoma Health Sciences Center	ADV
Mr. Gary Marrs	Oklahoma City Fire Chief	ADV
Mr. Melvin Mathals	District Chief, Virginia Beach, VA Fire Dept.	ADV
Mr. Mike McAuliffe	Ackerman McQueen	IDS
Mr. Fred McCann	Architect	DSN
Mr. Tom McDaniel	Kerr-McGee Corporation	ADV / COR / GVT Co-Chair
Ms. Brenda McDaniel	Community Volunteer	PFR
Mr. Dan McKinney	Victim's Family Member	FSL
Mr. David Medina	Oklahoma City Air Traffic Control	IDS
Ms. Sunni Mercer	Community Volunteer	ARC
Mr. Paul Meyer	Community Volunteer	ARC
Ms. Sandy Meyers	Community Volunteer	PFR
Ms. Gayle Miles-Scott	Community Volunteer	FIN

NAME	ORGANIZATION/CAPACITY	COMMITTEE/S
Mr. Jim Miller	Norman Transcript	PR
Mr. Roosevelt Milton	NAACP	ADV
Mr. Gracie Monson	Oklahoma Human Rights Commission	FSL
Mr. John Montgomery	Washington Rep, City of Oklahoma City	GVT
Mr. Vern Moore	Oklahoma City Public Schools	ADV / IDS
Mr. Rick Moore	Assistant to Mayor, City of Oklahoma City	GVT
Mr. James Moore	Oklahoma Health System	PR
Mr. Calvin Moser	Survivor	ADV / DSN
Dr. K. C. Mui	MUI Investment Services, Inc.	PFR
Mr. A. Paul Murrah, Jr.	Murrah Family Representative	ADV / IDS
Mr. Leslie Nance	Survivor	ADV
Ms. Barbara Naranche	Redland Council of Girl Scouts	IDS
Dr. Norman Neaves	Church of the Servant	IDS
Mr. Cu D. Nguyen	Community Volunteer	IDS
Ms. Polly Nichols	Survivor and Victim's Family Member	ADV / COR / IDS Co-Chair
Senator Don Nickles	U.S. Senator from Oklahoma	ADV / GVT
Mr. George Nigh	University of Central Oklahoma	ADV
Ms. Carolyn Norick	Community Volunteer	ARC
Ms. Kim O'Connor	Community Volunteer	IDS
Mr. Tim O'Connor	Associated Catholic Charities	ADV / COR / FSL Co-Chair
Mr. James O'Loughlin	Presbyterian Hospital	ADV

APPENDIX II: MEMBERSHIP OF MEMORIAL TASK FORCE

NAME	ORGANIZATION/CAPACITY	COMMITTEE/S
Mr. Harry Oakes, Jr.	Mountain Wilderness Search Dogs	ADV
Rabbi David Packman	Temple B'Nai Israel	ADV
Mr. Mike Parrish	Riverside, CA USAR Team	ADV
Ms. Carole Patton	Neighborhood Services Organization	ADV / FSL
Ms. Miki Payne-Farris	Community Volunteer	IDS
Ms. JoAnn Pearce	Kirkpatrick Center	DSN
Mr. John Perry	Oklahoman	ADV
Mr. Russell Perry	Black Chronicle Newspaper	ADV / PFR
Rev. John Petuskey	St. John's Parish	ADV
Mr. James A. Pickel	Smith & Pickel Construction	ADV / FIN
Mr. Peter Pierce, III	First National Bank of Bethany	ADV
Mr. Donnie Pitman	Community Volunteer	ADV
Chaplin Jack Poe	Chaplin, Oklahoma City Police Department	ADV
Mr. Bing Poh	Vietnamese American Community	ADV
Ms. Betty Price	Oklahoma State Arts Council	ADV / DSN
Mr. Byron Price	National Cowboy Hall of Fame	ARC
Mr. Jim Priest	McKinney, Stringer & Webster	FSL
Mr. Dennis Purifoy	Survivor	FSL
Mr. Fred Quinn	Quinn & Associates	DSN
Mr. Gene Rainbolt	BancFirst	ADV / COR / PFR Co-Chair
Mr. Jack Ramos	A.R.K Ramos	IDS

NAME	ORGANIZATION/CAPACITY	COMMITTEE/S
Rev. John Reed	Fairview Baptist Church	ADV
Ms. Joyce Reed	KWTV	ADV
Mr. George Reeder	TVR Communications	ADV / PFR
Ms. Mary Reneau	Community Volunteer	ADV / IDS
Mr. John Rex	American Fidelity	ADV / COR / FIN
Mr. Dick Reynolds	Reynolds Ford, Norman, OK	ADV
Ms. Anne Roberts	Oklahoma Institute of Child Advocacy	ADV / FSL
Mr. Marvin Rabinowitz	Grand Resources, Inc.	ADV / IDS
Mr. Don Rogers	Survivor	ADV / GVT / FSL
Ms. Florence Rogers	Survivor	ADV / COR/ FIN Co-Chair
Ms. Joyce Rogers	Survivor's Family Member	IDS
Ms. Edie Roodman	Jewish Federation of Greater Oklahoma City	ADV
Ms. Lil Ross	Community Volunteer	PFR
Mr. Charles Roundtree	Community Volunteer	PR / ARC
Dr. Bob Rundstrom	University of Oklahoma	ARC
Mr. Richard Rush	Oklahoma State Chamber of Commerce	ADV
Ms. Priscilla Salyers	Survivor	ADV
Mr. Rodney Sandburg	Community Volunteer	ADV
Mr. Mike Samis	Macklanburg-Duncan Company	ADV / DSN
Mr. Timothy Sartorius	American Red Cross	ADV
Ms. Lynn Saunders	Law Clerk, Federal Judge Miles-LeGrange	ADV / IDS

APPENDIX II: MEMBERSHIP OF MEMORIAL TASK FORCE

NAME	ORGANIZATION/CAPACITY	COMMITTEE/S
Captain Harold Schapelhouman	Fremont, CA USAR Team	ADV
Ms. Cheryl Scroggins	Victim's Family Member	ADV / FSL
Ms. Shirley Shanker	Community Volunteer	ADV / PFR
Mr. Paul Sheline	Community Volunteer	ADM
Ms. Beth Shortt	Leadership Oklahoma City	ADV / IDS
Ms. Jeane Smith	Community Volunteer	ADV
Mr. Lee Allan Smith	Ackerman McQueen	ADV / COR / PFR Co-Chair
Mr. Al Snipes	Snipes Insurance Agency	PFR
Ms. Marcia Spivey	Edmond, OK	ARC
Ms. Kim Stapleton	Downtown Now	PR / ARC
Mr. George Steimper	Jefferson County, OH	ADV
Ms. Phyllis Stough	Community Volunteer	DSN/ ADM
Mr. Wayne Stone	Bank of Oklahoma	FIN
Ms. Mary Streich	Community Volunteer	PPG
Chief Jim Strickland	Fairfax County VA Fire & Rescue	ADV
Ms. Glenda Talbot	Community Volunteer	ADM
Mr. Tim Tallchief	Native American Graduate College of Public Health	ADV
Mr. John Tassey	Veterans Affairs Medical Center	ADV
Mr. Zach Taylor	Association of Central Oklahoma Governments	GVT
Ms. Jane Thomas	Community Volunteer, Guthrie, OK	ARC
Mr. Ken Thompson	Victim's Family Member	PR

NAME	ORGANIZATION/CAPACITY	COMMITTEE/S
Mr. Phillip Thompson	Victim's Family Member	ADV / COR / FSL Co-Chair
Mr. Toby Thompson	Victim's Family Member	ADV / COR / FSL Co-Chair
Mr. Bill Thrash	Community Volunteer	ARC / PR
Dr. Bill Thurman	Oklahoma City Chamber of Commerce	ADV
Ms. Phillipa Tibbs	Community Volunteer	ADV
Mr. David Timberlake	Timberlake Construction Company	FIN
Mr. Jim Tolbert	First Oklahoma Corporation	ADV / DSN
Ms. Beth Tolbert	Community Volunteer	ADV / COR / DSN Co-Chair
Mr. Tom Toperzer	Fred Jones Jr. Museum of Art	ADV / COR / ARC Co-Chair
Mr. Ken Townsend	Boatmen's First National Bank of Oklahoma City	ADV / DSN
Ms. Kathleen Treanor	Victim's Family Member	ADV / COR / FSL Co-Chair
Ms. Pam Troup	St. Anthony Hospital North	PFR
Reverend Melvin Truiett, Sr.	Interfaith Disaster Recovery of Greater Oklahoma	ADV
Ms. Sissy Tubb	Children's Hospital	FSL
Mr. Be V Tu	Vietnamese American Community	ADV / COR
Mr. Charles Van Rysselberge	Oklahoma City Chamber of Commerce	ADV
Ms. Cheryl Vaught	Hammons, Vaught & Conner	ADV / COR / FSL Co-Chair
Ms. Helen VonFeldt	Community Volunteer	PFR
Ms. Barbara Vose	Community Volunteer	DSN
Mr. John Waldo	Leo Oppenheim & Co.	IDS
Mr. Kenny Walker	Walker Stamp & Seal Co.	ADV

APPENDIX II: MEMBERSHIP OF MEMORIAL TASK FORCE

NAME	ORGANIZATION/CAPACITY	COMMITTEE/S
Mr. Curt Wargo	New York Police Emergency Services Unit	ADV
Mr. Richard Webber	Webber Investment Company	ADM
Mr. Bud Welch	Victim's Family Member	ADV / GVT
Mr. William Welge	Oklahoma State Historical Society	ARC
Mr. Roy Wilkins	Survivor	PFR
Ms. Laurie Williams	WorldCom	IDS
Mr. G. Rainey Williams, Jr.	Kestrel Investment, Inc.	ADV / COR / PPG Co-Chair
Mr. Richard Williams	Survivor	ADV
Rev. Ted Wilson	Chaplain, Oklahoma City Fire Department	ADV
Chief Richard Wolfe	Special Operations Phoenix, AZ Fire Department	ADV
Mr. Pendleton Woods	Community Volunteer	ARC
Ms. Ann Workman	Community Volunteer	ADV
Ms. Katie Worsham	Survivor	ADV / FSL
Mr. Allen B. Wright	Chief of Staff, U.S. Congressman Frank Lucas	ADV / GVT
Ms. Kathy Wyche	General Services Administration	ADV / GVT
Ms. Janice Yeary	U.S. Courthouse	ADV
Mr. James Young	Bank IV	PPG
Mr. Charlie Younger	Community Volunteer	ADV
Ms. Becky Zurcher	Fred Jones Jr. Museum of Art	ADV / ARC

COMMITTEE LEGEND:

ADV: Advisory
COR: Coordinating
ADM:Administration
ARC: Archives
FIN: Budget/Finance
DSN: Design Solicitation
GVT: Government Liaison
IDS: Memorial Ideas Input
PF: Public Fundraising
PPG: Public/Private Grants
PR: Public Relations
VFS: Victims' Families/ Survivors

APPENDIX III:

ORGANIZATIONAL STRUCTURE OF MEMORIAL TASK FORCE

**MURRAH FEDERAL BUILDING MEMORIAL
TASK FORCE**

**P. O. Box 18390
Oklahoma City, Oklahoma 73154-0390**

**(405) 528-5575
(405) 236-8400**

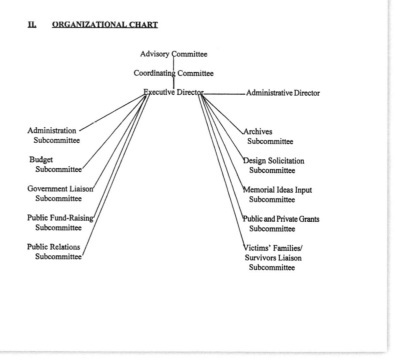

MURRAH FEDERAL BUILDING MEMORIAL TASK FORCE

I.   PURPOSE OF TASK FORCE

The Murrah Federal Building Memorial Task Force was appointed in July, 1995, by Oklahoma City Mayor Ronald J. Norick to create and administer a planning process resulting in a Memorial which will be enduring, appropriate and, most importantly, sensitive to the feelings of those most directly affected by the bombing. The Task Force is also responsible for providing funding for completion and possibly ongoing g administration and maintenance of the Memorial.

II.   ORGANIZATIONAL CHART

Advisory Committee

Coordinating Committee

Executive Director — Administrative Director

Administration Subcommittee

Budget Subcommittee

Government Liaison Subcommittee

Public Fund-Raising Subcommittee

Public Relations Subcommittee

Archives Subcommittee

Design Solicitation Subcommittee

Memorial Ideas Input Subcommittee

Public and Private Grants Subcommittee

Victims' Families/ Survivors Liaison Subcommittee

APPENDIX III: ORGANIZATIONAL STRUCTURE OF MEMORIAL TASK FORCE

III.   **TASK FORCE LEADERSHIP**

A.   **Advisory Committee:**

Chair: Robert M. Johnson
Vice-Chair: Karen Luke

B.   **Coordinating Committee:**
Chair: Robert M. Johnson
Vice-Chair: Karen Luke
Ex-Officio Members:
    Subcommittee Co-Chairs
Members at Large:
    Deborah Goodman, Ph.D.
    Frank D. Hill
    Jackie L. Jones
    Dr. William G. Thurman
    Be Van Tu

C.   Executive Director: Rowland Denman

D.   Administrative Director: Phyllis Stough

E.   Administrative Subcommittee:
    Chair: Rowland Denman

F.   Archives Subcommittee:
    Co-Chairs: Anita Arnold
        Tom Torperzer

G.   Budget Subcommittee:
    Co-Chairs: Linda Lambert
        John Rex

H.   Design Solicitation Subcommittee:
    Co-Chairs: William B. Cleary
        Beth Tolbert

I.   Government Liaison Subcommittee:
    Co-Chairs: Terry Childers
        Thomas J. McDaniel

J.   Memorial Ideas Input Subcommittee:
    Co-Chairs: Polly Nichols
        Sydney Dobson
        Jimmy Goodman

K.   Public Fund-Raising Subcommittee:
    Co-Chairs: Ann Alspaugh
        Barbara Kerrick
        Gene Rainbolt
        Lee Allan Smith

L.   Public and Private Grants Subcommittee:
    Co-Chairs: Jean Gumerson
        G. Rainey Williams, Jr.

M.   Public Relations Subcommittee:
    Co-Chairs: Jeanette Gamba
        Sam Armstrong Lopez

N.   Victims' Families/Survivors Liaison Subcommittee:
    Co-Chairs: Kathleen Treanor
        Kim Jones-Shelton
        Cheryl Vaught
        Phillip Thompson
        Toby Thompson
        Tim O'Conner

APPENDIX III: ORGANIZATIONAL STRUCTURE OF MEMORIAL TASK FORCE

IV. ALLOCATION OF TASKS

A. **Advisory Committee** - Responsible for: (i) coordinating and unifying the Memorial planning process to **allow all constituencies to participate in the process** and to express opinions and ideas; (ii) approving the design selection methodology based on Design Solicitation Subcommittee research and recommendation; (iii) adopting a Memorial Mission Statement consisting of a statement of objectives to be achieved by the completed Memorial, based on Reports of extensive public input received from the Victims' Families / Survivors Liaison and Memorial Ideas Input Subcommittees, (iv) providing input and assistance to the Coordinating Committee and the operating Subcommittees, (v) recommending to the Mayor and the City Council a Memorial Plan addressing the design, components, funding, administration and maintenance of the Memorial, and (vi) providing citizens' oversight during construction of the Memorial.

B. **Coordinating Committee** - Responsible for staff oversight and coordination of the Subcommittees as the executive committee of the Task Force and as the Board of Directors of the 501(c)(3) foundation established by the Task Force.

C. **Executive Director** - Responsible for (i) coordinating the day-to-day operational functioning of the Subcommittees listed below and (ii) preparing information for submission to the Coordinating Committee and Advisory Committee.

D. **Operating Subcommittees**

1. Administration Subcommittee - Responsible for: (i) development of a volunteer and employee loan program to provide such administrative assistance as the Advisory Committee and any of the Subcommittees may require, (ii) coordination of scheduling of such volunteers and loaned employees, and (iii) arrangements for office space and office supplies.

2. Archives Subcommittee - Responsible for: (i) determining location of all materials deemed important to such Subcommittee for possible incorporation into the Memorial and making arrangements for satisfactory cataloging, preservation and storage of the same; and (ii) documenting the memorialization process.

3. Budget Subcommittee - Responsible for: (i) development of a planning budget for the Task Force; (ii) economic feasibility analyses of the Memorial Plan Proposals of each of the proposal finalists selected by the Selection Panel (See Design Selection Subcommittee below) prior to the final decision by the Selection Panel, (iii) solicitation of input from National Park Service regarding maintenance plan and costs; and (iv) development of administration/maintenance budget and funding plan.

4. Design Solicitation Subcommittee - Responsible for: (i) research of the alternative design selection methodologies employed in the creation of other significant memorials and recommendation to the Advisory Committee of a design selection methodology and plan; (ii) identification of Project Advisor Candidates who have experience with other significant commemorative projects and recommendation to the Coordinating Committee of a candidate for such position; and (iii) administer the design selection process approved by the Advisory Committee following completion by the Advisory Committee of the Memorial Mission Statement

5. Government Liaison Subcommittee - Responsible for: (i) securing from GSA an agreement to donate the Murrah Federal Building block and all improvements thereon (including the underground parking facility) to the City of Oklahoma City, (ii) exploring the possibility of incorporating additional adjacent property into the memorial site, (iii) working out details of the Private Sector/City/State/Federal partnership, i.e. the role of each in planning, funding, development, construction, maintenance and administration of the Memorial and the collaboration to occur, (iv) exploring with the National Park Service the possibility of designation of the Memorial as a national monument to be maintained by the National Park Service, (v) working with the City of Oklahoma City to establish protective zoning for the area surrounding the Murrah Federal Building block, and (vi) acting as liaison between the Advisory Committee and government authorities during the planning and implementation process.

6. Memorial Ideas Input Subcommittee - Responsible for: (i) assuring widespread public participation in the Memorial planning process by creating and implementing a plan to extensively solicit input from all interested sectors of the public regarding objectives to be achieved by the creation of the Memorial, and (ii) preparing a report reflecting the memorial objectives expressed by the public.

7. Public Fund Raising Subcommittee - Responsible for developing, implementing and coordinating local, state and national fund raising campaign for cost of completion and, if necessary, establishment of an endowment for ongoing future administration and maintenance of the Memorial.

8. Public and Private Grants Subcommittee - Responsible for: (i) identifying of potential sources of public and private grants, and (ii) preparing applications for such grants and pursuing the same.

APPENDIX III: ORGANIZATIONAL STRUCTURE OF MEMORIAL TASK FORCE

9.   Public Relations Subcommittee - Responsible for: (i) informing the public
      of the opportunity for input into and participating in the Memorial planning
      process, and (ii) updating the public on a current basis regarding the status
      and progress of such planning process.

10.   Victims' Families/Survivors Liaison Subcommittee - Responsible for: (i)
      communicating with representatives of families of victims and survivors
      regarding their opinions and ideas relating to the Memorial, (ii) discussing
      with such families and survivors all sensitive issues relating to possible
      components of the Memorial, and (iii) preparing a report to the Advisory
      Committee reelecting the opinions and ideas of the families and survivors.

7236.JOHNSONR

APPENDIX IV:

MINUTES OF JULY 26, 1995, ORIENTATION MEETING OF MEMORIAL TASK FORCE

MURRAH FEDERAL BUILDING MEMORIAL TASK FORCE
ORIENTATION MEETING

St. Luke's Methodist Church
Wednesday, July 26, 1995

- - - - -

Agenda

I. **Welcome, Remarks & Introductions of Task Force Chair, Vice Chair, Executive Director & Subcommittee Chairs**

   Mayor Ronald J. Norick

II. **Overview of Memorial Task Force**

   Robert M. Johnson

   A. **Objectives:**

      1. Create and administer a planning process resulting in a recommendation to Mayor Norick and the City Council of a design for a Memorial which will be enduring, appropriate, non-exclusionary and, most importantly, sensitive to the feelings of those most directly affected by the bombing; and

      2. Provide funding for the completion and possibly ongoing administration and maintenance of the Memorial.

   B. **Organizational Structure:** The Task Force consists of an Advisory Committee, Ten Operating Subcommittees and a Coordinating Committee, each of which has a separate and clearly defined mission.

      1. **Advisory Committee.** The Advisory Committee is a very broad based coalition which should reflect all perspectives relating to he bombing. It is representative of all economic levels, ethnic backgrounds, racial origin, vocations, religious denominations, geographical locations and levels of involvement in the

-1-

aftermath of the bombing, including representatives of victims' families, survivors and a representative of each of the rescue teams. **The missions of the Advisory Committee will be:**

   a. <u>Provide broad based citizens' oversight</u> of the memorialization process;

   b. Review the alternative design selection methodologies and <u>designate the design selection approach to be employed by the Task Force</u>; and

   c. Most importantly, prepare a <u>Memorial Mission Statement setting forth the objectives to be achieved by the Memorial and whether the Memorial should consist of a symbolic memorial, an interpretive memorial or both</u>.

2. **Ten Operating Subcommittees:**

   a. **Administration** - Responsible for all administrative support of all components of the Task Force, including the development of an employee loan and volunteer program, office arrangements and supplies and meetings coordination.

   b. **Archives** - Responsible for:

      (1) identifying and properly preserving and storing of memorabilia relating to the bombing in order to keep open our options as to what might be incorporated into the Memorial,

      (2) considering the feasibility of assembling a traveling exhibit to serve as a temporary memorial, and

      (3) arranging for the documentation of the memorialization process.

-2-

APPENDIX IV: MINUTES OF JULY 26, 1995, ORIENTATION MEETING OF MEMORIAL TASK FORCE

c. **Budget** – As you would expect, the Budget Subcommittee will be the financial planning arm of the Task Force. Its most important function will conducting an economic feasibility analysis of the Memorial Design prior to recommending the selected design to the City.

d. **Design Solicitation** – Responsible for researching the alternative design selection methodologies, making a recommendation of a selection methodology to the Advisory Committee and administering the design selection process.

e. **Government Liaison** – Composed of private citizens and representatives of all levels of government, including City of Oklahoma City, Second Century, Governor's Office, Oklahoma Senate and House leadership, Oklahoma Attorney General, Senators Nickles and Inhofe, Congressman Lucas, General Services Administration and the Assistant to the President and Director of Intergovernmental Affairs;

Responsible for:

(1) arranging the <u>transfer of the Murrah block from GSA to the City</u> of Oklahoma City;

(2) working out <u>arrangements with GSA regarding the usage of the underground parking</u> – (604 spaces, 4 levels, approx 25% used by occupants of Murrah building and balance of the parking was used by occupants of Federal Court Building);

(3) <u>Establishing a public/private partnership</u> to clarify up front the role of the private sector and each

–3–

level of government in the planning, funding, development, construction, maintenance and administration of the Memorial;

(4) Working with local officials to <u>establish zoning of the surrounding area to protect the Memorial site;</u> and

(5) <u>Serving as liaison between the Task Force and government authorities during the planning and implementation process.</u>

f. **Memorial Ideas Input.** Very important public outreach committee which I will discuss in a moment regarding the description of planning process.

g. **Public Fund Raising and Public and Private Grants.** Two separate Subcommittees with a common goal of funding the cost of completion and perhaps establishing an endowment for the ongoing maintenance and administration of the Memorial.

h. **Public Relations.** Responsible for advising the public of the <u>opportunities for participation</u> in the memorialization process and for updating the public on a current basis of the <u>status of such process.</u>

i. **Victims' Families and Survivors.** Most importantly, a Subcommittee has been established to intensely <u>focus on the feelings and opinions of those most directly affected by the bombing.</u> All members of victims' families and survivors are invited to participate not only on this subcommittee, but also on the other subcommittees if they so desire. <u>You will recall that I said our objectives include the planning of a memorial which must be sensitive to the feelings of those most directly affected.</u> This Subcommittee is being co-chaired by

–4–

APPENDIX IV: MINUTES OF JULY 26, 1995, ORIENTATION MEETING OF MEMORIAL TASK FORCE

Phillip Thompson, whose mother was one of the final three victims recovered after the implosion of the building, Toby Thompson, whose brother was killed in the bombing, by Cheryl Vaught, a Red Cross volunteer and Tim O'Connor, Executive Director of Associated Catholic Charities, whose post bombing volunteer time was spent with families of the victims.

3. **Coordinating Committee and Executive Director.** The memorialization process will be kept moving and coordinated by the Coordinating Committee (consisting of the Subcommittee Chairs and 5 at large members) and by a very capable volunteer Executive Director.

C. **Planning Process.** - How do we progress from today to the selection of a design for the Memorial or Memorial Components?

1. **Hallmarks of the Process.** A number of us attended a recent symposium on memorials in San Jose, and the common thread of memorial projects which have encountered difficulties has been the lack of public participation. The hallmarks of the memorialization process will be: Listening and Public Participation.

2. Accordingly, the initial phase of the planning process will be public outreach, i.e. soliciting the feelings and opinions of all interested members of the public regarding what the Memorial should reflect and remember. Perhaps the dominant questions should be:

   a. What do you want to feel when visiting the Memorial?
   b. What do you want other adults and children to feel and learn when visiting the Memorial?

-5-

3. **When we speak of public outreach, what do we mean by "public"? Who is included?** There are concentric rings of impact from the bombing radiating out from:

   a. the families of victims and survivors,
   b. to those who were directly involved in rescue and relief efforts,
   c. and to all people across our state, nation and throughout the world whose hearts were impacted by the bombing.

Based on calls and correspondence received, the April 19 bombing shook the world. Hence, by "public" we are including all who were impacted, and order to assist in the healing process, we feel an obligation to listen all who want to be heard.

4. **How will the public outreach segment of the planning process be conducted?**

Solicitation of feelings and opinions as to what should be memorialized, that is, what should be reflected and remembered by the Memorial will be conducted by two of the Task Force Subcommittees.

   a. Victims' Families and Survivors Liaison will hold several meetings with all families of victims and survivors who desire to participate. The first of these meetings was held Monday evening. The relief agencies have been very protective (as they should be) of the confidentiality of the names and addresses of families and survivors, so we do not yet have a comprehensive list, but we are working to resolve such problem.

   b. The solicitation of feelings from the balance of the public will be administered by the Memorial Ideas Input Subcommittee. This Subcommittee will probably employ a number of means, including public

-6-

APPENDIX IV: MINUTES OF JULY 26, 1995, ORIENTATION MEETING OF MEMORIAL TASK FORCE

meetings, written surveys, teleconferencing and higher tech outreach.

5. **Memorial Mission Statement.** After the public outreach program is concluded in several months, reports will be prepared by the Victims' Families and Survivors Liaison and Memorial Ideas Input Subcommittees setting forth the results of their respective outreach programs. Such reports will be presented to the Advisory Committee, and the Advisory Committee will then prepare a Memorial Mission Statement setting forth the objectives to be achieved by the Memorial. I envision that the Memorial Mission Statement will become an integral part of the Memorial as the public's interpretation of the meaning of the Memorial.

6. **When will be the appropriate time to discuss the physical design of the Memorial components?** Until we complete the public outreach programs and the Memorial Mission Statement, the Task Force will not focus on physical design. After the Memorial Mission Statement is completed, the Design Solicitation Subcommittee will incorporate the Memorial Mission Statement into a Request for Design Proposals and distribute such Requests. The Requests will require a response consisting of both a Visual Design and a Statement of Explanation of Compliance With and Justification of Fulfillment of the Memorial Mission Statement.

7. **Selection of Physical Design.** Alternative design selection methodologies will be researched by the Design Solicitation Subcommittee and a report and recommendation will be made to the Advisory Committee at its meeting scheduled for 5:00 p.m. on September 19.

The normal selection methodology employed in major commemorative projects is a design competition judged by a

professional panel. IF a design competition is the approach selected by the Advisory Committee, we will recommend that prior to final selection by the professional panel, models of the finalist designs should be prepared to allow additional public comment regarding fulfillment of the Memorial Mission Statement.

8. **Importance of the Memorialization Process.** We must be realistic in our expectations as to the end result of this process, that is, our respective views of the Completed Memorial. Because at least any symbolic component of the Memorial will be an art form, opinions as to its perfection will vary; HOWEVER, I firmly believe that the Process of Memorialization will be more important than the end result. If the process is conducted in an open, caring, public participatory and non-commercial manner, as it must be, I believe we will form a strong consensus as to the process. **More Importantly,** if we administer the memorialization process appropriately, it will not only be a planning process, but it will be a major component of the healing process.

D. **Memorial Timeline Being Developed.** We are researching other memorialization projects, and as soon as we are comfortable that we have developed a realistic and achievable timeline, we will announce it. I agree that the development of such timeline is important and will be a key to moving this process along in an efficient manner.

E. **Distinction between North Downtown Design Workshop and Memorial Planning Process.** During the past several weeks a North Downtown Design Workshop has been is process under the sponsorship of the City of Oklahoma City, The National Endowment for the Arts and The Arts Council of Oklahoma City. The final presentations were made yesterday afternoon. The reason for mentioning the this Workshop is to clarify that while the Workshop has focused to some extent on the Murrah block,

-7-

-8-

300

APPENDIX IV: MINUTES OF JULY 26, 1995, ORIENTATION MEETING OF MEMORIAL TASK FORCE

it has only done so because of the
relationship and importance of the Memorial
to the redevelopment of the surrounding
area. The planning of the Memorial will
result from the Memorial Task Force process
outlined to you this afternoon.

F.   **Memorial Task Force Mailing Address:** P. O.
Box 18390, Oklahoma City, OK 73154-0390

G.   **Memorial Task Force Telephone Number:**
236-8400

H.   **Memorial Fund**

Federal Building Memorial Fund
Oklahoma City Community Foundation
P. O. Box 1146
Oklahoma City, OK 73101

III. **Comments, Questions and Answers**

IV.   **Meeting Schedule**

A.   **Advisory Committee**

1.   September 19, 1995 - 5:00 p.m. - St.
Luke's Methodist Church

a.   Subcommittee Reports
b.   Consideration of design selection
methodology

2.   November 14, 1995 - 5:00 p.m. - St.
Luke's Methodist Church

B.   **Subcommittee Meetings** - To be announced by
Subcommittee Chairs

V.   **Adjourn** Thank you for your attendance and your
willingness to participate. We are
adjourned.

-9-

MEMORIAL MISSION STATEMENT AND APPENDICES

Murrah Federal Building Memorial Task Force

Memorial Mission Statement

❦❦❦

Adopted **March 26, 1996**
Oklahoma City, Oklahoma

APPENDIX V: MEMORIAL MISSION STATEMENT AND APPENDICES

Murrah Federal Building
Memorial Task Force

Chairman
Robert M. Johnson

Vice-Chairman
Karen Luke

Executive Director
Rowland Denman

Subcommittee Co-Chairs

Administration
Rowland Denman
Doris Jones

Archives
Anita Arnold
Deb Farrell-Lynn
Tom Toperzer

Design Solicitation
Jackie I. Jones
Toby Thompson
Beth Tolbert

Families/ Survivors
Kim Jones-Shelton
Tim O'Connor
Phillip Thompson
Toby Thompson
Kathleen Treanor
Cheryl Vaught

Finance
Linda Lambert
John Rex
Florence Rogers

Government Liaison
Terry Childers
Kevin Gotshall
Thomas J. McDaniel

Memorial Ideas Input
Sydney Dobson
Jimmy Goodman
Polly Nichols

Public Fund Raising
Ann Alspaugh
LeAnn Jenkins
Barbara Kerrick
Gene Rainbolt
Lee Allan Smith

Public & Private Grants
Jean Gumerson
G. Rainey Williams, Jr.

Public Relations
Jeanette Gamba
Sam Armstrong Lopez
Kathleen Treanor

Administrative Director
Phyllis Stough

PREFACE

In the aftermath of the April 19, 1995, bombing of the Alfred P. Murrah Federal Building in Oklahoma City, Mayor Ron Norick appointed a 350-member Memorial Task Force charged with developing an appropriate memorial to honor those touched by the event. Members of the Task Force include family members of those killed in the bombing, survivors of the blast and volunteers with expertise in areas ranging from mental health, law and the arts, to fund-raising, business, communications and government.

From summer 1995 until spring 1996, members of the Memorial Task Force conducted a very intensive, deliberate and inclusive listening process to gather from families, survivors and the general public throughout the world ideas about what visitors to the bombing Memorial should feel and experience. Using comments gathered from numerous family and survivors meetings, general citizens meetings and thousands of written and Internet survey responses, the subcommittee responsible for drafting the Mission Statement met for weeks and revised the statement several times based upon comments from the Task Force as a whole.

The following Memorial Mission Statement was approved unanimously at a meeting of the Advisory Committee of the Memorial Task Force on March 26, 1996.

The Mission Statement will be the cornerstone document in shaping the meaning and guiding the design and development of the Memorial. It represents a remarkable community consensus document which evolved under the most difficult circumstances.

POST OFFICE BOX 18390 / OKLAHOMA CITY, OK / 73154-0390 / PHONE: (405) 236-8400

Murrah Federal Building Memorial Task Force
Memorial Mission Statement

We come here to remember
those who were killed, those who survived and those changed forever.
May all who leave here know the impact of violence.
May this memorial offer comfort, strength, peace, hope and serenity.

Context

Few events in the past quarter-century have rocked Americans' perception of themselves and their institutions, and brought together the people of our nation with greater intensity than the April 19, 1995, bombing of the Alfred P. Murrah Federal Building in downtown Oklahoma City.

The resulting deaths of 168 people, some of whom were children, immediately touched thousands of family members whose lives will forever bear the scars of having had those precious to them taken away so brutally.

Suffering with such families are countless survivors, including children, who struggle not only with the suffering around them, but with their own physical and emotional injuries and with shaping a life beyond April 19. Such losses and struggles are personal and, since they resulted from so public an attack, they also are shared with a community, a nation and the world.

But the story of the bombing does not stop with the attack itself or with the many losses it caused. The responses of Oklahoma's public servants and private citizens, and those from throughout the nation remain as a testament to the sense of unity, compassion, even heroism, that characterized the rescue and recovery following the bombing.

In the aftermath of the bombing, people of all colors, ages, religions and political philosophies reached out in love -- from co-workers, bystanders and professionals who appeared almost instantly to help at the site, to individuals thousands of miles away who sent letters of support or funds to provide for devastated families.

Within days of the bombing, the Mayor's office, the Governor's office, non-profit agencies and citizens of Oklahoma City began to receive suggestions, ideas and offers of donations related to the creation of a memorial.

1

APPENDIX V: MEMORIAL MISSION STATEMENT AND APPENDICES

Mindful of the far-reaching impact of the bombing and aware of the historic nature of the event, Oklahoma City Mayor Ron Norick appointed a 350-member volunteer task force charged with developing an appropriate memorial.

Specifically, the Task Force was called to: ensure that everyone could participate in the planning process; gather extensive input from families, survivors and the public about what visitors to the memorial should think, feel or experience; develop a mission statement for the memorial; carry out a design-solicitation process based upon objectives in the mission statement; and recommend to the Mayor and Oklahoma City Council a plan for design, construction, administration and maintenance of the memorial, including citizen oversight during the construction.

The Task Force includes 11 subcommittees, each responsible for researching and forming recommendations related to different components of the memorial development process. Reports from two such subcommittees are the foundation for this Mission Statement.

The Families and Survivors Liaison Subcommittee and the Memorial Ideas Input Subcommittee spent eight months gathering ideas from family members of those killed, survivors and the general public across America and throughout the world regarding what the bombing memorial should strive to accomplish.

Priorities identified through that idea-gathering process are outlined in detail in the two subcommittee reports which are summarized in the section of this Mission Statement entitled "Guidance: Themes." The full reports are available as appendices to this Mission Statement *(see Appendices A and B).*

By summarizing the reports as part of this Mission Statement, the Mission Statement Drafting Subcommittee wished to stress the importance of the public idea-gathering process in development of the Memorial and, most important, reinforce the families' and survivors' wishes in shaping the meaning of the memorial.

Guidance: Priorities

First and foremost, the Memorial shall honor and respect the work of the Families and Survivors Liaison Subcommittee and the Memorial Ideas Input Subcommittee, and shall reflect the priorities identified by the subcommittees in their reports.

Second, the Memorial shall comply with two resolutions passed by the Memorial Advisory Committee. These resolutions concern an information center and inclusion of a tree, and they are summarized in the section of this Mission Statement entitled "Guidance: Resolutions." Their full text is provided in Appendices C and D.

Third, the general site for the overall Memorial Complex *should* include the Murrah Building block, the south half of the Journal Record Building block, including the Oklahoma Water Resources Board Building and the Athenian Building, and Fifth Street between the two blocks.

Fourth, the Memorial Complex, and especially where the Murrah Building stood, is "sacred ground" -- a hallowed place deserving of the respect and solemnity associated with great loss. In that vein, families, survivors and others prefer that: the Memorial itself be located completely or partially on the spot where the Murrah Building stood; and the information center be located off the site of the Murrah Building, but within or very near the overall Memorial Complex.

Fifth, the Memorial itself or the site where the Murrah Building stood *must* incorporate the names of those who died (noting in some way, if the family desires, each victim who was carrying an unborn child). The Memorial or the site where the Murrah Building stood also *must* incorporate the names of survivors and must do so in a manner separate, distinct and apart from the tribute to and presentation of the names of those who died.

Finally, it is the wish of the Memorial Task Force that, after completion of the Memorial and Memorial Complex, the entire facility be designated as a National Monument to be operated and maintained by the National Parks Service. Such an arrangement is seen as the best way to ensure perpetual high-quality care for a Memorial Complex of national and historic significance.

Guidance: Themes

After eight months of conducting public surveys, community meetings and small group discussions to gather ideas about what the Memorial should evoke, Task Force members found that the hopes of the general public mirrored almost identically those outlined by the Families/Survivors Liaison Subcommittee.

The result is a description of what visitors to the Memorial Complex should feel, experience and encounter. Participants made a solid effort to avoid discussing what the Memorial should *look* like, feeling deeply that talented designers were better qualified to suggest meaningful ways to evoke feelings and create memorable experiences.

Families, survivors and the public wish for the Memorial Complex to be a place of:

- ☙ *Remembrance* -- The Memorial Complex should have on the site where the Murrah Building stood a beautiful universal symbol as a Memorial focusing on victims and survivors of the April 19 blast. The symbol should be enduring in its form and content, and it should be appropriate to the culture and environment of the Oklahoma City community. Visitors to the Memorial Complex should develop an understanding of victims and survivors as *individuals* with many roles -- family members, friends, co-workers and neighbors. The range of cultures, races and ages of those attacked should be evident.

- ☙ *Peace* -- The Memorial Complex should provide a quiet, peaceful setting where visitors have opportunity for reflection. Many participants suggest using natural elements, such as trees, flowers, gardens or water, to create a serene atmosphere.

- ☙ *Spirituality and Hope* -- The Memorial should be powerful, awe-inspiring and convey the sense of deep loss caused by the bombing. By the same token, it should evoke feelings of compassion and hope, and inspire visitors to live their lives more meaningfully. It should speak of the spirituality of the community and nation that was so evident in the wake of the attack.

2

3

304

APPENDIX V: MEMORIAL MISSION STATEMENT AND APPENDICES

Cherished Children -- Families, survivors and individuals across the globe agree that the Memorial Complex should include a special place for children. The Memorial Complex should have a component designed to reach kids on "their level," both physically and cognitively. The component should help children learn and feel something they can carry with them as they grow and should offer them assurance that the world holds far more good than bad.

Comfort -- The Memorial Complex should provide comfort to visitors and should ultimately offer an uplifting experience -- elevating the memory of the dead and survivors and, in some way too, the spirit of those who visit.

Recognition -- The Memorial Complex should include a tribute to those who helped. It should honor professionals who worked to rescue and treat survivors and to recover victims of the blast. Such recognition also should extend to the many volunteers who supported rescue, recovery and medical personnel by providing supplies, food and shelter, as well as emotional and spiritual support. Also, the tribute should honor the spirit of unity that characterized the response of the community and nation following the attack, and it should reflect the sense of pride such responses created. It is important that such a tribute in no way diminish the tragedy, but rather, that it offer an inspiring contrast between the brutality of the evil and the tenderness of the response.

Learning -- The Memorial Complex should include an information center that records important facts and observations about the bombing and teaches visitors never to forget the event or the people it touched. Educational information should include, among other elements, personal stories about those who died and those who survived *(see "Guidance: Resolutions" section for more detail)*; "before and after" information about the Murrah Building and surrounding areas; and the immediate aftermath of the blast. The educational area should tell visitors about the loss of a sense of innocence and security that can follow a terrorist attack. Such a learning center should be participatory and should instill an understanding of the senselessness of violence, especially as a means of effecting government change. It should convey the imperative to reject violence.

As much as possible, the Memorial Complex and, where appropriate, the Memorial itself must incorporate the themes outlined above.

The wishes of the Families/Survivors Liaison Subcommittee are to be given the greatest weight in the Memorial planning and development process. That has been a fundamental philosophy of the Memorial Task Force since its inception.

Ensuring that families and survivors are involved to the greatest degree feasible in development, design, funding, construction and maintenance of the Memorial is one way to honor those who died, those who survived and those who love them.

Guidance: Resolutions

Memorial Complex designs must comply with the two resolutions of the Memorial Task Force Advisory Committee. The first resolution pertains to incorporating biographies and photos of victims, and stories and photos of survivors within a Memorial information center. The second resolution relates to incorporating within the Memorial Complex the "Survivor Tree" located in the south portion of the Journal Record Building block.

Following are pertinent portions of each resolution. Complete text of the resolutions is provided in Appendices C and D.

November 14, 1995 Resolution:
Stories and Photographs of
Victims and Survivors

NOW, THEREFORE, IT IS RESOLVED THAT the Memorial Mission Statement will include a requirement that one of the components of the Memorial must be an information center, which, in part, would include a segment consisting of: (a) biographies of the victims written by the families of the victims and photographic representations of the victims, and (b) stories of the survivors written by the survivors and photographic representations of the survivors.

IT IS FURTHER RESOLVED THAT the Families/Survivors Liaison Subcommittee, in consultation with the Archives Subcommittee, develop guidelines for format and length of such biographies and stories for distribution to families of victims and survivors.

January 16, 1996 Resolution:
The Survivor Tree

NOW, THEREFORE, IT IS RESOLVED THAT the Memorial Mission Statement will include a requirement that one of the components of the Memorial must be the "Survivor Tree" located on the south half of the Journal Record Building block.

IT IS FURTHER RESOLVED THAT the Advisory Committee take steps to protect and preserve such Survivor Tree.

C:\wpdocs\murrah\mission.r
(approved by Advisory Committee 3/26/96)

4

131701.GOODMANJ

APPENDIX V: MEMORIAL MISSION STATEMENT AND APPENDICES

Murrah Federal Building Memorial Task Force
Memorial Mission Statement

[Appendix A]

FINAL REPORT of the
Families/Survivors Liaison Subcommittee
March 1, 1996

INTRODUCTION

The following report is an overview of the last 8 months of meetings of the Families/Survivors Liaison Subcommittee("FSL" or "Committee") the initial commitment that the FSL would be a part of every step of the process and anyone from this Committee would be urged and welcome to serve on any and all of the other subcommittees laid out in the initial structure of the Task Force. We began with a lot of anger and distrust and we have progressed to working as a family unit. Please accept this as a historical record of the process we have gone through to reach this point.

HISTORY

On July 17, 1995, the first meeting of the Families/Survivors Liaison Subcommittee met at the First Christian Church at 36th & Walker. Phillip Thompson and Toby Thompson facilitated the meeting and introductions of the respective committee chairs were made to a group of approximately 150 people. Bob Johnson came and explained the Task Force structure to the group and fielded questions from the floor. Mayor Norick also spoke to the families and survivors and assured them that they were necessary to the process and that over the course of the following months, the Committee chairmen would be organizing their committees and needed the names, addresses and phone numbers of any family/survivor who wished to be a part of the process.

The group then went into an open discussion of a list of Opportunities and Challenges that would face us over the course of the next few months. We recognized then that controlling our anger and keeping an open mind would be a true challenge. We saw a need to identify how we would be involved in the process, and how we would communicate between the various Task Force committees and families/survivors. We identified the need for a time line to set the mission statement and how we would keep an open mind and be objective. We reminded each other that we needed to be inclusive to all and that we needed to find the spirituality of the event. Reverence to the rescue was important to the process. We did not want to honor the criminals, or memorialize them in any way. We said that the need to listen and be respectful of each other was very important. We also identified a list of opportunities which later became the framework for the Survey that the Memorial Ideas Input committee used for its input. We concluded the meeting by setting the date of our next meeting of August 14, 1995.

At the August 14th meeting, we requested volunteers for each of the subcommittee. Several of the different committee chairs were there to take names of people interested in being on their committees. We spent time going over the materials from the previous meeting for those who could not attend. Philip Thompson issued a request for someone to do a database. Kathleen Treanor volunteered to do this for FSL and to try to produce a newsletter for the Memorial. We concluded this meeting by also identifying our next meeting date of September 18, 1995.

At the September 18th meeting we had sent our first newsletter with terrific response. The database had over 250 names at that time and we were still trying to identify names of survivors and victims families. A "Search for Survivors" was sent out to the local newspapers and response was coming in but we saw a greater need for the word of mouth spread for requesting names for the database. Feelings of anger and distrust ran high and we saw a need to draw more victims families/survivors into the Memorial Task Force. At that time we saw that it was of great importance to identify people from our group who were willing and able to serve as subcommittee chairmen on the other subcommittees and we started measures to identify those people. We concluded this meeting as usual with setting the next meeting date of October 16, 1995.

At our October 16th meeting, we began working in small group settings. We decided to use the smaller groups to promote intimacy and familiarity among victims families and survivors. This was the process we chose to use to put our feelings and concepts down on paper. Counselors came to act as facilitators and to allow us to speak freely without reservation and without distraction. They were the recorders at the different tables putting the committee's feelings into words. We also adjourned this meeting with the date planned for our next meeting, which was November 13, 1995.

At our November 13 meeting we continued with our group discussions on our feelings and interpretations of the Memorial. It was also brought to the attention of the committee that a compilation should be written by the victims families and survivors. Such material would be made available for review by any design team prior to submission of a proposed design for the Memorial. Also at this meeting a proposal from the Coordinating Committee was brought before the FSL by Bob Johnson. This proposal was that the stories of the victims as told by the families and the survivors as told by the survivors, and the photographs of the victims and survivors be included in any information center, as one component of the Memorial. This proposal was unanimously received by the FSL. This was also accepted with the stipulation that the Archives committee and the FSL come to an agreement as to content and length. A resolution setting forth the proposal was approved by the Advisory Committee on November 14, 1995. See attached Appendix "A" to this report.

The next meeting was held on December 11th. At this meeting we narrowed down the ideas and themes to the top five ideas in our small groups. From that we proceeded to our next meeting of January 8th.

The next meeting was held on January 8, 1996. From the five themes an overall trend was noticed. There were 20 things that were repeated in all the groups. So we had inadvertently

1

2

APPENDIX V: MEMORIAL MISSION STATEMENT AND APPENDICES

narrowed down our feelings and themes to these final 20 selections. The group used a multi-voting process using seven votes that they could place on any of the 20 themes as they wished. They were allowed, if they chose, to put all their votes on one selection or they could disperse their votes to several categories as they wished. This method was designed to allow participants to take ownership in the finalization process. This month it was also brought to our attention that a tree, which was a forgotten survivor of the blast, was still living. It was requested that we take measures to save the tree and incorporate it as a living element to the Memorial. This was also voted in unanimously. Hence we had identified the second element of the Memorial. The Survivor Tree. A resolution regarding The Survivor Tree was adopted by the Advisory Committee at its meeting on January 16, 1996.

At our February 19th meeting, from our voting the month before, we narrowed down our feelings to the top ten recurring themes, those being:

1. Focus on victims and survivors
2. Never forget/always remember
3. Quiet, peaceful, serene, sacred
4. Hope, spiritual
5. Something special for the children

6. Universal Symbol
7. Comforting
8. Sense of Pride
9. Educational (study of non-violence)
10. Loss of innocence/security

Also at the February 19 meeting, the Coordinating Committee presented the design selection methodology structure, which was adopted by the Advisory Committee on January 16, 1996, subject to review and approval by the Families/ Survivors Liaison Subcommittee. A copy of such design selection methodology is attached as Appendix B. After a discussion, the resolution was passed with a small addition. The addition would be that after the Evaluation Panel narrows the field down to 10 honorable mentions and 3 finalists, the families and survivors would be asked to view the final three and each participant would be asked to write comments on the three finalists. The Final Selection committee would then consider these written recommendations prior to selecting the winner. We ended the meeting by everyone writing down their individual feelings on the memorial. These will be compiled and submitted to the Design Solicitation Committee for the potential designers to read and know our feelings.

Therefore, after reviewing the many months of notes and statements written by the families and survivors, this Committee strongly believes that the Mission Statement should include the following: The Memorial should include a beautiful universal symbol that focuses on the Victims and Survivors. The Memorial Site should include a quiet, peaceful, serene and sacred place of learning located away from the "footprint" of the Alfred P. Murrah Building. It should teach us to never forget/always remember. The Memorial should memorialize those who are lost and remember those survived. There should be an area set aside for the children where they can learn and grow and be assured that there is more good in the world than bad. The Memorial should also include an information center, and one of the exhibits contained therein shall be the biographies of the victims (written by the families), the stories of the survivors (written by the survivors), and the photographs of the victims and survivors. The Memorial shall

also include information about those involved in the rescue effort which inspired a sense of pride in our state and fellow man. The Survivor Tree located north of N.W. 5th Street should be preserved as a part of the Memorial.

In conclusion, we respectfully submit our above recommendation to be included within the Mission statement for the Memorial in some form, however that may be.

The Families/Survivors Liaison Subcommittee

3

4

APPENDIX V: MEMORIAL MISSION STATEMENT AND APPENDICES

Murrah Federal Building Memorial Task Force
Memorial Mission Statement

[Appendix B]

FINAL REPORT OF
The Murrah Federal Building Memorial Task Force
Memorial Ideas Input Subcommittee
March 1, 1996

At 9:02 a.m. on April 19, 1995, the horror of domestic terrorism struck deeply into the heart of Oklahoma City--and all of our lives were immediately changed forever. The grief, loss and helplessness we individually and collectively suffered as a result of the bombing of the Alfred P. Murrah Federal Building, and from the mass murders of our family members, friends and fellow workers, was a suffering that no other American city had ever experienced. Our public servants and private citizens, along with those from other towns and cities throughout this great nation, responded quickly and effectively with acts of heroism and deeds of compassion. And the world seemed to marvel at the way in which Oklahoma City and the State of Oklahoma carried itself with dignity and generosity through this time of tragedy--coming to describe it as the "Oklahoma Standard."

Before the sun set on the day after the bomb exploded, the Oklahoma City Mayor's office, the Governor's office, directors of non-profit agencies, and citizens throughout the City began to receive suggestions and ideas, and offers of donations and assistance, about the creation of a memorial to be built in response to the bombing. The number of memorial ideas and specific design proposals being submitted by interested persons increased substantially over the next few weeks. When the process of dealing with the removal of the victims and the demolition of the building had been completed, and the initial mechanisms for delivering financial assistance to the victims' families and survivors had been instituted, Mayor Ron Norick was able to turn his attention to the memorial process.

In mid-July, Mayor Norick appointed the initial members of the Murrah Federal Building Memorial Task Force (the "Task Force"), chaired by Robert M. Johnson, with Karen Luke as its Vice Chair. The Task Force was charged to (I) coordinate and unify the Memorial process, so that all constituencies could participate in the process, (ii) obtain extensive input from the victims' families and the public about what the memorial should remember and what visitors to it should feel, think and experience, (iii) develop a Memorial Mission Statement of the objectives to be achieved by the completed Memorial, (iv) carry out the design solicitation process based on the objectives in the Mission Statement, and (v) ultimately recommend to the Mayor and the Oklahoma City Council a Memorial Plan addressing the design, components, funding, administration and maintenance of the Memorial, including citizens' oversight during the construction of the Memorial.

5

The Task Force was fortunate that several of its members had the opportunity to attend a national conference in San Jose, California in June on the development of memorials, which was sponsored by the National Association of Local Arts Agencies. They gained valuable insights into some of the most common of the potential pitfalls in any memorialization process. First, that the memorials which had the least acceptance and most opposition appeared to be those which lacked significant citizen/constituent involvement in the overall memorialization process. Second, that the memorialization process itself, if handled with sensitivity and inclusiveness, can be as positive and enduring as the final memorial eventually created. Third, that Oklahoma City was embarking on a process with the development of its memorial that no community had ever attempted before--while the emotions of grief, anger, despair and hopelessness still ran strongly through the families, friends and neighborhoods of those who had been attacked. Even before we knew individually or collectively how this tragedy had changed us in the deepest ways, we would begin the process of forging a community-wide effort to develop a memorial which would be fitting for and respectful of those who lost their lives in or were survivors of the attack, to their families, and to the City of Oklahoma City.

The Memorial Ideas Input Subcommittee was created as an integral part of the Task Force. Its initial task was to prepare a plan for the solicitation of ideas and opinions from the public regarding the values, themes and messages to be reflected by the Memorial--a plan that must create widespread public participation and help develop a sense of ownership by the public in the resulting Memorial. It was to present the plan to the Advisory Committee of the Task Force, implement the Plan after initial approval of its general concepts, and finally issue a report to the Advisory Committee reflecting the objectives and opinions expressed by the public, including recommendations as to the general objectives to be achieved in the creation of the Memorial.

The Co-Chairs of the Subcommittee are Sydney Dobson, Polly Nichols, and Jimmy Goodman. A list of active Subcommittee Volunteers is included in the Appendix to this report.

History of Subcommittee Meetings/Actions
The first meeting of the Subcommittee was held on August 17, 1995. The members were advised that the essential functions of the Subcommittee would be:

- to provide every opportunity possible for people to share their feelings and ideas about what the memorial should remember and represent

- to listen carefully and record accurately the responses received, and

- to maintain an approach of sensitivity and inclusiveness in all stages of the process.

All Subcommittee members understood from the first meeting that this report would be used to help develop a Memorial Mission Statement that the Design Solicitation

6

APPENDIX V: MEMORIAL MISSION STATEMENT AND APPENDICES

Subcommittee would use in the memorial design process. Consequently, the focus of the Subcommittee did not include obtaining input about the physical appearance and content of the memorial.

Based on the discussion at the initial meeting, the Co-Chairs decided to divide the Subcommittee's task into three working Subgroups: Community Meetings, Memorial Constituents, and Memorial Survey. Respectively, Beth Shortt, Barbara Naranche, and Larry Jeffries, Subcommittee members, agreed to chair these three Subgroups. The concentrated efforts of these three Subgroups formed the foundation of the Subcommittee's outreach and their respective reports are included in the Appendix to this report.

After the initial meeting held at 4:00 p.m., in the City Bank & Trust board room at Park Avenue and Robinson in downtown Oklahoma City, it was decided to make the time and place of the meetings convenient for the majority of the members. All further Subcommittee meetings were held at 5:15 p.m. in the Youth Services for Oklahoma County building at 201 N.E. 50th Street. We are especially grateful to Youth Services for accommodating our meeting needs with the generous donation of their space as needed. A total of eight Subcommittee meetings were held, with attendance varying from 40 to 3 participants. Separate Subgroup meetings were held at other times as necessary. The final Subcommittee meeting was held on February 27, 1996, at which time this report received final approval.

Community Meetings

The Community Meetings Subgroup was assigned the task to develop the format for, make the arrangements for, and publicize and coordinate the presentation of community meetings throughout the greater Oklahoma City area in order to help obtain public input about the Memorial. It made every effort to plan and publicize the community meetings so that they were as convenient as possible for the public--varying the geographic locations and times of the meetings. All meetings were held in buildings thought to be unintimidating to public access.

Publicity was coordinated through the Public Relations Subcommittee. Press releases about each meeting were sent to the local media, including newspaper, television and radio. In addition, several members of the Task Force were able to publicize the meetings during interviews with television and radio that were arranged by the Public Relations Subcommittee.

The meetings were staffed entirely by volunteers. Beth Shortt prepared all of the necessary written materials and facilitated each meeting. While total attendance was less than expected, the quality of the input and participation of those who did attend was excellent, and will be of great use in developing the Mission Statement. Regardless of the numbers who chose this particular medium, all who heard of the meetings did have the opportunity to participate in this way if they wished.

7

In summary, we feel that the results of the community meetings process are:

- The memorialization process has been made open to the public.

- Public input has been solicited and obtained.

- A process for obtaining individual input in a group setting has been tested.

- The quality of the input received is excellent.

- Those who participated appreciated the opportunity and benefited from the process.

A complete copy of the Subgroup Report is included in the Appendix to this Report.

Memorial Constituents

Memorial Constituents were defined as those groups of people who, by virtue of their experience with the bombing of the Murrah Federal Building, had a particular perspective to share. The Subcommittee agreed that these particular groups warranted a special contact to obtain their ideas. The Subgroup attempted to contact as many members of each constituent group as possible to encourage their input and their involvement in the process.

The Subgroup's objectives were:

- to encourage and gather input from each group of constituents about what they want visitors to the memorial to learn and feel

- to provide a variety of opportunities for those closely involved groups to voice their opinions about feelings the memorial should evoke, and

- to listen to and value each contribution made.

The Subgroup was gratified by the response of those who were contacted. Available methods to obtain the input included: the memorial survey, group meetings, focus groups for a smaller representative sample, and personal communication or conversation. In most cases, the memorial survey turned out to be the instrument used. In those instances, the responses of the various groups will be included in the compilation of all survey responses. The Subgroup believes that most of the targeted constituents were reached and offered the chance to have input in some manner. It feels that the process of sharing and the quality of the meetings and contacts with the Memorial constituents fulfilled their intended purposes, and the effort was successful and worthwhile. A complete list of the various memorial constituent groups included in this outreach is included in the Subgroup Report included in the Appendix to this Report.

8

APPENDIX V: MEMORIAL MISSION STATEMENT AND APPENDICES

Memorial Survey

The subcommittee Co-Chairs agreed that a survey could be an excellent tool to help achieve the goal of gathering ideas and feelings about what the memorial should remember and represent. They agreed to draft a survey for discussion at the first Subcommittee meeting on August 17, 1995.

To gain ideas about the contents of the survey, Subcommittee Co-Chairs attended the first Families and Survivors Subcommittee meeting on July 24, 1995 and listened to the ideas and feelings expressed by that group--which had been most deeply affected by the bombing. Their comments and ideas formed the basis for the survey's first draft.

A Memorial Survey Subgroup was formed

- To make certain that every person involved in the memorial process, especially the families and survivors, was given the opportunity to review and make suggestions for revision of the one-page draft survey;

- To solicit printing donors; and

- To plan and implement a worldwide distribution system.

With only minor changes, the final survey was essentially the same as the first draft. The survey received final approval in late November and the Subgroup turned its focus to printing and distribution.

Survey distribution methods were:

- Press releases to both print and electronic media (resulting in the survey being reprinted in   full in both local and Tulsa area newspapers);

- A homepage on the worldwide web Internet with local, national and international access;

- 17 U.S. Postal Service locations in the metro area;

- 12 Metropolitan Library branches; and

- The Memorial post box address where anyone could send a self-addressed, stamped envelope.

Survey results were tabulated by city, state, national, and international input. This will ensure that the input of the people of Oklahoma City may be clearly defined. In addition, handwritten comments were individually read and the written suggestions most often submitted were also summarized and included in the Subgroup's Report. The full

9

Memorial Survey Subgroup Report is included in the Appendix to this Report.

Summary of Public Input

The Subcommittee believes that the following principal themes consistently repeat themselves throughout the public suggestions as to what the Memorial should represent and remember:

- Remembrance of the individuals who were attacked on April 19, 1995--Visitors should learn their individual life stories, and leave the Memorial with a strong and clear sense of who they were/are--not just as names, but as individuals, and as our family members, loved ones, friends, neighbors and co-workers. The multicultural cross-section of those attacked should be acknowledged and recorded.

- Honoring those who helped--Many suggestions focused on honoring those who helped in response to the bombing, especially the rescue, medical and recovery workers. But participants also included, to a lesser extent, the many general citizen volunteers who acted in support of the rescue/recovery teams, and generously and freely provided them with the necessary supplies, clothing, food and shelter while they carried out their grueling tasks.

- Community--Without negating in any way the tragic loss the bomb caused, to record and commemorate the spirit of community and unity which characterized the reaction, locally and nationally, in response to the bombing.

- Serenity, Peacefulness and Reflection--Visitors should be able to encounter a space where they have the opportunity to experience serenity and peacefulness and engage in reflection. (Many suggested the use of natural elements such as trees, flowers, gardens, and water as a means of accomplishing this desired end.)

- Something for the Children--This addresses two different but related concepts: First, there should be some component which relates to children on their level, both physically and cognitively. From this they should feel and learn something which they will take away with them and remember for years to come. Second, some component of the memorial should openly and obviously be a special place or space which is just "for" the children.

- Historical/Educational--There should be a component to the Memorial which teaches and records the important historical facts, and resulting observations, about these events; including, for example, information about the Murrah Federal Building, the individuals who died, the survivors, the bombing and its immediate aftermath, the magnitude of the attack on people and property, the response, the area in the immediate vicinity before and after the bombing--and puts it all in the context of the futility and senselessness of domestic terrorism--killing government servants-- as a means of effecting political change in our nation. (Many thought that this could be on

10

APPENDIX V: MEMORIAL MISSION STATEMENT AND APPENDICES

a site separate from where the building was located.)

- Inspiration/Emotion--Many suggestions centered on a hope that the Memorial would be powerful and awe-inspiring, and that visitors would experience not only the various feelings of compassion, hope, peacefulness, and serenity, but also the sense of loss caused by this tragedy--and leave the Memorial personally inspired to live their lives in some meaningful way differently than they had intended before their visit.

- That the Memorial be spiritual, participatory and positive was also mentioned by a significant number of the participants.

Recommendations to Advisory Committee

The Subcommittee makes the following recommendations of the general objectives to be achieved in the creation of the Memorial:

- First and foremost, it must be sensitive to those most directly affected by the bombing, as the Task Force has always intended.

- Second, it should be enduring in its form and content, and appropriate to the unique and special Oklahoma City community in which it will be located.

- Third, it should incorporate as many of the above-summarized major themes, ideas and opinions suggested by the public as possible--keeping in mind that they must be compatible with the suggestions in the companion report being submitted by the Families and Survivors Subcommittee and the first two goals noted above.

- Fourth, that the remaining steps in the memorialization process continue to involve those most directly affected to the greatest extent feasible in all important aspects of the development, design, funding, construction and maintenance of the Memorial.

Parting Thoughts

In addition to the specific charge to be accomplished by the Subcommittee, the Co-Chairs and members present at the final meeting voted to share the following impressions with the Advisory Committee:

- Subcommittee members are grateful that the Families and Survivors Subcommittee was formed and has continued to meet and will prepare its own report about what the memorial should remember and represent. It is the belief of the Memorial Ideas Input Subcommittee that no one else could represent adequately this very special group so directly affected by the bombing.

- Subcommittee volunteers agreed that it was most important that every family member of a victim or bombing survivor be asked to participate, even though some did not want to participate in the process during this initial phase. For that same reason, the

11

Memorial Constituents Subgroup made every effort to solicit input from every group directly affected by or involved in the bombing.

- While general public participation in the input process was in some ways less than originally anticipated, the Subcommittee members believe that every person interested in sharing his or her ideas and feelings about the Memorial had that opportunity.

- At the Community Meetings, Subcommittee volunteers were touched by the grateful appreciation expressed by the people who did participate and had the opportunity to connect with other citizens and express their feelings. In addition, the Community Meetings served other purposes, and some victim's family members learned of the opportunity to participate in the Families and Survivors Subcommittee of the Task Force as a result of such meetings.

- Your Subcommittee Co-Chairs, and all Subcommittee members are deeply honored, and most proud, to have been given the chance to serve on this Task Force, and to help in some small measure to ensure that the Memorial created in and for Oklahoma City in response to the events of April 19, 1995 and following will be something that we can be proud of for decades to come.

12

APPENDIX V: MEMORIAL MISSION STATEMENT AND APPENDICES

Murrah Federal Building Memorial Task Force
Memorial Mission Statement

[Appendix C]

RESOLUTION

Adopted by Advisory Committee per Request of
Families / Survivors Liaison Subcommittee
November 14, 1995

Whereas, the Advisory Committee has responsibility for adoption of a Memorial Mission Statement setting forth the objectives to be achieved by the Memorial, which Mission Statement is scheduled for completion during the month of March, 1996;

Whereas, the Families/Survivors Liaison Subcommittee met on November 13, 1995, and unanimously voted to request a resolution of the Advisory Committee to include in the Memorial Mission Statement a requirement that one of the components of the Memorial must be an information center, which, in part, would include a living memorial segment consisting of: (a) biographies of the victims written by the families of the victims and photographic representations of the victims, and (b) stories of the survivors written by the survivors and photographic representations of the survivors; and

Whereas, the Advisory Committee has determined that it is appropriate to adopt at this time the following segment of the Memorial Mission Statement and to reserve for consideration in March, 1996 the remainder of the Mission Statement after the public outreach programs of the Families/ Survivors Liaison Subcommittee and the Memorial Ideas Input Subcommittee have been completed.

NOW, THEREFORE, IT IS RESOLVED THAT the Memorial Mission Statement will include a requirement that one of the components of the Memorial must be an information center, which, in part, would include a segment consisting of: (a) biographies of the victims written by the families of the victims and photographic representations of the victims, and (b) stories of the survivors written by the survivors and photographic representations of the survivors.

IT IS FURTHER RESOLVED THAT the Families / Survivors Liaison Subcommittee, in consultation with the Archives Subcommittee, develop guidelines for format and length of such biographies and stories for distribution to families of victims and survivors.

13

Murrah Federal Building Memorial Task Force
Memorial Mission Statement

[Appendix D]

RESOLUTION
Adopted by Advisory Committee Per Request
of
Families/Survivors Liaison Subcommittee
January 16, 1996

Whereas, the Advisory Committee has responsibility for adoption of a Memorial Mission Statement setting forth the objectives to be achieved by the Memorial, which Mission Statement is scheduled for completion during the month of March, 1996;

Whereas, the Families/Survivors Liaison Subcommittee met on January 8, 1996, and unanimously voted to request a resolution of the Advisory Committee to include in the Memorial Mission Statement a requirement that one of the components of the Memorial must be the preservation of a tree located on the south half of the Journal Record Building block, which tree has special symbolic meaning as a survivor of the bombing; and

Whereas, the Advisory Committee has determined that it is appropriate to adopt at this time the following additional segment of the Memorial Mission Statement and to reserve for consideration in March, 1996 the remainder of the Mission Statement after the public outreach programs of the Families/Survivors Liaison Subcommittee and the Memorial Ideas Input Subcommittee have been completed.

NOW, THEREFORE, IT IS RESOLVED THAT the Memorial Mission Statement will include a requirement that one of the components of the Memorial must be the "Survivor Tree" located on the south half of the Journal Record Building block.

IT IS FURTHER RESOLVED THAT the Advisory Committee take steps to protect and preserve such Survivor Tree.

-end-

C:\murrah\appendix.ms
[Appendices A-D to the Memorial Mission Statement -- approved by the Advisory Committee 3/26/96]

131696.GOODMANJ

INTERGOVERNMENTAL LETTER OF UNDERSTANDING

OKLAHOMA CITY MEMORIAL FOUNDATION

We come here to remember those who were killed, those who survived and those changed forever. May all who leave here know the impact of violence. May this memorial offer comfort, strength, peace, hope and serenity.

INTERGOVERNMENTAL LETTER OF UNDERSTANDING
October 28, 1996

420 North Robinson
Oklahoma City, Oklahoma 73102
(405) 235-3313
Fax: (405) 235-3315

THE WHITE HOUSE
WASHINGTON

March 7, 1997

It has been almost two years since the bombing of the Alfred P. Murrah Federal Building in Oklahoma City, but the memory of that terrible day is still fresh in the minds and hearts of all Americans.

We learned a lot about ourselves that day. We recognized that we are a family, that a cowardly terrorist attack on one American is an attack on us all. We were reminded that, despite our differences in outlook and background and politics, Americans still unite to help one another when tragedy strikes. And in the wake of that tragedy, we realized anew that the human spirit, blessed by hope and strengthened by determination, can rise above any adversity.

Now we have an opportunity to unite again around the citizens of Oklahoma City. I ask all Americans to join me in supporting the effort to establish a memorial on the site of the bombing. Together, let us transform that scarred square of earth into a fitting tribute to those who died, to those who survived, and to those whose lives have been changed forever by this devastating event. By honoring them, we can help to bring healing and create hope for a brighter, more secure future.

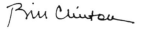

APPENDIX VI: INTERGOVERNMENTAL LETTER OF UNDERSTANDING

INTERGOVERNMENTAL LETTER OF UNDERSTANDING

PREMISE

This Letter of Understanding is intended to provide a framework that will enable the Murrah Federal Building Memorial Task Force (the "Task Force"), Oklahoma City Memorial Foundation (the "Foundation"), and representatives of the City of Oklahoma City (the "City"), the County of Oklahoma County, the State of Oklahoma (the "State") and the government of the United States (the "U.S. Government") to work together efficiently and respectfully in developing a National Memorial (the "Memorial") relating to the April 19, 1995, bombing in Oklahoma City, which will be appropriate, enduring and sensitive to those most directly affected by the bombing.

This document outlines the expectations and responsibilities each participant has related to development and ongoing maintenance of the Memorial. It reinforces the mutual commitment participants have to ensure that Memorial efforts are timely, non-political, productive and respectful of the needs of victims' families and survivors.

BACKGROUND

Few events in the past quarter-century have rocked Americans' perception of themselves and their institutions, and brought together the people of our nation more intensely than the April 19, 1995, bombing of the Alfred P. Murrah Federal Building in downtown Oklahoma City.

The resulting 168 murders immediately touched thousands of family members -- wives, husbands, children, brothers, sisters, parents -- whose lives will forever bear the scars of having had those precious to them taken away so brutally. Suffering with such families are hundreds of survivors who struggle not only with the suffering around them, but with their own physical and emotional injuries and with shaping a life beyond April 19. Such losses and struggles are personal and, since they resulted from so public an attack, they also are shared with a community, a nation and the world.

Just as reverberations from the blast shook people as far away as 50 miles, the effects of the crime reach across Oklahoma and throughout the nation. By its very nature as an attack on the American government and our public servants, the bombing was a violent assault on each American citizen. When friends, colleagues, neighbors and fellow citizens are brutalized, each of us is diminished.

Mindful of the far-reaching impact of the assault in the heart of Oklahoma City and the nation, and aware of the historic nature of the event, Oklahoma City Mayor Ron Norick appointed the 350-member volunteer Task Force charged with developing an appropriate Memorial. The Task Force, in turn, organized the Foundation to acquire funding for development of the Memorial.

Parties to this Letter of Understanding recognize that prior to Sept. 1, 1996, all Memorial planning activities occurred by operation of the Task Force, but, effective Sept. 1, 1996, the Task Force will be transformed into the Foundation, and all future Memorial planning activities will be conducted by the Foundation.

MUTUAL COMMITMENTS

Throughout the planning, design and construction of the Memorial, we, the undersigned participants, agree on behalf of ourselves and our organizations to:

1. Remain faithful to the ideal that the development of the Memorial shall be respectful, non-political and timely.

2. Recognize, respect and support the autonomy of the Task Force and the Foundation as non-profit, non-political organizations dedicated to creating and overseeing a Memorial development process that is sensitive, inclusive, collaborative, thorough and productive.

3. Recognize and respect the special role the local community has as the site of the 1995 bombing and as the home of the Memorial. While the crime has national and international implications, victims' families, survivors and residents of Central Oklahoma bore the brunt of the impact and rightly shall play a leadership role in planning and establishing a lasting Memorial.

4. Recognize that among the range of opinions, ideas and priorities expressed in the information gathering phase of the Memorial development process, those expressed by victims' families and survivors shall be given the greatest weight and highest degree of respect.

5. Recognize and abide by the Task Force Mission Statement adopted by the Advisory Committee of the Task Force on March 26, 1996.

6. Recognize as being final the design selection made pursuant to the design selection methodology adopted by the Task Force and an International Design Competition administered by the Task Force.

7. Recognize, respect and facilitate a Memorial development time line to be outlined by the Task Force.

- 2 -

314

8. Recognize the importance of working together to accommodate the Memorial design selected pursuant to the International Design Competition. For instance, should the selected design call for using a portion of the Murrah Building site, its plaza and/or acquiring a parcel of land near the site of the former Murrah Building, all participants agree to cooperate in making such efforts possible.

9. Recognize the importance of administering and maintaining the Memorial and surrounding sites with dignity and honor befitting the memories of those killed or injured in the blast. Signatories of this Letter of Understanding agree to cooperate with one another to ensure that such ongoing administration and maintenance of the Memorial is consistent, efficient and respectful.

10. Recognize that governmental and private financial assistance may be required to support the planning, design, construction and operation of the Memorial.

11. Recognize the work of the Task Force and Foundation as a unified effort to establish one Memorial commemorating the April 19, 1995, bombing and commit *not* to develop or take part in developing competing Memorial proposals without prior written consent of the Foundation.

12. Pursue Congressional Authorization for the completed Memorial Complex to be designated a National Monument to be operated and maintained by the National Park Service.

SPECIFIC COMMITMENTS
The following specific commitments are made:

1. The Task Force & Foundation agree to:

A. pursue the funding of both the planning and construction of the Memorial;

B. select the design of the Memorial through an International Design Competition pursuant to a design selection methodology adopted by the Task Force;

C. notify the General Services Administration (the "GSA") and the City when (1) the Foundation has selected the final Memorial design and (2) the Foundation is prepared to commence construction of the Memorial, so that GSA may deliver to whomever is ultimately going to maintain the property the deed to the land on which the Murrah Federal Building was located;

D. enter into a separate agreement with GSA providing for the use of the Murrah Federal Building Block Plaza as a part of the Memorial complex; and

E. oversee construction of the Memorial.

- 3 -

2. The City agrees to:

A. acquire the South half of the Journal-Record Building block for incorporation into the Memorial site and, if required by the Task Force, to raze the remains of the Oklahoma Water Resources Board building and Athenian building;

B. erect and maintain permanent-style fencing to the south half of the Journal-Record Building block, pending commencement of construction of the Memorial by adding fencing beginning at the northeast corner of the Athenian building fence going east to the sidewalk at Robinson Street, then south along the Robinson Street sidewalk to 5th Street. Such fencing shall contain two gates, one at each end of the closed portion of 5th Street, and shall allow, where safe, pedestrian access to the closed portion of 5th Street. Such fencing also shall be of the same style erected by the GSA surrounding the Murrah Building block;

C. honor the adopted Mission Statement of the Task Force as a community consensus guidance document, including the permanent closure of 5th Street by the City of Oklahoma City City Council by a unanimous vote on October 22, 1996;

D. pursue the adoption of the North Downtown Design Workshop and Urban Land Institute recommendations regarding protective zoning for the area surrounding the Memorial site;

E. receive from the Foundation notification that (1) the Foundation has selected the final Memorial design and (2) the Foundation is prepared to commence construction of the Memorial, and then, based upon GSA receiving similar notification from the Foundation, grant to the Foundation an agreement allowing the Foundation to construct the Memorial on the site; and

F. convey to the National Park Service the site of the Memorial and its associated improvements upon completion of the Memorial and final Congressional Authorization of the site as a National Monument to be operated and maintained by the National Park Service.

3. The State agrees to:

A. participate in a coordinated effort to facilitate, support and assist work of the Task Force and Foundation;

B. recognize Task Force and Foundation efforts to procure private funding for planning and construction of the Memorial, while standing ready to identify and possibly allocate State resources, if available, to assist in development of the Memorial;

- 4 -

APPENDIX VI: INTERGOVERNMENTAL LETTER OF UNDERSTANDING

C. endorse and assist efforts of the Task Force, Foundation and other signatories to procure designation of the Memorial as a National Monument and to secure U.S. Government funding to support the ongoing operation and maintenance of the Memorial;

D. provide the necessary professional archival assistance of the Oklahoma Historical Society, as requested by the Foundation, to collect, catalog and preserve artifacts related to the April 19, 1995, bombing for possible inclusion in the Memorial Information/Learning Center and Museum to be developed by the Foundation; and

E. make available to the Foundation all April 19, 1995, bombing artifacts received by any office or agency of the State of Oklahoma.

4. The GSA agrees to:

A. maintain protective fencing around the Murrah Federal Building block in good condition and maintain the landscaping and other improvements, including the vault and underground parking garage, on such block until such time as the former office building footprint of the Murrah Federal Building block is transferred by GSA for construction of the Memorial and to reroute any easements as may be required prior to such transfer;

B. upon receiving from the Foundation notification that (1) the Foundation has selected the final Memorial design and (2) the Foundation is prepared to commence construction of the Memorial, GSA shall deliver to whomever is ultimately going to maintain the property the deed to the land on which the footprint of the Murrah Federal Building was located;

C. enter into a separate agreement with the Foundation providing for the use of the Murrah Federal Building Block Plaza as a part of the Memorial complex. Further, the Murrah Federal Building Memorial Block Plaza, parking garage and vault will remain the property of the U.S. Government; and

D. provide warehousing facilities for storing artifacts regarding the bombing pending completion of the Memorial, and provide, as existing facilities permit, warehouse and office space with climates suitable for needs of the International Design Competition not to exceed current facility conditions.

- 5 -

5. U.S. Government representatives who are signatories to this Agreement agree to:

A. exercise their best efforts to cause the National Park Service to participate as a technical advisor to the Foundation, lending consultation and experience to help the foundation develop a Memorial appropriate for National Monument status and care.

6. All signatories to this Letter of Understanding acknowledge that:

A. this letter is not intended to create, nor does it create, any right or benefit, substantial or procedural, enforceable at law by a party against any body or agency represented as a signatory to the agreement or such body's or agency's instrumentalities, officers or employees, or any other person.

In witness whereof, the parties have executed this Letter of Understanding

on this __28th__ day of __October__, 1996.

- 6 -

APPENDIX VI: INTERGOVERNMENTAL LETTER OF UNDERSTANDING

The Intergovernmental Letter of Understanding was signed by the following:

Karen Luke, Vice-Chair

Robert M. Johnson, Chairman of the Board

Ronald J. Norick, Mayor

Frosty Peak, Councilmember, Ward One

Mark Schwartz, Councilmember, Ward Two

Jack W. Cornett, Councilmember, Ward Three

Frances Lowrey, Councilmember, Ward Four

Jerry W. Foshee, Councilmember, Ward Five

Ann Simank, Councilmember, Ward Six

Willa D. Johnson, Councilmember, Ward Seven

Guy H. Liebmann, Councilmember, Ward Eight

Zach D. Taylor, Executive Director

Stuart E. Earnest, Sr., Commissioner, District Three

Frank Keating, Governor

Mary Fallin, Lieutenant Governor

Keith Leftwich, President Pro Tempore Designee

Debbie Blackburn, Speaker of the House Designee

Don Nickles, Senator

James Inhofe, Senator

Steve Largent, U. S. Representative, First District

Tom Coburn, U. S. Representative, Second District

Bill Brewster, U. S. Representative, Third District

J. C. Watts, U. S. Representative, Fourth District

Ernest Istook, U. S. Representative, Fifth District

Frank Lucas, U. S. Representative, Sixth District

Leighton Waters, Acting Regional Administrator

William J. Clinton, President of the United States of America

APPENDIX VII

PRESENTATION TO THE CITY COUNCIL OF OKLAHOMA CITY REGARDING THE CLOSING OF FIFTH STREET

October 22, 1996

"Good afternoon, my name is Bob Johnson and I am the Chairman of the Oklahoma City Memorial Foundation appointed by Mayor Norick in June of 1995. The Foundation has 350 members who also were appointed by Mayor Norick. It is composed of victims' families, survivors, rescue and recovery workers and volunteers of all economic levels, walks of life, races, religions and geographic locations within the Oklahoma City metropolitan area and beyond. It truly draws from every quarter of our City.

"It has been more than a year since our first Task Force meeting last summer. We were charged with the responsibility to conduct the memorialization process in an open and inclusive manner that would assure widespread public participation, and we have done so.

"Last summer we began an open and inclusive listening process, conducted through round table discussions with victims' families and survivors, a written survey as to what a visitor to the completed memorial should feel, learn, experience and encounter, a survey on the internet, community town hall meetings and small focus group discussions. We have listened and we have learned. The culmination of such listening process was the adoption of a Memorial Mission Statement by an incredible unanimous vote of the victims' families and survivors committee and an equally incredible unanimous vote of the large, diverse Task Force. It is a remarkable document in that it reflects a strong consensus which evolved from a very diverse organization under a very open planning process intertwined with elevated raw emotions integral to the grieving process.

"The Mission Statement in part provides that the Memorial site shall consist of the Murrah Building block, the south half of the Journal Record Building block and that portion of Fifth Street that lies between the two blocks. So it is because of the Memorial Mission Statement that we are before you today.

"We must resolve the Fifth Street issue before we can commence an International Design Competition from which the Memorial Design will emerge. If we receive a positive response from you today, we are set to announce the design competition on November 14 by issuing a Call for Entries and publishing the Competition Guideline Materials around the world.

"I want to briefly discuss a few misconceptions regarding Fifth Street and the Memorial Site.

"One of the misconceptions held by some people is that we have the entire Murrah block with which to work. We will have less than 1/3 of such block, namely, the footprint of the former Murrah Building. Including the Murrah Building footprint, Fifth Street and the south half of the Journal Record Building block, we will have approximately 3 acres. For comparison, the Vietnam Memorial is placed on 5 acres. The proposed 3-acre site is also significantly smaller than the 22-acre park proposed by the Urban Land Institute to underscore the significance of our Memorial.

"A symbolic memorial of the size of the Vietnam Memorial, which is 500 feet long, would not fit on the footprint of the former Murrah Building as has been suggested. For those who have visited the Vietnam Memorial and felt the impact from such visit, I believe most would agree that such impact would be diminished tremendously if the Memorial were not situated in a serene setting.

"Secondly, some who oppose keeping Fifth Street closed have complained of the deterioration of the North downtown area. This is a concern with which we agree; however, a very high quality world class Memorial will serve as a catalyst to initiate the rebuilding of the surrounding area. We have been working with the property owners and area associations to make sure that we work together to not only create high quality within the Memorial site, but also in the district that surrounds the area. That is why the permanent closure of Fifth Street is supported by the lengthy list of businesses and property owners that we have provided to you. We also have provided you a chart that shows the property owners who support closing of Fifth Street and the property owners who are known to oppose such closing. So when statements are made that imply that a large number of area businesses and property owners in the area oppose the closing of Fifth Street, such statements are misleading.

"Another concern expressed by some who oppose the permanent closure of Fifth Street relates to traffic flow. It is important to note that based upon the Department of Transportation Ramp counts at the Fifth Street ramp to I-235 East of the site, the traffic count prior to April 19, 1995 was 8,799 cars per day and the count at the same ramp in October 1995 was 8,766 cars per day. Such counts confirm that the traffic continues to move at the same volume from the downtown area to the Fifth Street entrance ramp to I-235 and we also know that there is no traffic congestion in the Fourth, Fifth and Sixth Street area of downtown. Therefore, it is clear that traffic from west of the site has rerouted and continues to move without any interruption to the entrance to I-235. We also know from the Oklahoma City Planning Commission staff report that Fourth Street and Sixth Street will accommodate all existing traffic without modification if this one block segment of Fifth Street is permanently closed.

"Because of your important responsibilities here today, you have probably visited the site recently. Probably the first thing you noticed was the chain length fence that guards the Murrah Building site. Looking at it, you may have wondered why no one has removed the thousands of items left as tributes by visitors, but you should know that each week our Archives Curator and volunteers on the Archives Committee remove hundreds of items from the fence. Presently, we have approximately several thousand items that are being preserved in our archives collection pending a decision regarding the composition of the exhibit to be created in the Memorial Museum and a significant portion of those items have been removed from the fence.

"I have visited the site dozens of times and I am still amazed to see so many out of state cars, whose occupants have stopped to pay tribute. What is important to understand is that each item left on the fence represents someone's life that has been touched by what happened on and along Fifth Street. Have you ever stood there and read the messages that are left on the fence? If you haven't, I hope you will. What you will see is that there is not a corner of the earth that hasn't responded to what happened to all of us. The area we are discussing is already an international memorial. Our research shows that more than 400,000 visitors went to the site the first year.... and the number will grow upon completion of the Memorial.

"With all these comments as background, there are three primary reasons underlying the Memorial Mission Statement for the importance of the permanent closure of Fifth Street:

"First, it was the site of the recovery of many of the victims of the tragedy that impacted the world and the site of the remarkable, selfless and courageous rescue and recovery effort during the aftermath of the bombing. How can we separate the death of an individual on the south side of Fifth Street from the victim on the north side of Fifth? We cannot say that the near-death injuries suffered in the Journal Record Building are less important than the pain inflicted on the Murrah Building survivors.

"Secondly, as stressed by the Memorial Mission Statement, the Memorial is to represent a place of serenity and peace. We cannot achieve this goal with a street running through the middle of the Memorial Complex, whether it is four lanes or two lanes as suggested by the Traffic Commission staff.

"Thirdly, the Memorial Mission Statement process that included citizens from all areas, segments, races and walks of life in our community should create a legacy for the solution of community problems, but such legacy will not be realized if the resulting consensus reached on March 26th is not respected.

"In closing, you know that the bombing of the Murrah Federal Building on April 19, 1995 was a pivotal moment in the history of the United States. Our perceptions of ourselves as Americans, our unique sense of national security within our shores changed forever. Your lives also changed forever that day. You have heard our Mission, to remember those who were killed, those who survived and those changed forever. Please do not forget the Memorial's mission is also to educate people about the senselessness and impact of violence and about the Oklahoma Standard for responding. How you respond to this Fifth Street issue today will tell the world what the Oklahoma Standard really is. Let's show the world that we are still a unified people working together to build a world class Memorial of which everyone will be proud.

"Just as we all benefitted from your leadership during the aftermath of the bombing, we respectfully request your leadership today in keeping this one block of Fifth Street permanently closed so that an appropriate and enduring Memorial can be created in a peaceful and serene setting. Thank you."

ABC 39, 133
Abraira, Steve 284
Ace Aerial Photography 6
Ackerman McQueen 26
Ackerman, Ann 284
Ackerman, Ray 284
Ackerman, Ray A. 284
Afghanistan 209
Alderton, Jonie 284
Aleman, Lucio, Jr. 276
Alexander, Don H. 31, 284
Alexander, Teresa Antionette 276
Alfred P. Murrah Federal Building,
    Oklahoma City viii, 2, 6-11, 13-15,
    18, 21-22, 26, 28, 31, 35, 40-41,
    44-45, 48, 52-53, 58, 66, 79, 83,
    87, 92, 94-95, 129, 139, 160, 187,
    220; Plaza 92, 94-95, 160; snack
    shop 10
Allen, Ann 284
Allen, Richard A. 276
Allen, Ted L. 276
Almon, Miss Baylee 276
Alspaugh, Ann 284, 294
Althouse, Diane E. (Hollingsworth)
    276
"Amazing Grace" 168
Ambassadors' Concert Choir xvii, 160

America's Kids Day Care 6-7, 44
American Academy of Arts and
    Sciences, Cambridge, MA 100
American Academy, Rome, Italy
    100
American Association of Museums
    (AAM) 207
American Institute of Architects
    99-100
American Medical Association 22-
    23; Medal of Valor 22-23
American Planning Association 99
American Red Cross 31, 43; Board of
    Directors 43
American Society of Landscape
    Architects 99; President's Award
    99
Ames, IA 105
Anderson, Fred 284
Anderson, Rebecca Needham 23,
    201, 276
Anthony, Nancy 284
Arafat, Yasser 24
Aragon, Joelda 284
Argo, Pamela Cleveland 276
Arkansas 164
Arnold, Anita xvii, 284, 294
Arts Council Oklahoma City 44-45, 129

Ash, Michael J. 284
Associated Press Bureau 39
Association of Central Oklahoma
    Governments 75, 85
Athenian Building, Oklahoma
    City 91
Atkins, Hannah 138, 284
Australia 24, 39, 98
Avery, Saundra G. (Sandy) 276
Avillanoza, Peter R. 276

Bahamas 98
Bailey, Clark xv, 284
Bailey, Keith 284
Bailey, Paul 284
Ballard, Currie 284
BancFirst, Oklahoma City 141
Banks, Marcela 284
Barry, John E. 284
Battle, Calvin 276
Battle, Peola 276
Bays, Mark 79, 163
BBC 39
Beckelman, Laurie 106-108
Belgium 98
Bell, Bill xvi
Bell, Danielle Nicole 276
Bell, Deniece 284

Bell, William M. "Bill" xvi, 284
Beltram, Ed 284
Bennett, Clayton I. 41, 284
Benson Loyd 284
Bentley, Sally 284
Benton, Leonard 284
Berenbaum, Michael 46
Berg, Sven 104, 110, 179
Berlin, Germany 104, 110
Berry, M. T. 169, 179
Biddy, Oleta C. 276
Bishop, Pat 284
Bitsche, Ray xv, 55, 284
Black Chronicle, The 41
Blackburn, Bob xvii, 55, 284
Blackburn, Debbie 284, 317
Bland, Shelly D. 276
Blanton, Andrea Yvette 276
Blaschke, Shirley 284
Bloomer, Maureen 284
Bloomer, Olen Burl 276
Bockus, Bruce xv, 284
Boggs, Wade 23
Bogle, Ron 284
Bohanon, Ann 285
Bohanon, Richard L. 284
Bolden, Lola 276
Boles, James E. 276

Bolivia 98
Bolte, Mark Allen 276
Bonney, Natalie 285
Booker, Casandra Kay 276
Borden, Frank 285
Boss, Ruth 285
Boston Globe, The 99
Boston Marathon, Boston, MA 250
Boston Red Sox 23
Boston, MA 250
Bowers, Carol Louise 277
Bozalis, John R. 23, 285
Bradley, Peachlyn 277
Brady, Woodrow Clifford "Woody"
    277
Brake, Mike xviii
Branstetter, Brian 105
Brawner, Lee B. 285
Brazil 98, 209
Bread, Philip 285
Brewster, Bill 86, 317
Bridges, Anita 285
Brokaw, Tom 26, 245-246
Bross, William J. 285
Brown, Ben 285
Brown, Cynthia L. 277
Browne, Cherly 285
Broxterman, Paul Gregory Beatty 277

Bruce, Gabreon D. L. 277
Brummett, Larry 138
Bryant, Charles 285
Bullard, Joe Van 285
Bunster-Ossa, Ignacio 106-108
Burgess, Kimbery Ruth 277
Burke, Edmund 25
Burkett, David Neil 277
Burns, Donald Earl, Sr. 277
Bush, George W. 139, 201-205, 207
Bush, Laura 201-202
Butterworth, Joanna xviii
Butzer, Hans 104, 110, 112, 114-119, 133, 179
Butzer, Torrey 104, 110, 112, 114-119, 133, 179

Cain, Bernest H., Jr. 285
Cambridge, MA 99
Campbell, Gini Moore xviii
Campbell, Robert 99-100, 102-103
Canada 24, 98
Canadian Broadcast Network 39
Carr, Karen Gist 108, 169, 277
Carr, Tommy 285
Carrillo, Michael 277
Carter, Jimmy 262
Casper, J. Kyle 105

Castillo, Charles 285
Catalon, Sherman 285
Cate, Jean 285
Catholic Charities of Oklahoma City 44, 75
Cavanaugh, Linda 142
CBN 39
CBS 39
Cerny, Sam 285
Chavez, Zackary Taylor 277
Cheney, Dick 141, 221
Chicago, IL 39
Childers, Terry 285, 294
Chinese TV Network 39
Chipman, Robert N. 277
Chumard, Robert L. 285
Churchill, Winston 51, 256, 261
City of Oklahoma City 6, 11-13, 40-41, 47, 79, 84-85, 91, 93; Council 85, 91-94
Clark, Earnestine xvi, 151, 285
Clark, James C. 285
Clark, John 12
Clark, Kimberly Kay 277
Clark, Margaret L. "Peggy" 277
Clay, Nolan 237
Clayton, Milford 285
Cleary, William B. "Bill" 70, 285, 294

Clinton, William J. "Bill" 24-25, 33-34, 37, 77, 83, 110-111, 135, 164, 169, 175-177, 179, 313, 317
Clowers, Dennis 285
CNN 39
Coburn, Tom 86, 317
Cole, John xvii, 75, 106-108, 169, 179, 285
Cole, Sam 285
Collier, Chet 215-216
Comey, James 27
Compton, Dennis 31
Concord, MA 244
Coniglione, Thomas 285
Cook, John 138
Cook, Kaye L. 285
Cooper, Anthony Christopher, II 277
Cooper, Antonio Ansara, Jr. 277
Cooper, Dana LeAnne 277
Cooper, Lee 285
Cope, Cynthia 285
Corbett, Luke xvii, 106-108, 112, 138, 142, 226, 228, 285
Cornett, Jack W. 85, 317
Coronado Heights Elementary, Oklahoma City 147
Cortina Productions 237
Costa Rica 98

Cottingham, Harley Richard 277
Cousins, Kim R. 277
Coverdale, Aaron 108, 169, 277
Coverdale, Elijah 108, 169, 278
Coyne, Jaci Rae 278
Crain Communications of Chicago 39
Cregan, Katherine Louise 278
Crossings Community Church, Oklahoma City xvii
Crowe & Dunlevy xiv, 31; Guardian Angel Fund 31
Crowell, Lisa 285
Cummings, Douglas R. 285
Cummings, Elcena 285
Cummins, Richard (Dick) 278
Curry, Steven Douglas 278

Dade County, FL 11
Daily Oklahoman, The 8, 21, 25, 41, 44, 196
Dallas, TX 26, 46, 105, 137
Dalton, Deborah 45, 285
Dana, Khalil 285
Daniel, Jim 285
Daniels, Brenda Faye 278
Davis, Benjamin Laranzo 278
Day, Diana Lynne 278
de Weldon, Felix 51

Deaver, Nancy 285
Declaration of Independence 266
DeMaster, Peter L. 278
DeNegri, Talita 205-206
Denman, Rowland xiv, 70, 93, 163, 182-185, 226-227, 285, 294
Denmark 98
Denny, James 286
Department of Housing and Urban Development (HUD) 7
Design Museum, London, England 99
Deveroux, Castine Brooks Hearn 278
Devon Energy Corporation 271
Devore, Marion 286
Dillon, Chris 286
Dillon, Paul 286
Dobson, Sydney xvii, 58, 75, 102-103, 107, 286, 294
Douglas, Tiana 286
Douglas|Gallagher (DG) 193, 195
Downey, Ray 286
Driver, Gregory N., II 279
Dulaney, Tom 286
Duncan, Ann-Clore 240
Earnest, Stuart E., Sr. 85, 286, 317
Easton, Gary 286
Eaton, K. M. 286

Eaves, Tylor Santoi 278
Eckenstein, Ed 286
Eckles, Ashley Megan 55, 278
Eckstein, Mary Ann xviii
Edmond Evening Sun 41
Edmond Life & Leisure 41
Edmondson, W. A. Drew 286
Edwards, Carl E. 286
Egypt 209, 263
Eisenhower, Dwight D. 18, 255
El Pais Service (Spain) 39
Elkins, Ronald C. 286
England 98
European Union 24
Exhibit Concepts 193, 198, 237

Fairfax County, VA 11
Fallin, Mary 85, 286, 317
"Fanfare for the Common Man" 169
Faulkner, William 268
Federal Bureau of Investigation (FBI) 13, 27
Federal Emergency Management Agency (FEMA) 11, 13, 15, 29, 31, 47, 86, 188
Federal Employees Credit Union 31, 45, 170
Federal Times 39

Fennell, Patricia B. 286
Fentriss, Suzie 286
Ferguson, Sarah 80
Ferrell-Lynn, Deb xvii, 286
Ferrell, Don 139, 205, 286
Ferrell, Susan Jane 139, 205, 278
Fields, Carol June "Chip" 278
Finley, Kathy A. 278
First Christian Church, Oklahoma City 31
Fisher, Judy J. (Froh) 278
Fleischaker, Pam 286
Florence, Linda Louise 7, 278
Floyd, Marca 286
Forsyth, Don 286
Foshee, Jerry W. 85, 317
FOX Network 39
France 24, 26, 39, 98
Fried, Helene 97, 100, 102-103, 106-107
Fritzler, Don 278
Fritzler, Mary Anne 278
Fudge, Chip 286

Gallagher & Associates 237
Gallagher, Patrick 237
Gamba, Jeanette xv, 286, 294
Garrett, Tevin D'Aundrae 278
Garrison, Gene 286

Garrison, Laura Jane 278
"Gates of Reflection" 117
Gentling, Steve J. 286
Genzer, Jamie (Fialkowski) 279
Georgia 165
Germany 98
Gesner, Marshall 286
Gibson, Charles 133
Gibson, Gilbert 286
Gigger-Driver, Sheila R. 279
Gill, Vince 142
Gilmore, Joan 286
Gist, Jeannine xvii, 106 108, 164, 169-170, 179, 196, 202, 286
Gist, Karen *see Karen Gist Carr*
Givens, Charles 286
Gobin, Jack 286
Goebel, Kathi 286
Goebel, Kay xv, 55, 286
Gonzales, Sam 10-11, 13, 286
Good Morning America 39, 133
Goodacre, Glenna 1
Goodman, Deborah "Debby" 45, 286, 294
Goodman, Jimmy xv, xvii, 45, 58, 70, 75, 286, 294
Goodson, Margaret Betterton 279
Gore, Al 133, 159-160

Gottshall, Cheryl 286
Gottshall, Kevin "Lee", II 279, 286
Governor's Mansion, Oklahoma 33
Graham, Billy 33, 35-37; Evangelical Association 35
Greenberg, Alan 286
Gresham, Loren 286
Griffin, Ethel L. 279
Griffin, Gloria 228, 231
Groban, Josh 256
Grubbs, Marty xvii
Guam 98
Guatemala 98
Guernsey & Company 193
Guiles, J. Colleen 279
Gumerson, Jean 287, 294
Guthrie, OK 53
Guzman, Randolph A. 279

Haag, Richard 99-100, 103
Haiti 210
Hale, Marcia L. 287
Hale, Sue xvi, 41, 196, 287
Hall, Fred J. 287
Hall, Tom xvii, 106-108
Halliburton 141, 221
Hamilton, Robert Browning 261
Hammon, Cheryl E. 279

Hampton, Debbie 287
Hampton, Patty 287
Hanno Weber & Associates, Chicago, IL 104
Hannon, Steve 259
Hansen, Jon 287
Hanska, Mariana 287
Hanson, Steve 287
Hard Copy 39
Harding, Ronald Vernon, Sr. 279
Hargis, Burns 229, 231
Harlow, James G., Jr. 287
Harper, Penny 287
Harris, Nick 287
Hartman, Daniel 287
Harvard University, Cambridge, MA 99
Hawthorne, Thomas Lynn, Sr. 279
Hayden, Jeff 287
Healey, Mamie 169
Heath, Paul xvii, 106-108
Hefton, Dick 41, 287
Henderson, Joyce 287
Herbster, Lawrence 41, 287
Herrington, Susan 105
Hess, Kathleen 104
Hibbard, Ray 41, 287
Higginbottom, Doris "Adele" 100, 279

Hightower, Anita Christine 279
Hill, Carolyn 287
Hill, David 216
Hill, Ed 196, 203
Hill, Frank xv, 226, 228, 231, 287, 294
Hill, Thomas 216
Hillmann & Carr 193, 195, 237
Hodges, Thompson Eugene
    "Gene", Jr. 279
Hogan, Dan 92
Hogan, Randy 287
Holland, Peggy Louise 279
Hollis, Douglas 106-108
Holmes, Elizabeth 287
"Holy Ground" 160, 168
Holzberlein, Ann 287
Hooper, Charles 287
Hoover, Ann 287
Horton, LeAnn 287
Housley, Linda Coleen 279
Houston, TX 99
Howard, George Michael 279
Howell, Hilda Pattie 287
Howell, Wanda Lee 279
Hozendorf, George 112
Hudson, Cliff 287
Hudson, Effie 287
Huff, Amber Denise 279

Huff, John 287
Huff, Robbin Ann 279
Humphreys, Kirk 159, 169, 172, 201
Hunter, Dick 287
Hunter, Steven 287
Hupfeld, Stanley 287
Hurlburt, Charles E. 279
Hurlburt, Jean Nutting 279
Hyde, Sue Ann 287

Ice, Paul D. 279
India 209
India 24, 98
Inhofe, James 85, 317
Investors Business Daily 39
Ireland 209
Irish Times, The 113
Israel 25, 98, 263
Istook, Ernest 86, 317
Italy 98
Iwo Jima, Japan 51

Jack, Judy 287
Jackson, Andrew 209
Japan 26, 98, 209
Japanese News Network 39
Jayroe, Jane 287
Jefferson, Thomas 266

Jeffries, Larry 287
Jenkins LeAnn 287
Jenkins, Christi Yolanda 280
Jennings, Marty 287
Jewell, Kirk 41, 287
Johnson, Brent xviii
Johnson, Carlos 287
Johnson, Gennie 287
Johnson, Gennie x, 112, 181
Johnson, Glen 288
Johnson, Herb 288
Johnson, Norma "Jean" 280
Johnson, Raymond "Lee" 280
Johnson, Robert M. "Bob" ix-217,
    226-227, 240, 252-262, 288,
    294, 317
Johnson, Steve 214
Johnson, Willa D. 85, 317
Johnstone, William "Bill" 44, 288
Jones-Shelton, Kim xv, xvii, 55, 75,
    288, 294
Jones, Doris 164, 168, 288
Jones, Jackie xv, 44-45, 97, 107, 129,
    131, 288, 294
Jones, Larry James 280
Jones, Lynne 288
Jones, Will 288
Joseph, Romel 210

Journal Record Building, Okla-
    homa City 91-92, 100, 151, 174,
    192, 194
Joy-Sizemore, Diane 288
Juilliard School, The, New York
    City, NY 210
Justes, Alvin 66
Justes, Alvin J. 280

Kahane, Brianna 210
Kaspereit, Carol 288
Kates, Ben 288
Katsafanas, Bill 41, 288
Keating, Cathy xiii, 33-34, 43, 55,
    60-63, 110, 112, 159, 169
Keating, Frank viii, xiii, 31, 33-34,
    43, 51, 63, 85, 110, 112, 141-142,
    148, 159, 169, 172, 201, 317
Keener, Wanene 288
Keller, Ed 288
Kelley, Judy 112
Kennedy, Blake Ryan 280
Kennedy, John F. 46
Kennedy, John xvii, 45, 75, 288
Kenya 209
Kernke, Joe, Jr. 288
Kerr-McGee Corporation 43-44,
    108, 138, 141-143, 146

Kerr, Lou 288
Kerrick, Barbara 56, 288, 294
KFOR-TV xi, 41, 214
Khalil, Carole Sue 280
Kight, Marsha 288
Kight, Tom 133, 288
Kilgore, Kenneth xvii
Kilpatrick, John 288
Kimker, Klaholt 288
King, Jill 288
King, Martin Luther, Jr. 266, 269
Klenzie, Robbie 288
KOCO-TV 10, 41
Koelsch, Valerie Jo 280
Kreymborg, Ann 280
Krodel, Mary 288
Krodel, Nancy 147
Kuehner-Chafey, Rona Linn 280
Kuhlman, Lee Ann 288
KWTV 41, 187

Lambert, Linda xv, 45, 139, 226-227,
    288, 294
Langsam, Janet 129
Lanzone, Dale 288
Largent, Steve 86, 317
Las Vegas, NV 250
Lauderdale, Teresa Lea Taylor 280

Law, James W. 26
Lawton, V. Z. 288
Le Monde (France) 39
Leadership Oklahoma City 75
Leadership Square, Oklahoma City, OK 193
Leasure-Rentie, Mary 280
Ledger, Randy 288
LeFebvre, Paul 288
Leftwich, Keith 85, 288, 317
Lehmbeck, Barney 288
Leinen, Kathy Cagle 280
Lenz, Carrie Ann 168, 280
Lenz, Michael James, III 168, 280
Leonard, Donald Ray "Don" 280
Leonard, Frances 208
Lerup, Lars 106-108
Levy, Harrison 288
Levy, Lakesha Richardson 280
Liebmann, Guy H. 85, 317
Liebmann, Judy 288
Lincoln, Abraham 264, 266
Lindsey, Kay 288
Linenthal, Edward T. 89, 258
Lippert Bros., Inc. General Contractors 192, 237
Lissau, Bill 288
Livermore, Ed 41, 288

Locus Bold Design, Berlin, Germany 104
Loftis, James 288
Logan, J. Duke 288
Lokey, Bill 288
London Daily Express 39
London Daily News 39
London Sunday Times 39
London, Dominique Ravae (Johnson) 280
London, England 99, 164
Long, Bob xvi, 31, 289
Long, Lauren xviii
Long, Rheta Bender 280
Lopez, Dave xvii, 106-108, 289
Lopez, Sam Armstrong xv, 289, 294
Lorenz, Robert 289
Lorton, Bob 41, 289
Los Angeles Cultural Affairs Commission 99
Los Angeles, CA 11
Loudenslager, Michael L. 280
Love, Tom 289
Lowrey, Frances 85, 317
Lucado, Max 257
Lucas, Frank 86, 317
Luke, Karen x-xi, 19, 43-44, 85,
    106-107, 159, 177, 196, 218-223, 226-227, 289, 294, 317
Luster, Aurelia Donna 280
Luster, Robert Lee, Jr. 280

Mahoney, Dan 289
Maloan, Yvonne
Malone, Yvonne 75, 100, 102-103, 221
Maroney, Mickey B. 281
Marrero, Abe 289
Marrs, Gary xvi, 10-11, 13, 18, 29, 39, 139, 164, 171, 196, 208, 289
Martin, James K. 281
Martinez, Gilbert X. 281
Mathais, Melvin 289
Mayor's Prayer Breakfast, Oklahoma City 6, 18
McAuliffe, Mike 289
McCann, Fred 289
McCarthy, James A., II 281
McCullough, Kenneth Glenn 281
McDaniel, Brenda 112, 289
McDaniel, Tom xv, 43-44, 83, 112, 139, 142, 209, 289, 294
McGonnell, Betsy J. (Beebe) 281
McGraw, Dan 26
McKinney, Dan 289
McKinney, Linda G. 281

McLoud, OK 164
McNeil Lehrer News 39
McRaven, Cartney J. 281
McVeigh, Timothy 273
Meacham, Jon 263-270
Medearis, Claude Arthur 281
Medina, David 289
Meek, Claudette (Duke) 281
Meet The Press 261

Oklahoma City National Memorial & Museum 168 Pennies Campaign 147 148; Archives Committee 53; Called2Change 209; Capital Campaign xv; Children's Area 92, 129-131, 165; Commitment Statement 163; Community Choir 169, 179, 207; Conscience Committee 240; Construction Committee 184, 192; Content Committee 193, 196; dedication xii, 162-181, 186-189, 200-211; Design Evaluation Panel xv, 102-103; Design Selection Committee 70-71, 98, 106-108; Design Solicitation Committee 70, 97; Evaluation Panel 70-71, 99-105, 108; Fence Moving Ceremony, The 160-161; Fence, The 52-54, 133, 160-161; Field of Empty Chairs 124-125, 160, 164-167; Fifth Street Sub-Committee 93; Final Report 57, 59, 75; Foundation 53, 86, 91-92, 94-95, 108, 110, 116, 136, 139, 141, 146, 161, 184, 195, 220; Foundation Board of Directors 108, 136-137; Fundraising Committee 146, 221; Gallery of Honor 188-189, 199; Gates of Time 77, 122-123, 164, 203; Government Liaison Committee 83, 137; groundbreaking xii, 158-161; Ideas Input Committee xv, 58-59, 75; Intergovernmental Letter of Understanding 03-09, 94-95, 313-317; Marathon "Run to Remember" 215-217; Mission Statement 57, 74-77, 80, 87, 91-94, 97, 118-119, 131, 135, 138, 146, 157, 163, 168-169, 187, 221, 226, 302-312; Mission Statement Drafting Committee xvi-xvii, 74-77, 151; National Memorial 135-136, 138-139, 173; Oklahoma Standard ix, xviii,

2, 20-31, 188, 244, 247, 262, 271, 274; Organizing Group 44-45, 48; Orientation Meeting 72, 76; Pennies for My Mom Campaign 147-148; Prayer Service 33-37, 55, 110, 175, 188; Promontory Wall 36; Reflecting Pool 123, 164, 172, 181; Rescuers' Orchard 133; Slab 13-15, 44; Survivor Definition Committee xvi, 151, 156-157; Survivor Tree 36, 78-81, 126-127, 133, 163, 250, 254; Survivor Wall 128-129; Task Force xi, 41, 43-59, 66-67, 69-73, 75, 79, 85-89, 97, 141, 187, 257, 284-301; Task Force Advisory Committee 48, 75-76, 79, 87, 94, 187; Task Force Coordinating Committee 48, 70; Trust 137-139, 156; Uncover Discover Stem Lab 240; Victims' Families and Survivors Liaison Committee 45, 55, 57, 66-67, 73, 75-76, 100, 110, 196
Menlo Park, CA 11
Mercer, Sunni 45, 289
Merrell, Frankie Ann 133, 281
Mexico 98
Meyer, Paul 289

Meyers, Sandy 289
Mid-Southwest Foodservice Convention and Exposition 28
Miles-Scott, Gayle 289
Miller, Derwin W. 281
Miller, Jim 41, 289
Milton, Roosevelt, 289
Mitchell, Eula Leigh 281
Moggridge, Bill 99-100, 102-103
Monson, Gracie 289
Montgomery County, MD 11
Montgomery, John 289
Moore, James 289
Moore, Rick 289
Moore, Vern 289
Morris, Paul 97
Moser, Calvin xvii, 106-108, 289
Moss, John C., III 281
Mount Suribachi, Iwo Jima, Japan 51
Mui, K. C. 289
Murrah Federal Building see Alfred P. Murrah Federal Building
Murrah, A. Paul, Jr. 289
Murrah, Alfred P. 47, 51; family 47
Myriad Botanical Gardens 6
Myriad Convention Center 28-30

Nance, Leslie 289
Naranche, Barbara 289
NASA 250
National Assembly of Local Arts Agencies 45; Symposium on Commemoration 45
National Endowment for the Arts 100; Mayors Institute for City Design 100
National Organization of Minority Architects 99
National Park Service (NPS) 135-139, 173, 181, 194, 234; Intermountain Region 139
National Pulse Memorial & Museum, Orlando, FL 117
NBC xi, 26, 39, 261
Neaves, Norman 289
Netherlands, the 98
Neville, Pam 196
New Hampshire 165
New Jersey 164
New Mexico 99
New Victorian School, Haiti 210
New York City, NY 11, 39, 104-105, 260
New York Times, The 39, 263
New York Yankees 23
Newberry-Woodbridge, Ronota

Ann 281
News 4 New York 39
News Limited of Australia 39
Newsweek Magazine 23
Newtown, CT 250
Nguyen, Cu D. 289
NHK Japanese Television 39
Nichols Hills Elementary, Nichols Hills, OK 202; Varsity Choir 202
Nichols, Larry 271-274
Nichols, Polly xv, 58, 100, 103, 112, 136, 141, 144-149, 221, 226, 228, 271, 289, 294
Nickles, Don 85, 135, 159, 169, 173, 289, 317
Nigh, George 289
Nix, Patricia Ann 281
Norick, Carolyn 289
Norick, Ronald J. "Ron" xi, xiii-xiv, xvii, 10-11, 13, 16-19, 33, 36, 39, 43-44, 46, 48, 50-51, 66, 70-72, 85, 91, 106-108, 110, 112, 141, 148, 159, 170, 172, 274, 317
Norman Transcript 41
Norway 98

"O God, Our Help In Ages Past" 169
O'Connor, Kim 289

O'Connor, Tim xv, xvii, 44, 55, 75, 289, 294
O'Loughlin, James 289
O'Toole, Fintan 113
Oakes, Harry, Jr, 290
Oakland, CA 164
Oklahoma Blood Institute 21
Oklahoma City Beautiful 47, 75
Oklahoma City Chamber of Commerce 44
Oklahoma City Community Foundation 44, 47; Murrah Federal Building Memorial Fund 44
Oklahoma City Industrial and Cultural Facilities Trust 91-92
Oklahoma City National Memorial Act of 1997 95, 137
Oklahoma City Philharmonic 169
Oklahoma City Planning Commission 93-94
Oklahoma City Police Department 12, 40-41
Oklahoma City Thunder 244, 246
Oklahoma City Traffic Commission 93
Oklahoma City University xi
Oklahoma City, OK viii-251
Oklahoma County Medical Society 22-23

Oklahoma County Newspapers Inc. 41

Oklahoma Department of Agriculture, Food and Forestry 79

Oklahoma Foundation for Excellence 100

Oklahoma Hall of Fame Publishing xviii

Oklahoma Historical Society xvii, 55

Oklahoma House of Representatives 85-86; Senate 85-86

Oklahoma Medical Research Foundation 44

Oklahoma Publishing Company 8, 14, 33, 41, 54, 56, 161

Oklahoma Restaurant Association 28-30

Oklahoma Southwestern Bell 108

Oklahoma Standard ix, xviii, 2, 20-31, 188, 244, 247, 262, 271, 274

Oklahoma State Fairgrounds, Oklahoma City 33; Jim Norick Arena 33

Oklahoma Water Resources Building, Oklahoma City, OK 91, 187, 193

ONEOK 138

Orange County, CA 11

Orlando, FL 250

Oslo, Norway 250

Outlive Your Life 257

Packman, David 290

Palestine Liberation Organization 24

Parker, Jerry Lee 281

Parrish, Mike 290

Patton, Carole 290

Payne-Farris, Miki 290

PBS 179

Peak, Frosty 85, 317

Pearce, JoAnn 102-103, 290

Pentagon, Washington, D.C. 260

Perry, John 41, 290

Perry, Russell 41, 290

Petuskey, John 290

Philadelphia, PA 99

Phoenix, AZ 11

Pickel, James A. 290

Pierce, Peter, III 290

Pierson, Gary 229, 231

Pitman, Donnie 290

Poe, Jack 290

Poh, Bing 290

Ponder-Moore, Carmen 206-207

Portland, OR 97

Potter, Dustin xviii

Prayer of Saint Francis of Assisi, The viii-ix

Presidio, The, San Francisco, CA 135; Trust 135

Presti, Sam 242-247

Price, Betty 290

Price, Byron 290

Pride-Wells, Michaele 99-100, 102-103

Priest, Jim 290

Promontory Wall 36

Puerto Rico, Commonwealth 98, 209

Puget Sound, WA 11

Pulitzer Prize 99, 263

Pulse Night Club, Orlando, FL 250

Purifoy, Dennis 290

Quebec, Canada 164

Queen Elizabeth II 24

Quinn, Fred 290

Rabin, Yitzhak 24

Rabinowitz, Marvin 290

Radcliff, Crystal 102-103, 106-107

Rainbolt, H. E. "Gene" 141, 290, 294

Ramos, Jack 290

Randolph, Jill Diane 281

Rankin, Beverly 59

Rao, Narasimha 24

Rauch, Stephanie 24

Reed, John 290

Reed, Joyce 41, 290

Reeder, George 290

Reeder, Michelle A. 281

Rees, Terry Smith 281

Reneau, Mary 290

Reno, Janet 159, 169, 174

Rex, John 290, 294

Reyes, Antonio C. "Tony" 281

Reynolds, Dick 290

Rice University, Houston, TX 99; School of Architecture 108

Rice, Condoleezza 201

Richels, John 229, 231

Ricks, Bob 13

Ridley, Kathryn Elizabeth 282

Rigney, Trudy Jean 282

Riley, Joanne 196

Ritchie, Kimberly xvii, 106-108

Ritter, Claudine 282

Roberts, Anne 290

Rogers, Don 290

Rogers, Florence 164, 170, 290

Rogers, Joyce 290

Rome, Italy 100

Ronald Reagan Presidential Library, The 238

Roodman, Edie 290

Rosas, Christy 66, 282

Ross, Bob 230-231

Ross, Lil 290

Rossant, James 104-105

Roundtree, Charles 290

Royal College of Arts, London, England 99

Rundstrom, Bob 290

Rush, Richard 290

Russert, Tim 261

Russia 24

Sacramento, CA 11

Salyers, Priscilla xvii, 75, 169, 179, 290

Samis, Mike 290

San Fransico, CA 97

San Jose, CA 45

Sandburg, Rodney 290

Sanders, Brooklynn 31

Sanders, Mike 31

Sanders, Savanna 31

Sanders, Sonja Lynn 31, 282

Sandys, Edwina 51
Santos, Adèle Naude' 99-100
Sartorius, Timothy 290
Satellite City 40-41
Saunders, Lynn 290
Schapelhouman, Harold 291
Scheihing, Bill 229, 231
Scherr, Richard 104-105
Schwartz, Mark 85, 317
Schweitzer, Albert 258
Scroggins, Cheryl xvii, 106-108, 291
Scroggins, Lanny Lee David 108, 282
Seattle, WA 99
Seidl, Clint 147-148, 160
Seidl, Kathy Lynn 147, 160, 282
Sells, Leora Lee 282
Shanker, Shirley 291
Shanksville, PA 117, 260
Sheline, Paul 291
Shepherd, Karan Howell 282
Shortt, Beth xvi, 75, 151, 221, 291
Simank, Ann 85, 139, 317
Singapore 98
Sixth Floor Museum, The, Dallas, TX 46, 137
Skramstad, George xvii
Slovenia 98

Smith, Chase Dalton 282
Smith, Colton Wade 282
Smith, Jaune Quick-To-See 99-100, 102-103
Smith, Jeane 291
Smith, Lee Allan xvi, 146, 291, 294
Smith, Shawntel 148, 169
Snipes, Al 291
Sohn, Victoria (Vickey) L. 282
Sonic Corp. xi, 142
South Africa 99
Spain 39, 209
Spivey, Marcia 291
Spreiregen, Paul 69-73, 97
St. Luke's United Methodist Church, Oklahoma City xvi-xvii, 31, 49, 76
Stanford University, Stanford, CA 99
Stanford, CA 99
Stankard, Mark 105
Stanton, Robert 159, 169, 173
Stapleton, Kim 291
Stastny, Don 97, 100, 106-107
Steiniper, George 291
Steiver, Jerry 45
Stewart, John Thomas 282
Stiefmiller, Helen xviii

Stone, Wayne 291
Stough, Phyllis xiv, 291, 294
Stratton, Delores (Dee) 282
Streich, Mary 291
Strickland, Jim 291
Swanson, Art 215
Sweden 39
Swedish News Service 39
Switzerland 98

Talbot, Glenda 291
Tallchief, Tim 291
Tang, Ann Cong 285
Tapia, Emilio 282
Tassey, John 291
Taylor, Steven 230-231
Taylor, Zach D. 83, 85, 291, 317
Teleflora 148
Texas 165
Texas A & M University, College Station, TX 117; Bonfire Memorial 117
Texter, Victoria Jeanette 282
"The National Anthem" 169
Thomas, Charlotte Andrea Lewis 282
Thomas, Jane 53-54, 196, 291
Thomas, Mary xvii

Thompson, Ken 291
Thompson, Michael George 55, 100, 282
Thompson, Phillip xiii, xv, xvii, 19, 45, 55, 58, 64-67, 73, 75, 106-108, 112, 168, 291, 294
Thompson, Toby xvi-xvii, 45, 55, 100, 102-103, 112, 291, 294
Thompson, Virginia M. xiii, 45, 55, 66, 108, 282
Thrash, Bill 291
Thurman, William G. "Bill" 44, 291, 294
Tibbs, Phillipa 291
Timberlake, David 291
TIME Magazine 39, 179
Titsworth, Kayla Marie 282
"To Remember" 179, 207
Tolbert, Beth xv, 97, 102-103, 107, 291, 294
Tolbert, Jim 291
Tomlin, Rick L. 282
Toperzer, Tom xvii, 291, 294
Townsend, Ken 291
Treanor, Kathleen xvi-xvii, 55, 75, 112, 168, 291, 294
Treanor, LaRue A. 55, 283
Treanor, Luther H. 55, 283

Treanor, Michael 112
TripAdvisor 207; Top 10 Museums 207
Troup, Pam 291
Truiett, Melvin, Sr. 291
Tu, Be Van 291, 294
Tubb, Sissy 291
Tulsa World 41
Turley, Jonathan 213, 215
Turner, Larry L. 283
Turpen, Mike 230-231
Twain, Mark 89, 257

U. S. Bureau 39
U. S. Constitution 173, 266
U. S. Department of Interior 137
U. S. Department of Justice 174
U. S. General Services Administration (GSA) 92, 94-95
U. S. Government—General Services Administration 86
U. S. Marine Corps Iwo Jima Memorial, Washington, D.C. 51
U. S. News & World Report 26, 39
U. S. Senate Subcommittee on National Parks, Historic Preservation and Recreation 135-139
Unfinished Bombing: Oklahoma

City in American Memory, The 89, 258
United Flight 93 266
United Kingdom 24, 209
United Nations 24, 51
United States Holocaust Memorial Museum, Washington, D.C. 46
United Way 47
University of Oklahoma, Norman, OK 110; College of Architecture 110
University of Pennsylvania, Philadelphia, PA 99
Urban Search and Rescue (USAR) 11, 13; Task Forces 11
USA Today 39

Valdez, Jules A. 283
Van Ess, John Karl, III 283
Van Rysselberge, Charles 291
Vaught, Cheryl xv, xvii, 44, 55, 75, 103, 107, 112, 196, 291, 294
Vermont 165
Vietnam Veterans Memorial, Washington, D.C. 69, 118-119; Women's Memorial 51
Virginia Beach, VA 11
VonFeldt, Helen 291
Vose, Barbara 291

Wade, Johnny Allen 283
Waldo, John 291
Walker, David Jack 283
Walker, Kenny 93, 291
Walker, Robert N., Jr. 283
Wall Street Journal, The 39, 88
Wallace, Kim 10
Wargo, Curt 292
Washburn, Raymond 10
Washington Post, The 39, 97
Washington, D.C. 46, 51, 69, 72, 80, 213, 260
Waters, Leighton 86, 317
Watkins, Hardy xvi, 163, 188, 190-199
Watkins, Kari ix, xi-xiii, 2-3, 19, 62, 102-103, 106-107, 112, 164, 196, 220, 224-241
Watkins, Wanda Lee 283
Watts, J. C., Jr. 86, 317
Weaver, Michael D. 283
Webber, Richard 292
Weber, Hanno 104
Welch, Bud xvii, 83, 93-94, 106-108, 112, 292
Welch, Julie Marie 83, 108, 283
Welge, William 292
Westberry, Robert G. 283

Westchester County Arts Council, NY 129
Whicher, Alan G. 283
White House, Washington, D.C. 77, 80, 110-112, 136, 164, 176; Oval Office 110; Press 39
Whittenberg, Jo Ann 283
Wilkins, Roy 292
Williams, Frances "Fran" Ann 283
Williams, John Michael 92
Williams, Laurie 292
Williams, G. Rainey, Jr. 292, 294
Williams, Richard xvi-xvii, 57, 75, 100, 100, 102-103, 106, 112, 139, 151, 154 157, 196, 202, 292
Williams, Scott D. 283
Williams, W. Stephen 283
Wilson, Clarence Eugene, Sr. 283
Wilson, Ted 292
Winchester, Susan xvi, 230-231, 240
Wisdom Community 259
Witt, James Lee 13
Wolfe, Richard 292
Wood-Chesnut, Sharon Louise 283
Woods, Pendleton 292
Workman, Ann 292
World Charities Fund 48

World Organization of China Painters 129
World War II 266
Worldwide Television News 39
Worsham, Katie 292
Worton, Tresia Jo "Mathes" 283
Wright, Allen B. 292
Wyche, Kathy 292

Yeary, Janice 292
"You Raise Me Up" 256
Young, Buddy 86
Young, James 292
Youngblood, John A. 283
Younger, Charlie 292

Zurcher, Becky 292